THE ILLUSTRATED DIRECTORY OF
KNIVES
DAGGERS &
BAYONETS

THE ILLUSTRATED DIRECTORY OF
KNIVES
DAGGERS &
BAYONETS

A VISUAL ENCYCLOPEDIA OF EDGED WEAPONS FROM AROUND THE WORLD, INCLUDING KNIVES, DAGGERS, BAYONETS, MACHETES AND KHANJARS, WITH OVER 530 PHOTOGRAPHS

Dr TOBIAS CAPWELL

southwater

This edition is published by Southwater,
an imprint of Anness Publishing Ltd,
Blaby Road, Wigston,
Leicestershire LE18 4SE
Email: info@anness.com

www.southwaterbooks.com
www.annesspublishing.com

If you like the images in this book and would like to investigate using them for publishing, promotions or advertising, please visit our website www.practicalpictures.com for more information.

ETHICAL TRADING POLICY
At Anness Publishing we believe that business should be conducted in an ethical and ecologically sustainable way, with respect for the environment and a proper regard to the replacement of the natural resources we employ.

As a publisher, we use a lot of wood pulp to make high-quality paper for printing, and that wood commonly comes from spruce trees. We are therefore currently growing more than 750,000 trees in three Scottish forest plantations: Berrymoss (130 hectares/320 acres), West Touxhill (125 hectares/305 acres) and Deveron Forest (75 hectares/185 acres). The forests we manage contain more than 3.5 times the number of trees employed each year in making paper for the books we manufacture.

Because of this ongoing ecological investment programme, you, as our customer, can have the pleasure and reassurance of knowing that a tree is being cultivated on your behalf to naturally replace the materials used to make the book you are holding.

Our forestry programme is run in accordance with the UK Woodland Assurance Scheme (UKWAS) and will be certified by the internationally recognized Forest Stewardship Council (FSC). The FSC is a non-government organization dedicated to promoting responsible management of the world's forests. Certification ensures forests are managed in an environmentally sustainable and socially responsible way. For further information about this scheme, go to www.annesspublishing.com/trees

Publisher: Joanna Lorenz
Editorial Director: Helen Sudell
Project Editors: Sarah Doughty, Hazel Songhurst and Hannah Consterdine
Assistant Editor: Cynthia McCollum
Contributing authors: Jonathan Barrett, Peter Smithurst and Frederick Stephens
Photography: Gary Ombler (Armouries) and David Cummings (Berman)
Designer: Alistair Plumb
Art Director: Lisa McCormick
Production Controller: Christine Ni

Designed and produced for Anness Publishing by the Bridgewater Book Company Limited.

Previously published as part of a larger volume, *The Illustrated Encyclopedia of Knives, Daggers and Bayonets*

With special thanks to the Royal Armouries, Leeds in England and the Berman Museum of World History, Alabama in the United States. Also grateful thanks for the assistance of Hermann Historica Auctioneers, Munich and Wallis & Wallis auctioneers, Lewes, England.

PUBLISHER'S NOTE
Although the advice and information in this book are believed to be accurate and true at the time of going to press, neither the authors nor the publisher can accept any legal responsibility or liability for any errors or omissions that may have been made.

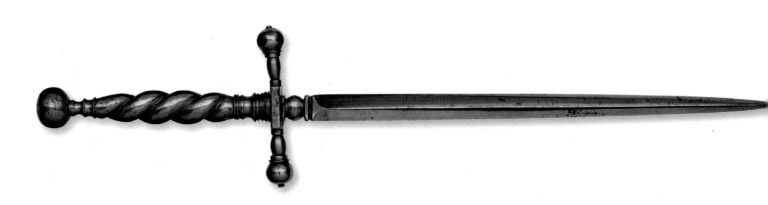

Contents

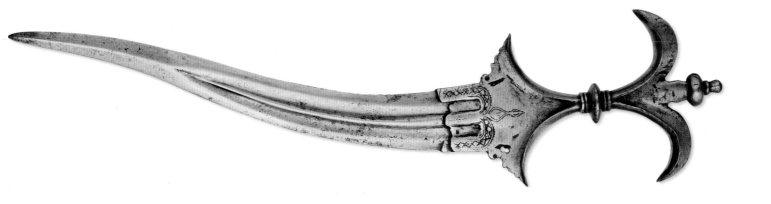

Introduction

From the sharp flints with which primitive humans defended themselves to the carbon-steel bayonets carried by modern soldiers, the fighting knife's history is a complex tale of technical ingenuity, artistic virtuosity and brutal violence. Like its larger cousin the sword, this lethal edged weapon expressed the wealth and taste of its owner. But it was also a vital last resort – easy to carry, quick to draw and always at the fighting man's side.

Butt cap   Spacer   Strong stabbing point

About the book

Knives, daggers and bayonets come in an incredible variety of forms, depending on their historical period and origin. Covering edged weapons shorter than a sword, this catalogue details some of the most important weapons from around the world and throughout history, along with information about their manufacture and use. Arranged chronologically and by geographical area, each of the weapons has a description and a specification listing its country of origin, date and length.

Design of knives, daggers and bayonets

This first section shows how each style of blade is specially designed for its purpose and has evolved to be both aesthetically pleasing and fit for use in its own specific situation. Cross-section diagrams show that each has its own unique shape and point which dictate its strength and power.

Decoration

Not just a weapon, knives and daggers have also been seen as a status symbol, whereby the style and precious metals used on the hilt and blade served as an indicator of the wearers' social standing. Here the main methods of applying the intricate and sometimes brilliantly coloured designs are explained in detail and illustrated with genuine examples.

RIGHT King Henry VIII (1491–1547) is portrayed in this portrait by Holbein wearing a gilded dagger as part of his courtly dress. The dagger was an essential fashion accessory for medieval and Renaissance men.

ABOVE Highland dress dirk, Scottish, *c.*1868. The word "dirk" is usually applied to the long fighting knife of the Scottish Highlanders – of which this is a late example – and to certain classes of military dress dagger.

RIGHT Soldiers of the Brazilian army, 1830s. Socket bayonets such as the one carried here quickly found their way into all modern armies throughout the world following their introduction in the 18th century.

Early daggers and fighting knives

Our story begins well over a million years ago. The earliest sharpened tools were fashioned by knapping flints into sharp shapes. Four millennia later, alloyed metals were developed. Bronze remained the mainstay of technology until iron became available 2,000 years later. Iron was being produced in large quantities by Roman times, when soldiers were armed with the feared pugio dagger and gladius sword.

Medieval and Renaissance daggers

The daggers of the first medieval knights were probably similar to small Viking and Saxon handsaxes. Like the knight's sword, these daggers acquired cruciform hilts and often double-edged blades.

From before the 11th until after the 16th century, the dagger was an essential battlefield weapon. It was also carried in civilian life for self-defence because, until the 16th century, swords were not worn with everyday dress. When the long, heavy-bladed civilian rapier came into fashion, the dagger became its parrying aid. But by the early 1600s sword blades were lighter and could be used rapidly to attack and defend. The parrying dagger was discarded, and daggers declined as fashion accessories.

Bayonets from the 17th to the 21st century

The earliest Bayonne daggers were probably not bayonets at all but rather ordinary daggers made in southwestern France. In order to transform a musket into a spear for close-quarters combat, soldiers started jamming daggers into the muzzles of weapons. The plug bayonet was born – a short-lived design, since it was impossible to fire the weapon with the bayonet in place. This was replaced by the socket bayonet, which became the standard issue.

Mechanized warfare in the 19th century meant that fighting forces became more diversified. One consequence was more varieties of bayonet, including unwieldy sword bayonets that, though impractical, remained in use through the 1800s. By the 20th century bayonets had begun to revert to their dagger-like origins; most soldiers now carry some form of knife bayonet, which is both an all-purpose tool and a weapon.

Daggers in Africa and Asia

In Africa, fighting knives and daggers assumed exotic, uniquely creative forms. Although important as weapons, many were also status symbols and forms of currency. Turning east, we encounter the dagger culture of the Middle East, where the Arab jambiya remains an essential part of formal male dress. We continue into Persia, where daggers are often superlative jewellery objects, rivalled only by the work of the Mughals from northern India.

In the Far East, the Japanese produced the tanto and aikuchi, smaller companions of the fabled katana sword of the samurai. Our journey ends in the South Pacific with the Indonesian kris, prized by European collectors since the 17th century, purported to have magical powers and felt to embody the spirit of the region.

BELOW Ottoman Turkish knife, 17th century. The finest Persian and Turkish daggers were usually forged of watered steel – giving strength and elasticity to the blade – and fitted with jade, ivory or crystal hilts.

Watered steel blade from Persia or India

Jade hilt from Turkey

Design of knives, daggers and bayonets

The creation of an aesthetically pleasing and successful fighting knife, dagger or bayonet involves a number of considerations. Foremost of these is the intended method of use of the weapon. The size and shape of the blade are of primary importance here – for example, stabbing daggers require a slender blade, while daggers intended to be used in rapier combat need to be strong – although the balance and proportions of the weapon also contribute to its effectiveness for a particular use.

Types of knives and daggers

Stabbing

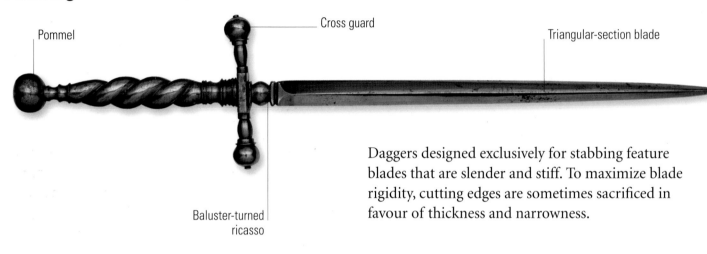

Pommel

Cross guard

Triangular-section blade

Baluster-turned ricasso

Daggers designed exclusively for stabbing feature blades that are slender and stiff. To maximize blade rigidity, cutting edges are sometimes sacrificed in favour of thickness and narrowness.

Cut and thrust

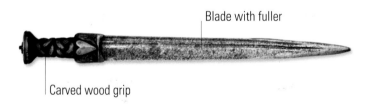

Blade with fuller

Carved wood grip

Most fighting knives and daggers are designed for both stabbing and slashing. These functions must be carefully balanced – a knife cannot do both perfectly.

Parrying

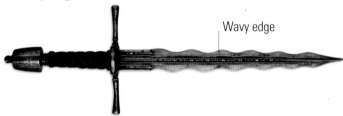

Wavy edge

Daggers designed to be used in rapier combat have to be large and strongly built, so that they can stand up to blows from opposing sword blades.

Folding

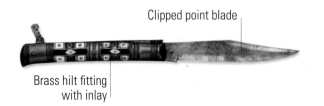

Clipped point blade

Brass hilt fitting with inlay

Fighting knives which have blades folding down into the handle are easy to carry about one's person. They usually have single-edged blades.

Push

Wide double-edged blade

Stag-horn grip

Push daggers are more unusual, perhaps because their method of use – a punching action with the blade projecting in front of the fist – is so specific.

African sickle blade

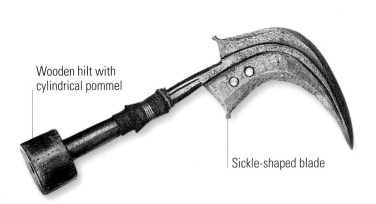

Wooden hilt with cylindrical pommel

Sickle-shaped blade

Large fighting knives with C-shaped blades are rare but not unknown; the cutting edge is on the concave side. These knives are often used to strike hammer-like blows with the point.

African throwing knife

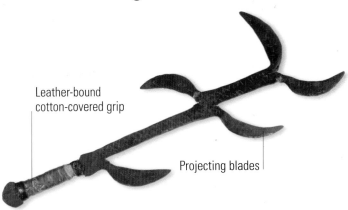

Leather-bound cotton-covered grip

Projecting blades

Single-blade throwing knives rely on the thrower accurately judging distance and rotation in the throw. Multi-bladed versions are designed to produce a blade-strike, whatever the point of impact.

Parts of a dagger and scabbard

The precise ways in which edged weapons are constructed varies tremendously. Likewise, the exact parts that make up a knife or dagger, and the names of those parts, depends on how and where the weapon has been built. Shown below are some of the basic elements that make up most forms of dagger and fighting knife.

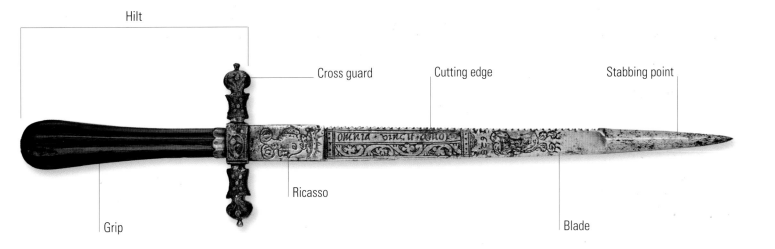

Hilt

Cross guard

Cutting edge

Stabbing point

Ricasso

Grip

Blade

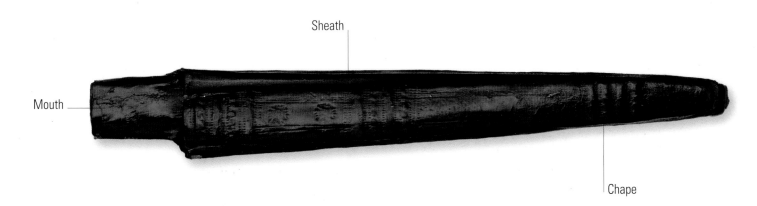

Sheath

Mouth

Chape

Types of bayonets

Plug

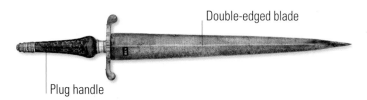

Double-edged blade

Plug handle

The earliest bayonet was simply a cross-hilt dagger with the handle tapered down so that it could be jammed into the end of the musket.

Socket

Socket

Narrow stabbing blade

The socket bayonet fitted around the muzzle, with the blade slung underneath to the side, allowing the musket to be fired with the bayonet fixed.

Sword

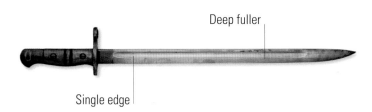

Deep fuller

Single edge

Sword bayonets were the result of an effort to combine the reach of a long blade with a hilt, allowing use as an independent weapon.

Knife

Short, double-edged blade

Assymetric guard

The knife bayonet was introduced in the late 19th century. Here the bayonet returned to its origins, coming to resemble a small all-purpose dagger again.

Parts of a bayonet

Bayonet terminology varies depending on the type of bayonet as, unlike most other small-edged weapons, different types of bayonet feature specific mechanical components – for example the devices for attachment to the firearm. Some of the most essential 19th- and 20th-century terms are given below.

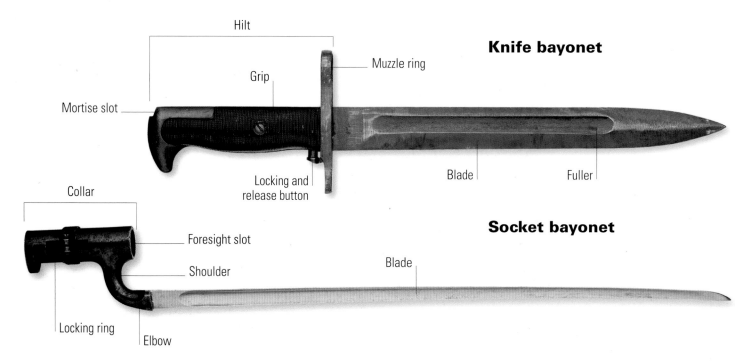

Hilt

Grip

Mortise slot

Collar

Muzzle ring

Knife bayonet

Blade

Fuller

Locking and release button

Foresight slot

Shoulder

Blade

Socket bayonet

Locking ring

Elbow

Types of blades

The form of the blade of an edged weapon determines everything about it – its method of use as well as the effects it can produce. The blade shape also gives the weapon its particular identity or "personality", bringing aesthetic attractiveness as well as deadly functionality.

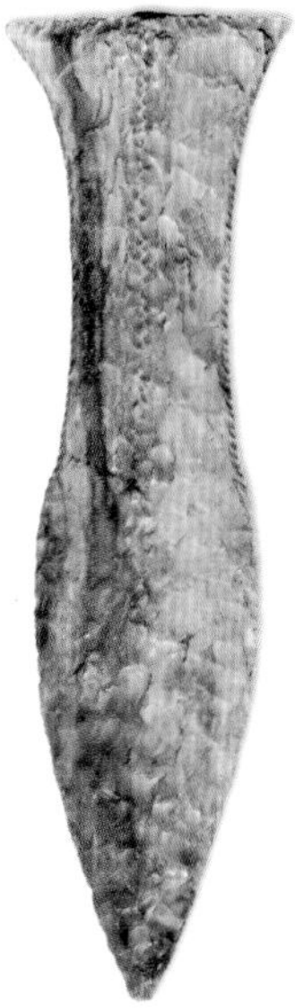

Leaf

Mechanical blade

Triangular

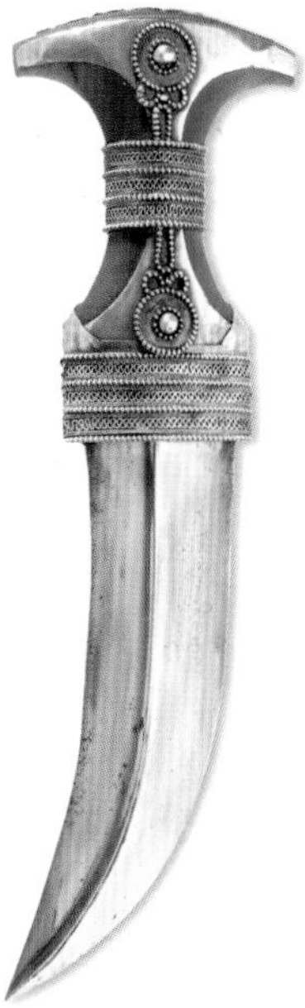

Double-edged curved

Double-edged straight

Thrusting

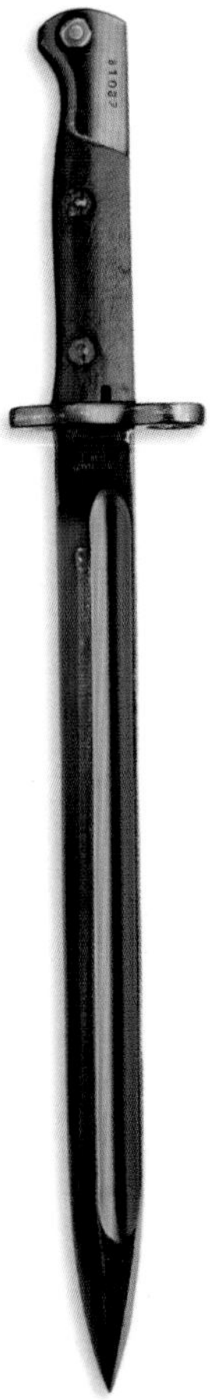

Single-edged straight

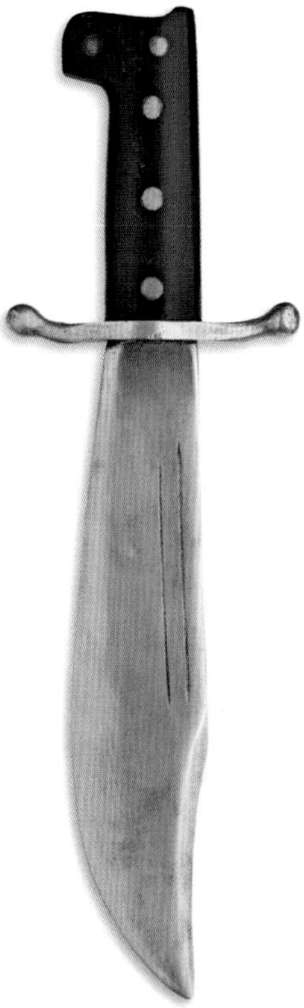

Single-edged with false edge

Single-edged curved

Variable section blade

Blade cross-sections

The cross-section shape of the blade of any edged weapon plays an essential role in determining the way in which that weapon performs. It determines whether the weapon is dedicated to one use, being better suited either to cutting or thrusting, or conversely, whether it is intended to provide a decent level of general effectiveness in both forms of attack. Cross-section shapes vary enormously; there are a small set of basic shapes, each of which has formed the basis for the development of more complex designs.

Basic blade sections

Flattened oval or lenticuler

This is one of the most ancient blade sections, found on flint knives of *c.*2000BC and earlier. The middle of the blade is kept thick to retain strength, while each side is smoothly tapered down to the two cutting edges.

Spined flat section

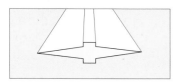

Blades with a simple flat section, though straightforward in design and easy to make, are very weak and therefore very rare. Most flat-sectioned blades of the Bronze Age, for example, have a specially thickened, straight-sided medial spine, to prevent the blade from simply collapsing on impact.

Wedge section

All single-edged or "backed" blades are of wedge section, with the thick unsharpened back providing the blade's strength and rigidity. The design is typically found on the early medieval scramasax, as well as on many medieval "cutting" daggers.

Diamond section

This is an excellent shape for daggers and knives intended primarily for stabbing because it provides very high rigidity at the cost of the cutting edges. Cutting edges can be retained with the flattened diamond section, but the decreased taper sacrifices some of the spine thickness.

Square section

A more extreme move towards an exclusively thrusting capability, with no edges of any sort. It's ideal for stabbing but the lack of a cutting edge is somewhat limiting.

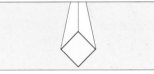

Triangular section

Another dedicated thrusting design, the triangular section is conceived to perform like the square section blade but with a reduced overall weight. For this reason it is commonly found on socket bayonets of the 18th and 19th centuries.

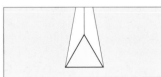

T-section

The T-section is an unusual variation of the wedge-section concept. The thickness of the back has been ground almost entirely away, leaving only a narrow shelf. This is a design unique to certain types of Indo-Persian peshkabz.

More complex sections

By the Medieval Period, blades started to develop with more than one cross-section. For example, the base of the blade might be made in a rectangular section to provide maximum strength at the guard; the middle of the blade could be shaped into a wedge section to give a long cutting edge; while the forward part might use a flattened diamond section to create a sharper point and better thrusting capability. These blades made up of more than one cross-section also reflect light in an interesting way.

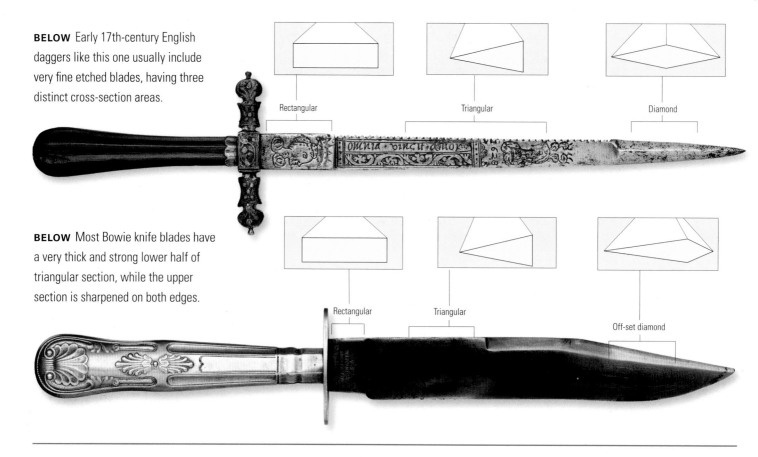

BELOW Early 17th-century English daggers like this one usually include very fine etched blades, having three distinct cross-section areas.

Rectangular   Triangular   Diamond

BELOW Most Bowie knife blades have a very thick and strong lower half of triangular section, while the upper section is sharpened on both edges.

Rectangular   Triangular   Off-set diamond

The fuller

Maintaining strength while reducing weight is important in blade design. The fuller is key to this. A shallow groove down a blade's length reduces its weight but does not weaken it. By the Medieval Period most blades had fullers, either down the middle or offset. The fuller was never a "blood-groove", nor did it make the weapon easier to pull out of an enemy's body. It was simply a way of optimizing weight. Some blades have multiple fullers – some very shallow and wide, others very narrow and quite deep.

Single-fullered flattened diamond section

One of the most common blade cross-sections, this design is found on many types of edged weapon. One of the simplest ways to reduce the weight of a double-edged blade is the addition of a fuller running down its centre line on both sides.

Offset fullered wedge section

This is another very common design, one that takes some of the weight out of the thick back of the blade while retaining overall strength.

Multi-fullered wedge section

A very elegant blade-type that is generally only found on certain types of wide-bladed fighting knife, such as some forms of the Nepalese *kukri*.

Multi-fullered flattened diamond section

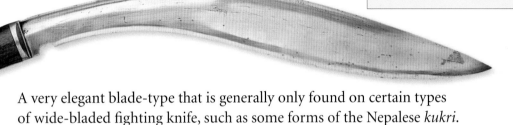

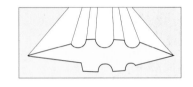

This very large group appears in many diverse variations. Some display only two or three shallow broad fullers, while others involve up to five very narrow and deep grooves, to the point where the overall cross-section before fullering is lost.

Hollow-ground triangular section

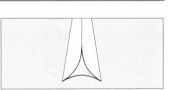

A hollow-ground blade involves one or more fullers that have been widened to take up the whole width of the blades' surface. Hollow-ground triangular sections are found on many socket bayonet patterns.

Cruciform section

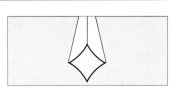

Found on several 19th-century bayonet types, this design is almost never used on any other sort of edged weapon; blades of this type are comparatively difficult to make and the benefits are minimal.

Decorations

Many decorative techniques were available to the makers of edged weapons, some spread by the export of the weapons themselves, others by the migration of their creators. The type and extent of the decoration was determined by the financial means of the person commissioning it, meaning that weapons were generally viewed as important indicators of social status. Most decorative processes were practised by specialists; decoration was almost never carried out by the weaponsmith himself. The finest and most beautiful weapons are often those that have been decorated by means of more than one process.

Engraving

Decorative silver finish

Engraved swastika on chape

A sharp graving tool is used to trace a design by cutting channels or furrows directly into a metal surface. In Europe this process was used throughout the Medieval and Renaissance Periods, although by the 15th century it had been largely superseded by etching, which was less difficult and time-consuming.

Etching

Fluted dudgeon wood grip

Long double-edged blade

Etched decoration to blade

This is a process of producing a design on metal by "biting" it away with acid. The surface to be etched is covered with an acid-resistant coating (the "resist"), usually a wax or varnish. The design is then scraped out in the resist with a graving tool. When the object is washed in acid, the exposed design becomes permanently etched into the metal. In "raised" etching the design is painted on to the metal surface in the resist substance, leaving the background exposed. This produces a very bold three-dimensional effect.

Steel-chiselling

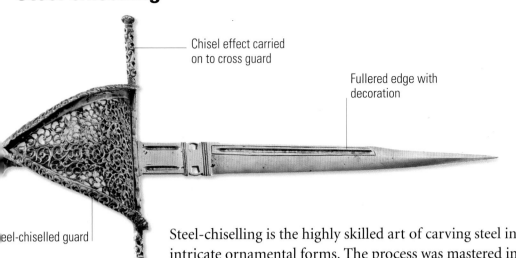

Chisel effect carried on to cross guard

Fullered edge with decoration

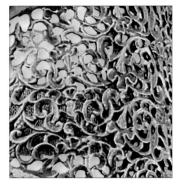

Intricate steel-chiselling

eel-chiselled guard

Steel-chiselling is the highly skilled art of carving steel into intricate ornamental forms. The process was mastered in Renaissance Europe, where it was used to decorate the hilts of fine swords and daggers, as well as the locks of firearms.

Punchwork

Punched and scratched decoration

Grip spike

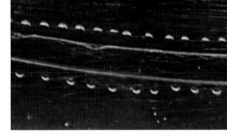

Punched decoration along the blade

A technique usually called *pointillé* is perhaps the simplest form of punchwork. This involves the formation of patterns on a surface by means of lightly punched dots, sometimes of varying sizes and depths. More complex effects were produced through the use of shaped punches.

Enamelling

Not to be confused with paint that is sometimes called enamel, true enamel is a brilliantly coloured vitreous substance applied in the form of a powder and heated until it begins to melt, coalescing into a smooth, glassy surface. Enamel is obviously very delicate and easily broken and is therefore usually found only on weapons intended purely for decorative or ceremonial use.

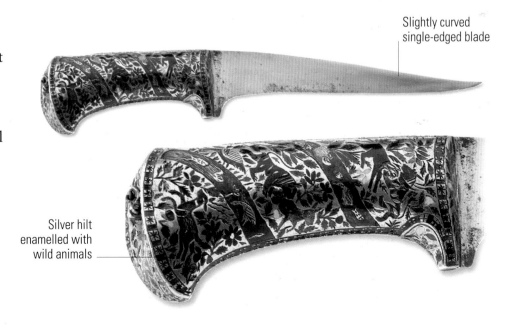

Slightly curved single-edged blade

Silver hilt enamelled with wild animals

Blueing

When highly polished steel is heated, it changes colour, passing through darkening shades of blue, until it reaches purple and black. If a particular temperature can be maintained for a certain period of time, the colour produced will remain after the steel cools. The rich tints produced with heat processes – "blueing" – were often used to decorate the hilts of edged weapons.

Wood grip covered with ray skin

Fire- or mercury-gilding

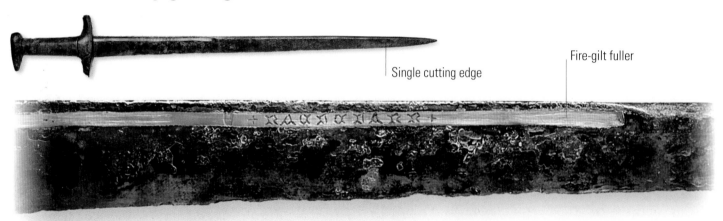

Single cutting edge

Fire-gilt fuller

This is perhaps the most common traditional way of applying gold to steel. An amount of gold dust was first mixed with mercury. The gold dissolved in the mercury forming an amalgam or paste-like mixture. This substance was then applied to the steel surface. The piece was then heated to boil or "fume" off the mercury, leaving the gold permanently bonded to the steel. The same technique could also be used to apply silver to steel.

Encrustation

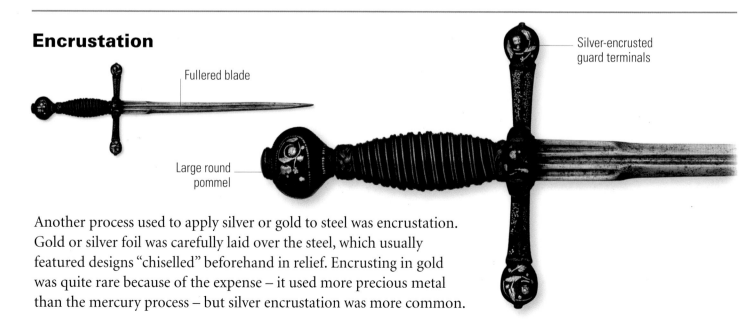

Fullered blade

Silver-encrusted guard terminals

Large round pommel

Another process used to apply silver or gold to steel was encrustation. Gold or silver foil was carefully laid over the steel, which usually featured designs "chiselled" beforehand in relief. Encrusting in gold was quite rare because of the expense – it used more precious metal than the mercury process – but silver encrustation was more common.

Inlay

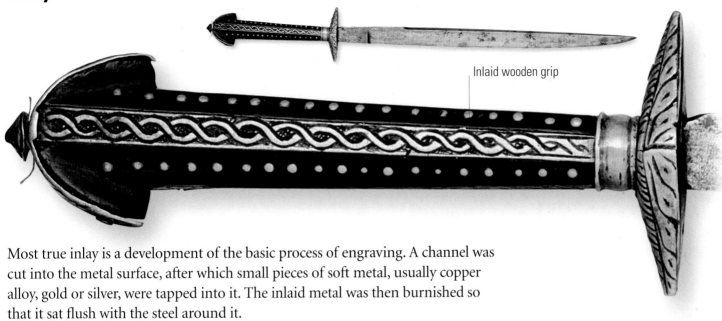

Inlaid wooden grip

Most true inlay is a development of the basic process of engraving. A channel was cut into the metal surface, after which small pieces of soft metal, usually copper alloy, gold or silver, were tapped into it. The inlaid metal was then burnished so that it sat flush with the steel around it.

Damascening

Damascening inlay

The use of the term "damascening" in English dates to at least the 16th century. True damascening is a form of inlay, wherein the precious metal, usually gold, is laid into a channel having a cross-section shaped like an upside down "Y". This technique was much rarer than "false" damascening with which it is often confused.

False or Counterfeit Damascening

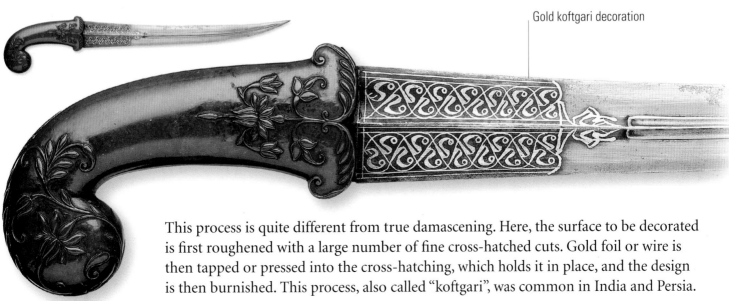

Gold koftgari decoration

This process is quite different from true damascening. Here, the surface to be decorated is first roughened with a large number of fine cross-hatched cuts. Gold foil or wire is then tapped or pressed into the cross-hatching, which holds it in place, and the design is then burnished. This process, also called "koftgari", was common in India and Persia.

Stone Age blades

For thousands of years the only edged weapons available to prehistoric peoples were simple stone hand axes. These were grasped in the palm and used to strike overarm cutting blows. Over 2000 centuries, these tools slowly began to take on a more recognizable blade shape. Some of the finest flint knives were made as recently as 1500BC, after which point they were rendered obsolete by bronze weapons.

Palaeolithic hand axe, 300,000BC

This quartzite hand axe is a rare example of the precision knapping skills of Palaeolithic humans. The cutting edge is placed at a right angle to the line of direct force, and the butt has been shaped with a few perfect knap-strikes to sit comfortably in the palm.

Cutting edge

DATE	300,000BC
ORIGIN	PALAEOLITHIC
LENGTH	17.8cm (7in)

Palaeolithic hand axe, 100,000–60,000BC

This flint core axe shows a very important development, for the maker's intention seems to have been to create a weapon or tool with a more prominent point. It is not in any sense a true stabbing blade, but the fact that a point will more effectively focus the force of a blow into a small area seems here to be well understood. The point and cutting edge have been skillfully pressure-flaked. Their patterns combined with the smooth white cortex produce a very beautiful sculptural effect.

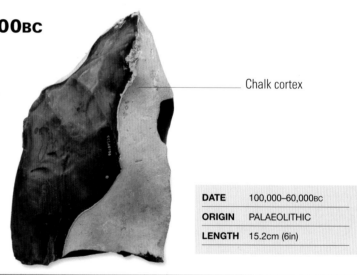

Chalk cortex

DATE	100,000–60,000BC
ORIGIN	PALAEOLITHIC
LENGTH	15.2cm (6in)

Neolithic chisel, 6000–3000BC

Tip

Long, narrow shape

As the skills of the flint-knapper became more advanced, tools could be shaped into more specialized forms. This Neolithic mottled flint chisel has taken on a form that is much more blade-like, being much longer and narrower in comparison to earlier tools.

DATE	6000–3000BC
ORIGIN	NEOLITHIC
LENGTH	17cm (6.75in)

Dagger of the Iceman

This small dagger was among a number of perfectly preserved objects found with "Ötzi the Iceman", an extraordinarily well-preserved natural mummy of a Chalcolithic (Copper Age) man who died c.3300BC in the Ötztal Alps on the Italo-Austrian border. When he died, possibly of an arrow wound in his shoulder or a blow to his skull, the Iceman's body froze in glacial ice and was there preserved until its discovery in 1991.

The dagger is made of a short flint blade and a handle of ash wood. The scabbard is woven from fibrous plant bark. This is the fighting weapon of a man whose death was a direct result of violence; the blade still bears traces of the blood of one of the Iceman's enemies.

Flint blade

Wood handle

Plant bark scabbard

ABOVE Perhaps the most extraordinary aspect of this weapon is the fact that it survives with all of its organic material elements intact.

Bronze Age dagger, c.1800–1500BC

Cutting edge

DATE	c.1800–1500BC
ORIGIN	BRONZE AGE
LENGTH	11.4cm (4.5in)

This late flint dagger, made as the use of metal was becoming more widespread, is a good example of a fully-fledged bladed weapon. Two pressure-flaking techniques have been used; larger flakes have been removed to form the grip, while much finer, tiny pieces have been taken away to create the edges of the razor-sharp blade.

Bronze Age dagger, 1600BC

Imitation stitching

DATE	1600BC
ORIGIN	BRONZE AGE
LENGTH	18cm (7.1in)

This beautiful weapon, typical of the best "Dagger Age" pieces, is a direct copy of a bronze knife. An impressive detail is the zigzag ridge that runs down the grip – an imitation of the stitching on the leather grip of this weapon's bronze counterpart.

Ancient Egyptian knives and daggers

The dagger had become a common weapon among ancient Egyptians long before the Early Dynastic Period (*c.*3150–2686BC). Fine flint daggers were produced, the best-known being cleaver-like ceremonial knives. Few Old Kingdom (2686–2134BC) daggers are known. More survive from the Middle (2040–1640BC) and New (1570–1070BC) Kingdoms, usually fitted with copper, bronze, or in a few cases, gold blades.

Egyptian ceremonial knife blade, *c.*3000BC

Pressure-flaked pattern

Handle was positioned here

This object is one of several ceremonial knife blades dating from the Predynastic Period in Egypt (*c.*5000–*c.*3100BC). It is now less recognizable as a knife because of the loss of its handle. Weapons of this type are in fact very beautiful works of art, the wavy patterns on the blade created with great skill by a master flint-knapper.

DATE	c.3000BC
ORIGIN	EGYPTIAN
LENGTH	18cm (7.1in)

Egyptian dagger, New Kingdom, *c.*1570–1085BC

Grip scales lost

Multi-fullered blade

This bronze dagger from the 18th, 19th or 20th Dynasty is comparable to weapons from Bronze Age Europe and Asia. The blade is quite wide for its length, the hilt ergonomically shaped and stepped on its outer edge to hold the missing grip scales. In these ways it is similar to bronze daggers from ancient Persia.

DATE	c.1570–1085BC
ORIGIN	EGYPTIAN
LENGTH	unknown

Egyptian knife, New Kingdom, *c.*1570–1085BC

Rounded point

Wooden grip

The wooden grip of this New Kingdom dagger may be original. It is fitted to a short blade of bronze, the profile of which shows it to be a serviceable cut-and-thrust weapon. The point may have become rounded due to wear, although it could have been made so. A rounded but razor-sharp tip would still slash flesh and split bone.

DATE	c.1570–1085BC
ORIGIN	EGYPTIAN
LENGTH	unknown

Egyptian thrusting dagger, New Kingdom, *c.*1570–1085BC

Narrow
stabbing blade

Large, mushroom-
shaped pommel

DATE	*c.*1570–1085BC
ORIGIN	EGYPTIAN
LENGTH	unknown

This spike-like weapon was designed for stabbing. But unlike later stabbing knives and stilettos of the Early Modern Era in Europe (*c.*1500–1800), to which it is not dissimilar, this dagger is made not of hardened steel but of softer bronze. To strengthen it, the smith has gracefully flared the blade just above the grip.

Egyptian funerary dagger, New Kingdom, *c.*1370–1352BC

Hunting scenes in relief

Enamel
decoration

Solid gold blade

DATE	*c.*1370–1352BC
ORIGIN	EGYPTIAN
LENGTH	31.8cm (12.5in)

Only Egyptian royalty could afford daggers with blades of pure gold. This ornately decorated solid gold weapon armed the boy-king, Tutankhamun, for the afterlife. A dagger and sheath of solid gold were also found among the tomb effects of Queen Ahhotpe, mother of Ahmosis I, founder of the 18th Dynasty of the New Kingdom during which Tutankhamun reigned.

Egyptian funerary dagger, New Kingdom, *c.*1370–1352BC

Iron blade

Enamelled bands

Palmette
ornamentation

DATE	*c.*1370–1352BC
ORIGIN	EGYPTIAN
LENGTH	34.3cm (13.5in)

The iron blade of Tutankhamun's second dagger may seem plain compared to the gold of its companion, but it is even more precious. Its composition is 97 per cent iron and three per cent nickel. This means it is meteoric iron, very rare and more valuable than gold. The pommel is rock-crystal and the hilt is decorated with enamel.

Bronze Age edged weapons

For 2,000 years bronze was the most advanced metal available. Despite the fact that bronze work hardens, weapons made out of this alloy still had to be designed to take account of its softness and propensity to deform during use. Most bronze daggers are relatively short with a sharp taper to help maintain rigidity, a requirement often enhanced by a strong medial ridge running down the blade.

French Bronze Age dagger, 1800–1500BC

Cylindrical grip

Densely ridged blade

This fine bronze dagger was found at Mirabel in France, and dates from the French Early Bronze Age, 1800–1500BC. The triangular blade, the edges of which are decorated with a number of ridges and grooves, is riveted to a separate hilt. Daggers of this type may have inspired the cinquedea of Renaissance Italy.

DATE	1800–1500BC
ORIGIN	FRENCH BRONZE AGE
LENGTH	27cm (11in)

Luristan dagger, 1200BC

Hilt block

Grip scale recess

This beautiful dagger is one of many found at Luristan. It is elegantly designed to make the best use of the material while minimizing the effects of its limitations. The sharply tapered blade is strengthened with quite a wide medial ridge, whilst the thick, crescent-shaped hilt block strengthens the top of the grip against breakage.

DATE	1200BC
ORIGIN	LURISTAN (IRANIAN)
LENGTH	41.5cm (16.3in)

European knife blade, 1200–1000BC

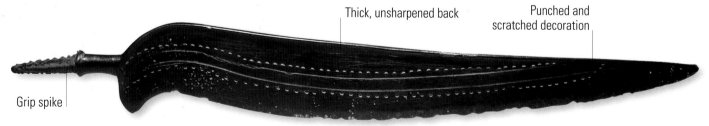

Thick, unsharpened back

Punched and scratched decoration

Grip spike

This long blade demonstrates a different approach to the problem of how to build a sound edged weapon out of bronze. The strength and rigidity derive not from a steep taper and thick medial ridge, but from the overall thickness of much of the blade and its wedge-shaped section, with a thick back and single cutting edge.

DATE	1200–1000BC
ORIGIN	EUROPEAN
LENGTH	30cm (11.8in)

Luristan dagger, 1200–800BC

Finger grooves

Narrow blade

DATE	1200–800BC
ORIGIN	LURISTAN (IRANIAN)
LENGTH	27cm (11in)

This fine bronze dagger is another Luristan find. Dating from 1200–800BC, it falls within the Ancient Persian Iron Age. The finely shaped handle is designed to fit perfectly into the hand, with finger grooves for a comfortable grip. It was also originally fitted with grip scales of wood or some other organic material.

Weapons from Luristan

Some of the largest groups of Bronze Age objects ever found come from sites in Luristan (also Lorestan), in what is now northwestern Iran. Excavations in the 20th century uncovered tools, ornamental objects and very large numbers of weapons made by the ancient semi-nomadic people who lived in this mountainous part of the Middle East. Along with many swords, axes and spearheads, the weapons included a great many daggers, cast in bronze and usually fitted with

grip scales of wood, horn or bone. Some of the best bronze daggers from Luristan in fact probably date from the Iranian Iron Age, c.1200–650BC, although many others have been found that belong to the Iranian Bronze Age, c.3500–1250BC.

BELOW Many ruined settlements like this one are preserved all over northwestern Iran, and have been extensively excavated yielding a large number of weapons, tools and other objects.

Daggers of the Classical World

We often imagine Greek and Roman warriors armed with shining bronze arms and armour. It is, however, important to remember that iron was well known by this time. Bronze and iron coexisted as weapons materials for centuries. Bronze was harder than early iron, but iron was cheaper. Almost all Roman weapons had iron blades. Roman smiths also made use of a new alloy of iron and carbon: steel.

Hallstatt "antennae" dagger, *c.*750–450BC

"Antennae" pommel

Damaged "antennae" guard

DATE	c.750–450BC
ORIGIN	HALLSTATT CULTURE
LENGTH	unknown

This classic Hallstatt "antennae" dagger is an excellent example of its type, not only because of the distinctive form of the hilt but also because it is made of iron. The Hallstatt were the first Bronze Age Europeans to master this metal.

Villanovan dagger and scabbard, 600–300BC

Wheel chape

Triple-button pommel

This exquisite Villanovan dagger, from tomb 11 at the Necropolis at Villanueva de Teba, is a beautiful example of the best ornamented bronze-work. The aesthetic influence on later Roman pugios is also apparent in the banded construction of the scabbard and in the overall proportions of the weapon.

DATE	600–300BC
ORIGIN	VILLANOVAN
LENGTH	unknown

English or German dagger and scabbard, 600–300BC

Bronze-banded scabbard

The design of this iron-bladed dagger is associated with southern Germany. It closely resembles the Roman pugio and may be one of its precursors. It was found in the River Thames, but was most likely imported into Britain rather than made there. The bronze-banded scabbard is probably the work of a local metalworker.

DATE	600–300BC
ORIGIN	ENGLISH/GERMAN
LENGTH	35.6cm (14in)

Roman pugio and scabbard, AD100

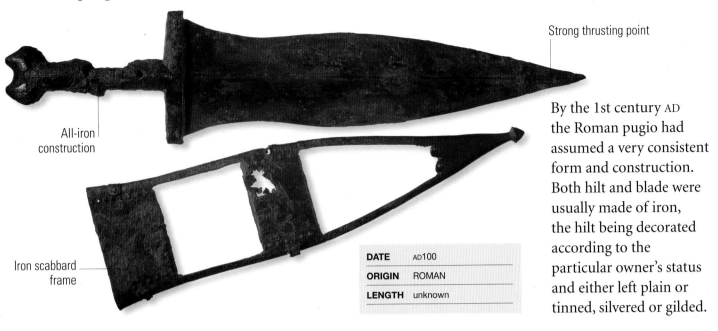

Strong thrusting point

All-iron construction

Iron scabbard frame

DATE	AD100
ORIGIN	ROMAN
LENGTH	unknown

By the 1st century AD the Roman pugio had assumed a very consistent form and construction. Both hilt and blade were usually made of iron, the hilt being decorated according to the particular owner's status and either left plain or tinned, silvered or gilded.

Roman pugio, AD100

Medial ridge

Wheel pommel

DATE	AD100
ORIGIN	ROMAN
LENGTH	26.5cm (10.4in)

This worn, bent example has a less pronounced point than many other examples, but otherwise it is fairly typical, having a narrow medial ridge running down the whole length of the blade. The grip displays the usual central swelling and wheel pommel, while the guard is decorated with incised lines and beading.

Roman officer's pugio, c.AD100–300

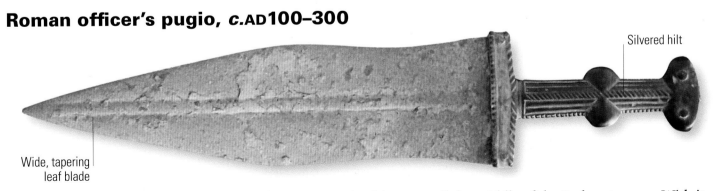

Silvered hilt

Wide, tapering leaf blade

DATE	c.AD100–300
ORIGIN	ROMAN
LENGTH	unknown

Pugios of this type remained in use until the middle of the 2nd century AD. With its silvered and finely worked hilt, it is clear this weapon belonged to a Roman officer, a centurion or perhaps a navarch. The decorative rope motif on the grip may indicate an association with a commander in the Roman Navy. This dagger survives in exceptional condition, one of the finest remaining Roman examples.

Daggers of the Medieval Period

The dating of the Medieval Period is very difficult. Working exclusively in the context of weapons history, it is possible to consider the Medieval Period, or "Middle Ages", as beginning with the collapse of the western Roman Empire in the 5th century (the Early Medieval Period, often wrongly called the "Dark Ages"), continuing through the early 14th century (the "High" Middle Ages), and ending sometime in the 15th century (the "Late" Middle Ages). Daggers developed a great deal during these ten centuries.

Central European scramasax blades, 500–600

Wide, unsharpened back

Tang

Asymmetric, stabbing point

Cutting edge

Although they are now in a heavily corroded "excavated" condition, these two Early Medieval sax blades still give a very good impression of their original shape. The wide, thick-backed form, ideal for cutting and slashing, angles sharply down in the upper third to form a very long stabbing point. It is not surprising that this impressive, multifunctional design remained popular throughout central, northern and western Europe for nearly 1,000 years.

DATE	500–600
ORIGIN	CENTRAL EUROPEAN
LENGTH	26cm (10.2in)

English cross-hilt dagger, *c.*1200–1300

Up-curving pommel arms

Down-curving guard

Double-edged blade

This classic High Medieval dagger carries a distinctive type of pommel, made essentially as a mirror of the cross guard. Medieval daggers of this type recall the "anthropomorphic" designs of the Hallstatt and La Tène Celts. A number of these daggers survive, many of which have been found in London. The type is probably not exclusively English and was undoubtedly also popular on the Continent.

DATE	*c.*1200–1300
ORIGIN	ENGLISH
LENGTH	30.5cm (12in)

English cross-hilt dagger, 1400

Square-section point

Copper-alloy hilt

DATE	1400
ORIGIN	ENGLISH
LENGTH	29cm (11.4in)

The guard and pommel of this fine dagger are made of a copper alloy instead of iron or steel. The missing grip may have been covered with a colourful textile. The blade is purely for stabbing, although the bladesmith has gone to some trouble to shape it into a more elegant form than a simple square-section spike. The blade's deeply fullered lower half transitions gracefully into the square-section upper half.

English or Scottish cross-hilt dagger, *c.*1300–1400

Drooping guard

Wheel pommel

Sharply tapered blade

DATE	c.1300–1400
ORIGIN	ENGLISH/SCOTTISH
LENGTH	33.8cm (13.3in)

Although its blade is relatively short, its narrowness and very sharp taper indicate that this dagger is undoubtedly what medieval people would recognize as a *couteau à pointe*, or "stabbing knife". The guard is of an interesting type, the arms drooping diagonally down towards the blade and swelling towards the ends. The guard block also extends down to sit flush with the wooden grip, which like those of most other surviving medieval daggers is not lost. Guards very similar to this are one of the characteristic features of Scottish medieval swords, of which this may be a diminutive.

German cross-hilt dagger, late 15th century

Variable-section blade

Pierced guard

DATE	late 15th century
ORIGIN	GERMAN
LENGTH	44cm (17.3in)

This very ornate dagger probably dates from the very end of the Medieval Period and may be of German origin. The pommel and guard are of copper alloy. The blade is especially interesting in that along its length the cross-section changes four times, beginning with a double-edged section at the guard to single-edged a few centimetres above the guard, and alternating back and forth to the point.

Rondel daggers

By the middle of the 14th century the rondel dagger was becoming the most fashionable type worn by all classes, both in war and for self-defence in daily life. Some have single-edged blades, while others are stabbing tools, the blades being merely long steel spikes. The disks or rondels were constructed of diverse materials – wood, horn, copper alloy, iron or steel – and can vary greatly in diameter. Nevertheless, they always grip the user's hand tightly, giving a solid seat for a powerful downward thrust.

English rondel dagger, c.14th century

Small rondel guard

"Teacosy" pommel

This weapon was found in the River Thames in London. It shows one of the characteristic features of the earliest forms of rondel dagger: while the guard is composed of a metal disk, the pommel is not, but is instead a heavy half-round "tea cosy" form found on many 12th- and 13th-century swords.

DATE	c.14th century
ORIGIN	ENGLISH
LENGTH	unknown

The suicide of Lucretia

Since weapons rarely survive in pristine, undamaged condition, it is vital to look at depictions of weapons in art. Most artists attempted to represent weapons as faithfully as possible. They can be seen as the artist himself saw them – bright, polished, with all decoration intact. Some artistic themes are very useful to weapons researchers. In the study of daggers, the tragic subject of Lucretia, a semi-mythical Roman noblewoman, is especially relevant. Her rape and subsequent suicide by stabbing was thought to have led to the foundation of the Roman Republic. Botticelli, Raphael and many other artists painted pictures of her, and these works usually include excellent renderings of daggers from the artist's time, usually of a very high quality to emphasize Lucretia's noble status.

RIGHT Lucretia supposedly stabbed herself to death after being dishonoured by the son of the last king of Rome. The popular outrage that followed brought the overthrow of the ancient Roman monarchy.

English (?) rondel dagger fragment, *c.*1400

Engraved geometric decoration

Fire-gilt surface

DATE	c.1400
ORIGIN	POSSIBLY ENGLISH
LENGTH	9.6cm (3.8in)

This broken piece of gilt metal is the grip and pommel of a once extremely fine rondel dagger, undoubtedly the weapon of a knight. The ornate geometric decoration is typical of knights' daggers as depicted on English funerary effigies of the late 14th and early 15th centuries. The squared, four-petal flower motif on the pommel is especially common in late medieval English metalwork; the same pattern was used to decorate copper-alloy boxes, candlesticks and armour.

English or Scottish rondel dagger, 15th century

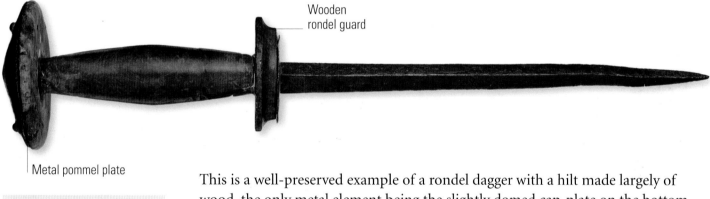

Wooden rondel guard

Metal pommel plate

DATE	15th century
ORIGIN	ENGLISH/SCOTTISH
LENGTH	35.4cm (13.9in)

This is a well-preserved example of a rondel dagger with a hilt made largely of wood, the only metal element being the slightly domed cap-plate on the bottom rondel. The stout, lozenge-section blade has no cutting edges; attacks were delivered with the point exclusively. The good quality of the blade is indicated by its mark – a letter "I" standing on a letter "O", inlaid in copper alloy.

English (?) rondel dagger, 15th century

Long, single-edged blade

Original wooden grip

DATE	15th century
ORIGIN	POSSIBLY ENGLISH
LENGTH	51.6cm (20.3in)

Its considerable length indicates that this dagger is undoubtedly a weapon of war, made long to pierce with lethal effect the multilayered armour of plate, mail and textile worn at the time. The metal rondels are quite thick and of a comparatively small diameter. Also unusual is the original wooden grip – the grips of most medieval daggers have long since rotted away, leaving only the exposed tang.

English rondel dagger, 15th century

Wooden grip

Forward-curving back

This small dagger is interesting because the original wooden grip survives, as do the wooden rondels which are capped with metal washers. Also, the single-edged wedge-section blade is unusual in that the back curves gently forward towards the cutting edge as it tapers to the point. This specimen was found in the River Thames in London under Southwark Bridge.

DATE	15th century
ORIGIN	ENGLISH
LENGTH	unknown

German rondel dagger, *c.*1500

Thick spike blade

Triple-lobed guard

The copper-alloy hilt of this weapon is unusual in that the guard, rather than being a simple disk – like that fitted to the end of the tang – is formed into three knobs, or lobes. This form is very similar to certain types of German, so-called "landsknecht" daggers fashionable in the early to mid-16th century. The thick, heavy blade is triangular in section and entirely suited to such common medieval fighting techniques as stabbing blows to the opponent's skull.

DATE	*c.*1500
ORIGIN	GERMAN
LENGTH	34cm (13.4in)

English rondel dagger, *c.*1510

Small rondel guard

Heavy fluted pommel

Strong medial rib

This late rondel dagger was found in the River Thames near Southwark in London. The heavy iron pommel is unusual and recalls the earliest forms of rondel dagger which had similar rounded pommels instead of the wide disk. The dagger was discovered along with the remains of its leather scabbard, and two small byknives for eating and other utilitarian purposes.

DATE	*c.*1510
ORIGIN	ENGLISH
LENGTH	unknown

Baselards

There was considerable variation in the size of baselards, some being small daggers, others short swords. The hilt always displays the distinctive I-shape, being two plates of wood sandwiching the tang, which is forged to the same shape. The small dagger baselards were most common in Italy during the late 14th and early 15th centuries. The longer sword baselards were closely associated with Germany and Switzerland.

European baselard dagger, *c.*1400

Medial ridge

Finger grooves

DATE	c.1400
ORIGIN	EUROPEAN
LENGTH	33.3cm (13.1in)

The smaller dagger version of the baselard seems to have appeared first, the longer versions appearing later. This example is for the most part representative of late 14th- and early 15th-century baselards, apart from the ergonomic finger grooves carved into the guard and pommel cross pieces, which are perhaps more atypical.

English long baselard, *c.*1490–1520

Fire-gilt fuller

Asymmetrical pommel

Single cutting edge

DATE	c.1490–1520
ORIGIN	ENGLISH
LENGTH	68.2cm (26.9in)

This rare English baselard indicates that the long type was popular outside Switzerland and Germany. It is an excellent cut-and-thrust blade. The hilt includes an asymmetrical pommel with an extended forward section; this allowed the user to make deadly whipping cuts, using his little finger as a fulcrum.

Swiss or German long baselard, 1520

Double-edged blade

Symmetrical wooden hilt

This standard early 16th-century baselard features the more usual symmetrical hilt, the cross guard being slightly wider than the pommel, which in this case has been widened into a roughly lenticular form. Unlike the English example above, this weapon is fitted with a plain, double-edged blade of flattened diamond section.

DATE	1520
ORIGIN	SWISS/GERMAN
LENGTH	unknown

Ballock daggers

Often referred to as "kidney" daggers even today, the form of these uniquely recognizable knives makes their true inspiration fairly obvious. While ballock knives shocked Victorian scholars of weapons into renaming them, to the medieval mind the open and public display of a phallic icon was not necessarily erotic at all. Rather it may have been an apotropaic defence intended to ward off evil.

English or Scottish ballock dagger, 14th century

Lobe rivet

Copper-alloy spacer

This ballock dagger clearly foreshadows the dudgeon daggers of the 17th century. It is a very early example of the placement of a metal spacer between the top of the lobes and the base of the blade. The spacer is secured by means of two rivets, one passing through each lobe, a method found on most surviving dudgeon daggers.

DATE	14th century
ORIGIN	ENGLISH/SCOTTISH
LENGTH	25.1cm (9.9in)

English ballock dagger, 15th century

Metal pommel button

This very long 15th-century example already looks something like its late 17th-century descendant, the Scottish Highland dirk. The hilt appears to be carved out of some very hard root or bogwood, while the thickly backed, single-edged blade is similar to the later Highland dirk blades in terms of its size and proportions.

DATE	15th century
ORIGIN	ENGLISH
LENGTH	29.2cm (11.5in)

English or Scottish ballock dagger, 15th century

Copper-alloy base plate

Shaped to scabbard

Like many examples of its type, this flared-base ballock dagger is fitted with a copper-alloy base plate. This plate is not only a convenient opportunity for incised decoration; it also provides a secure seat for the end of the tang, which passes down the centre of the wooden grip and out through a hole in the base plate, to be peened over, thus holding hilt and blade together.

DATE	15th century
ORIGIN	ENGLISH/SCOTTISH
LENGTH	39cm (15.4in)

English or Scottish ballock dagger, 15th century

Flaring grip | Toothed spacer

DATE	15th century
ORIGIN	ENGLISH/SCOTTISH
LENGTH	36.5cm (14.4in)

The lobes of ballock daggers with flared, trumpet-like grips are generally smaller in proportion to the blade than those of daggers with bulbous ends, the lobes of which are usually significantly wider than the base of the blade. This example also has a metal spacer between lobes and blade, with teeth above and below the blade to ensure a snug fit in the scabbard. The flared trumpet hilt appeared in the 15th century and remained popular into the 16th century. It may have been intended to provide a platform similar to that of the rondel dagger, allowing a firmer grip.

English or Scottish ballock dagger, 15th century

Carved testicular lobes

DATE	15th century
ORIGIN	ENGLISH/SCOTTISH
LENGTH	unknown

This fairly standard ballock hilt, carved in the usual way from a single piece of wood, is fitted to a noteworthy single-edged blade. In its form and especially its point, the blade closely resembles the earlier medieval dagger of the type called in textual sources *couteau à tailler*, or "cutting knife", the single sharpened edge of which curves gently upward towards the straight, unsharpened back to form an asymmetric point, not unlike that of a typical kitchen knife.

English (?) ballock dagger, 15th century

Hollow-ground diamond section | Triangular section

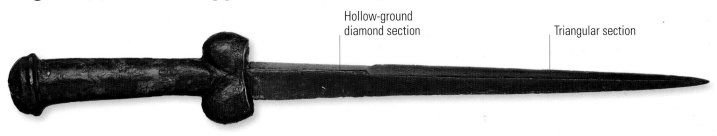

DATE	15th century
ORIGIN	POSSIBLY ENGLISH
LENGTH	34.7cm (13.7in)

This purposefully lifelike ballock hilt, the grip slightly curved, is fitted to a remarkable blade. The lower third of the blade is of a standard triangular construction, but it changes quite suddenly, and the upper two-thirds of the blade consists of a skilfully hollow-ground diamond section. This produces a blade that is extremely strong at the base but still narrow enough at the point to slide with ease between the ribs of an enemy. Elaborate blades like this are rare on ballock daggers, being perhaps more commonly found with rondel hilts.

Daggers of the Renaissance

The 16th century was an important turning point in the history of weapons. While traditional fighting methods, with swords, daggers and staff weapons, were still essential, new gunpowder-weapon technology was evolving rapidly. As the 1500s progressed, edged weapons started to become less important on the battlefield. But in civilian life they became much more significant. Duelling became common, and the dagger formed an integral part of most self-defence, or "fencing", systems of the time.

Italian ear dagger, *c.*1500

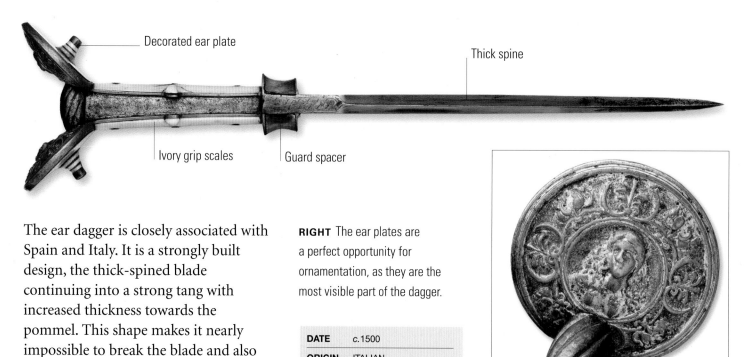

Decorated ear plate

Thick spine

Ivory grip scales

Guard spacer

The ear dagger is closely associated with Spain and Italy. It is a strongly built design, the thick-spined blade continuing into a strong tang with increased thickness towards the pommel. This shape makes it nearly impossible to break the blade and also perfectly balances it, making it seem feather-light in the hand.

RIGHT The ear plates are a perfect opportunity for ornamentation, as they are the most visible part of the dagger.

DATE	*c.*1500
ORIGIN	ITALIAN
LENGTH	unknown

German rondel dagger, early 16th century

Offset blade

Beaded rondel guard

This weapon is a good example of a late rondel dagger, the final form that this type assumed before falling out of use around the middle of the 16th century. It displays two key improvements that were made to the rondel dagger design around 1500: the rondel guard has been folded down at a 90-degree angle on the side, allowing it to rest against the body during routine wear. In addition, the blade is not located centrally in the guard but is offset towards its folded section; this also helps the weapon to rest flat against the hip.

DATE	early 16th century
ORIGIN	GERMAN
LENGTH	36cm (14.2in)

German "Landsknecht" dagger, 16th century

Copper alloy hilt

Circular katzbalger
S-guard

Strong, double-edged blade

DATE	16th century
ORIGIN	GERMAN
LENGTH	unknown

This exquisite and typologically important dagger is a very rare example of one made in the same style as the legendary *katzbalger* ("cat-fighter") short swords of the feared German and Swiss mercenaries known as Landsknechts. Hilts of this type were made not only for Landsknecht daggers and short swords, but also for their famous giant two-handed swords. The key features are the circular guard composed of a single bar forged into a tight S-shape, the slightly tapered grip flaring towards the pommel area and the small beaks on either side of the pommel.

Saxon side-ring dagger, *c.*1570

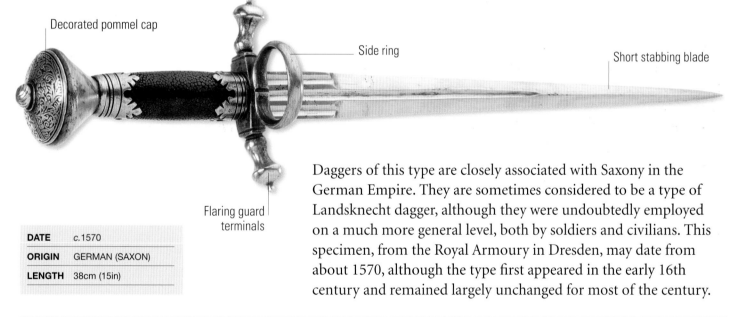

Decorated pommel cap

Side ring

Short stabbing blade

Flaring guard
terminals

DATE	c.1570
ORIGIN	GERMAN (SAXON)
LENGTH	38cm (15in)

Daggers of this type are closely associated with Saxony in the German Empire. They are sometimes considered to be a type of Landsknecht dagger, although they were undoubtedly employed on a much more general level, both by soldiers and civilians. This specimen, from the Royal Armoury in Dresden, may date from about 1570, although the type first appeared in the early 16th century and remained largely unchanged for most of the century.

Italian cross-hilt dagger, late 16th century

Narrow, single-edged blade

Inlaid wooden grip

Copper-alloy guard

DATE	late 16th century
ORIGIN	ITALIAN
LENGTH	37.2cm (14.6in)

This is a very curious form of cross-hilt dagger, quite unlike most other Renaissance designs. The very fine inlaid handle includes an integral pommel. The guard is very narrow in proportion to the length of the blade, which is quite extreme. The profile of the blade seems to be a forerunner to later types of Mediterranean fighting knife, especially the navaja.

Cinquedeas

Because their blades tend to be short and narrow, almost all forms of dagger are stabbing and slashing weapons. They cannot be used to deliver cutting blows, as their smallness rules out any sort of concussive potential. A unique exception to this rule, the cinquedea, appeared in the mid-15th century in Italy. Many cinquedeas could be described either as a dagger or short sword. They were designed primarily for dealing blows with their sharp edges rather than the point. Therefore the blade was usually very wide.

Italian short cinquedea, *c.*1500

Filigree handle inserts

Thick spine

Short dagger blade

The range of sizes in which cinquedeas were made was very wide. Although many are quite long and very effective as short cut-and-thrust swords, others, like this one, are quite small. The broad, sharply tapered blade, with its thick central spine, is ideally suited to thrusting. Here an ancient Bronze Age idea has been improved upon through its rendering in hardened steel.

DATE	c.1500
ORIGIN	ITALIAN
LENGTH	42cm (16.5in)

Italian short cinquedea, *c.*1500

Boomerang-shaped guard

Full-size hilt

Copper-alloy pommel cap

Short, sharply tapered blade

Although it is in an excavated condition, this elegant little weapon is an excellent example of the smaller form of cinquedea. The hilt is designed in the usual way for this style, being the same size as most of the larger forms, and has a copper-alloy pommel cap. The small but fearsome blade displays a needlelike reinforced point. This weapon was once in the collection of the British arms and armour scholar Charles Alexander, Baron de Cosson (1843–1929).

DATE	c.1500
ORIGIN	ITALY
LENGTH	37cm (14.5in)

Italian cinquedea, early 16th century

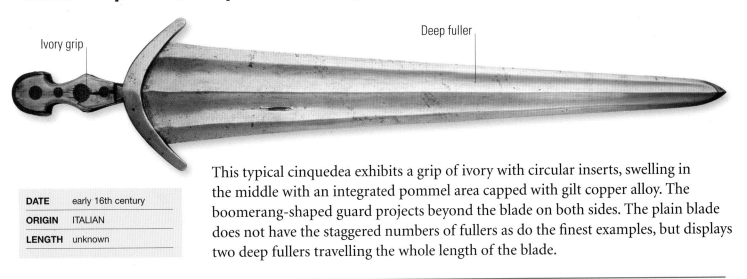

Ivory grip

Deep fuller

DATE	early 16th century
ORIGIN	ITALIAN
LENGTH	unknown

This typical cinquedea exhibits a grip of ivory with circular inserts, swelling in the middle with an integrated pommel area capped with gilt copper alloy. The boomerang-shaped guard projects beyond the blade on both sides. The plain blade does not have the staggered numbers of fullers as do the finest examples, but displays two deep fullers travelling the whole length of the blade.

North Italian cinquedea, early 16th century

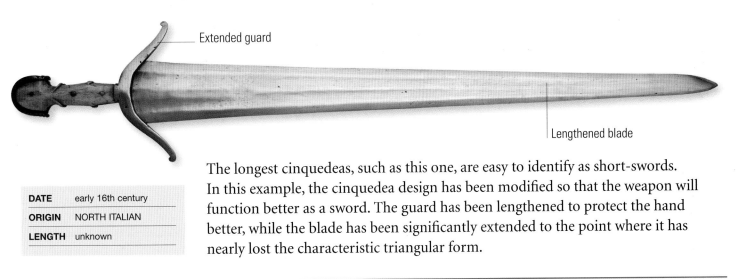

Extended guard

Lengthened blade

DATE	early 16th century
ORIGIN	NORTH ITALIAN
LENGTH	unknown

The longest cinquedeas, such as this one, are easy to identify as short-swords. In this example, the cinquedea design has been modified so that the weapon will function better as a sword. The guard has been lengthened to protect the hand better, while the blade has been significantly extended to the point where it has nearly lost the characteristic triangular form.

Replica cinquedea, 19th century

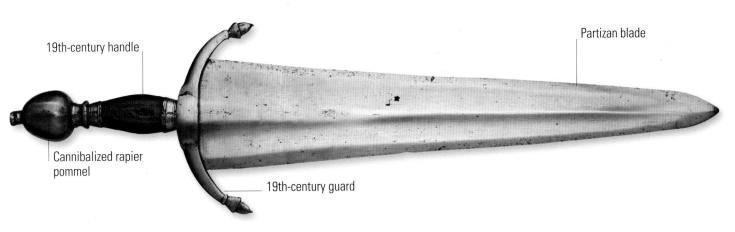

Partizan blade

19th-century handle

Cannibalized rapier pommel

19th-century guard

DATE	19th century
ORIGIN	UNKNOWN
LENGTH	unknown

Cinquedeas were very popular with 19th-century collectors. Their desirability led to a flood of fakes. Some were complete fabrications, others made up of original parts. This one has been constructed using a 16th-century rapier pommel, a 19th-century grip and guard, and the blade of a 16th- or 17th-century staff weapon.

"Side ring" parrying daggers

By the second half of the 16th century, rapier fencing almost always required a parrying dagger held in the left hand. Until the mid-17th century, parrying daggers were almost always of the "side ring" type, having a simple cross guard onto which was attached a metal ring that protected the outside of the hand. Parrying daggers were often decorated to match their rapiers, although very few matching sets survive.

German parrying dagger, late 16th century

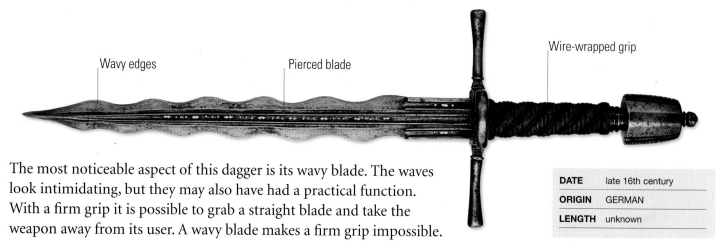

Wavy edges

Pierced blade

Wire-wrapped grip

The most noticeable aspect of this dagger is its wavy blade. The waves look intimidating, but they may also have had a practical function. With a firm grip it is possible to grab a straight blade and take the weapon away from its user. A wavy blade makes a firm grip impossible.

DATE	late 16th century
ORIGIN	GERMAN
LENGTH	unknown

English parrying dagger, late 16th century

Very worn blade

Heavily pitted surface

Fluted pommel

This rare English parrying dagger was found in the River Thames in London. After several hundred years underwater, the surface is now heavily pitted, but the fluted pommel and guard are still recognizable. This was a weapon of quality, although unusually it lacks a side ring.

DATE	late 16th century
ORIGIN	ENGLISH
LENGTH	unknown

German parrying dagger, *c.*1600

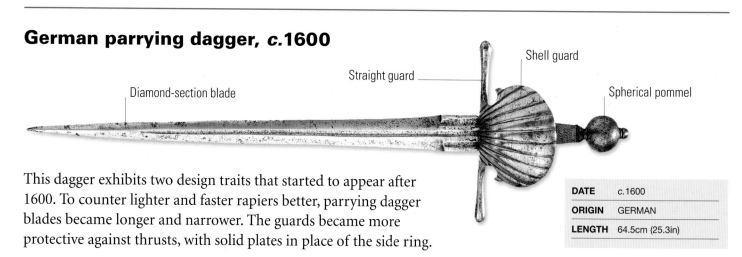

Shell guard

Straight guard

Spherical pommel

Diamond-section blade

This dagger exhibits two design traits that started to appear after 1600. To counter lighter and faster rapiers better, parrying dagger blades became longer and narrower. The guards became more protective against thrusts, with solid plates in place of the side ring.

DATE	c.1600
ORIGIN	GERMAN
LENGTH	64.5cm (25.3in)

German parrying dagger, *c.*1600

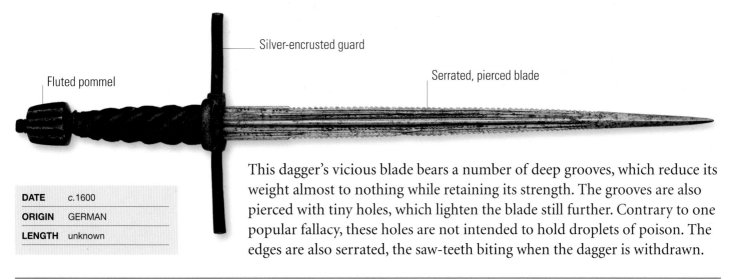

Fluted pommel

Silver-encrusted guard

Serrated, pierced blade

DATE	c.1600
ORIGIN	GERMAN
LENGTH	unknown

This dagger's vicious blade bears a number of deep grooves, which reduce its weight almost to nothing while retaining its strength. The grooves are also pierced with tiny holes, which lighten the blade still further. Contrary to one popular fallacy, these holes are not intended to hold droplets of poison. The edges are also serrated, the saw-teeth biting when the dagger is withdrawn.

German parrying dagger, *c.*1600

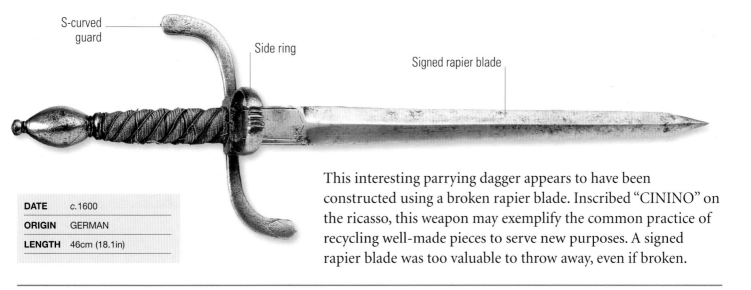

S-curved guard

Side ring

Signed rapier blade

DATE	c.1600
ORIGIN	GERMAN
LENGTH	46cm (18.1in)

This interesting parrying dagger appears to have been constructed using a broken rapier blade. Inscribed "CININO" on the ricasso, this weapon may exemplify the common practice of recycling well-made pieces to serve new purposes. A signed rapier blade was too valuable to throw away, even if broken.

Italian left-handed dagger, *c.*1600

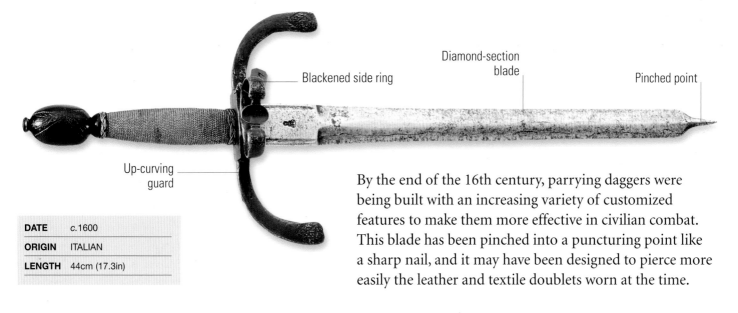

Blackened side ring

Diamond-section blade

Pinched point

Up-curving guard

DATE	c.1600
ORIGIN	ITALIAN
LENGTH	44cm (17.3in)

By the end of the 16th century, parrying daggers were being built with an increasing variety of customized features to make them more effective in civilian combat. This blade has been pinched into a puncturing point like a sharp nail, and it may have been designed to pierce more easily the leather and textile doublets worn at the time.

Spanish sword-catcher, *c.*1600

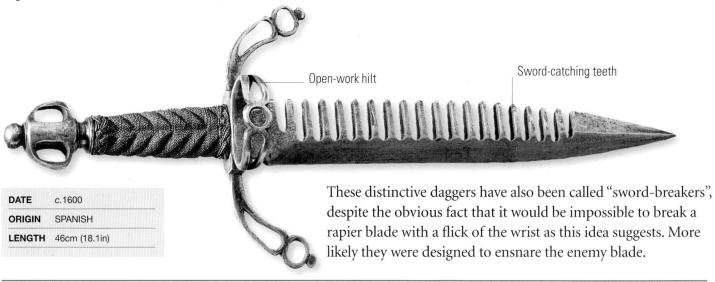

Open-work hilt

Sword-catching teeth

DATE	c.1600
ORIGIN	SPANISH
LENGTH	46cm (18.1in)

These distinctive daggers have also been called "sword-breakers", despite the obvious fact that it would be impossible to break a rapier blade with a flick of the wrist as this idea suggests. More likely they were designed to ensnare the enemy blade.

English parrying dagger, blade dated 1608

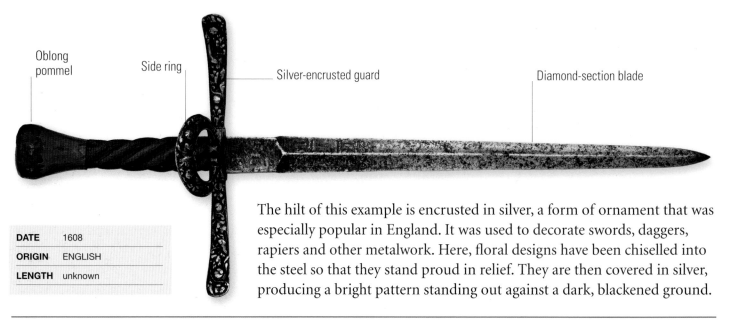

Oblong pommel

Side ring

Silver-encrusted guard

Diamond-section blade

DATE	1608
ORIGIN	ENGLISH
LENGTH	unknown

The hilt of this example is encrusted in silver, a form of ornament that was especially popular in England. It was used to decorate swords, daggers, rapiers and other metalwork. Here, floral designs have been chiselled into the steel so that they stand proud in relief. They are then covered in silver, producing a bright pattern standing out against a dark, blackened ground.

German parrying dagger, *c.*1610

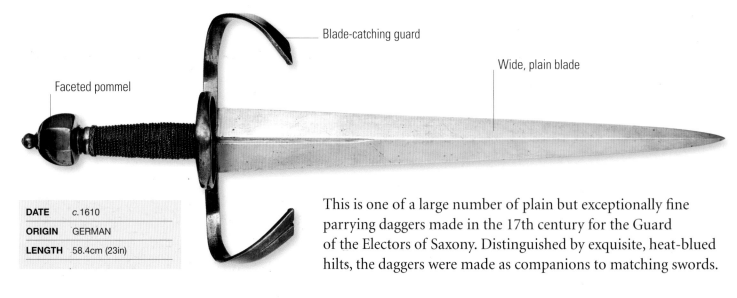

Blade-catching guard

Wide, plain blade

Faceted pommel

DATE	c.1610
ORIGIN	GERMAN
LENGTH	58.4cm (23in)

This is one of a large number of plain but exceptionally fine parrying daggers made in the 17th century for the Guard of the Electors of Saxony. Distinguished by exquisite, heat-blued hilts, the daggers were made as companions to matching swords.

English parrying dagger, early 17th century

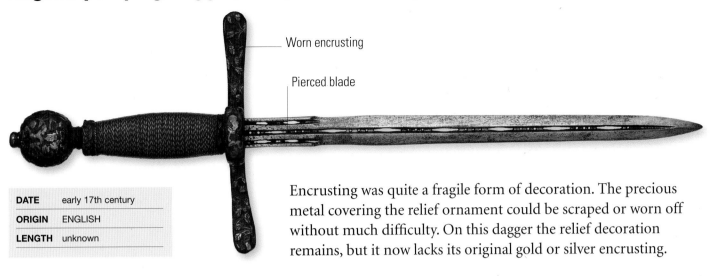

Worn encrusting

Pierced blade

DATE	early 17th century
ORIGIN	ENGLISH
LENGTH	unknown

Encrusting was quite a fragile form of decoration. The precious metal covering the relief ornament could be scraped or worn off without much difficulty. On this dagger the relief decoration remains, but it now lacks its original gold or silver encrusting.

German (?) parrying dagger, *c.*1600–20

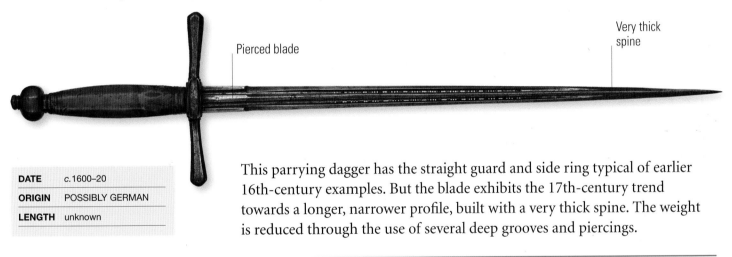

Pierced blade

Very thick spine

DATE	c.1600–20
ORIGIN	POSSIBLY GERMAN
LENGTH	unknown

This parrying dagger has the straight guard and side ring typical of earlier 16th-century examples. But the blade exhibits the 17th-century trend towards a longer, narrower profile, built with a very thick spine. The weight is reduced through the use of several deep grooves and piercings.

English dagger, *c.*1610–25

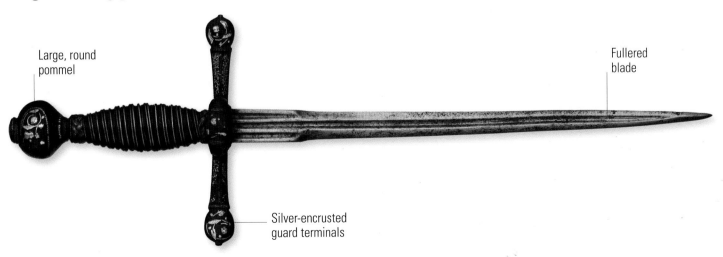

Large, round pommel

Fullered blade

Silver-encrusted guard terminals

DATE	c.1610–25
ORIGIN	ENGLISH
LENGTH	unknown

The style of the English hilt of this dagger is typical of the Jacobean period (1603–1625). The large, rounded pommel and straight cross guard with large, knob-like terminals, as well as the encrusting in silver, is typical of English taste of the early 17th century. The same design features are also found on contemporary dress swords.

17th-century main-gauche daggers

Main gauche simply means "left hand", and is therefore no more specific a term than "parrying dagger". It originally denoted a dagger that was meant for rapier and dagger fencing, as opposed to more general uses, as well as self-defence. However, over time it has come to be applied more specifically in English. Today it is used, rightly or wrongly, to refer to this quite late class of Italo-Spanish fencing dagger.

Spanish main-gauche dagger, *c.*1640

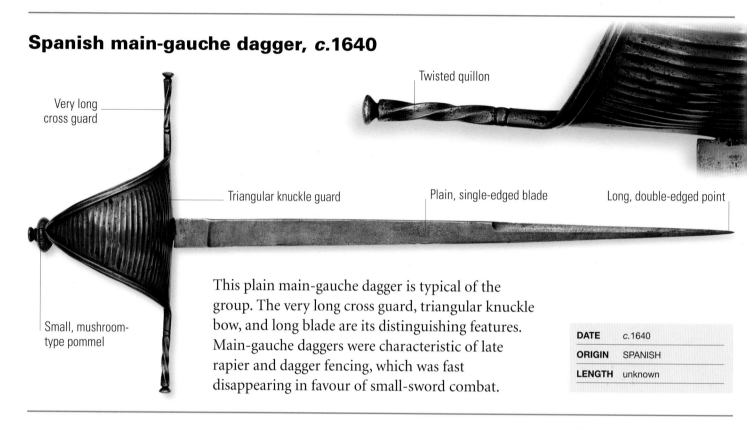

Very long cross guard

Twisted quillon

Triangular knuckle guard

Plain, single-edged blade

Long, double-edged point

Small, mushroom-type pommel

This plain main-gauche dagger is typical of the group. The very long cross guard, triangular knuckle bow, and long blade are its distinguishing features. Main-gauche daggers were characteristic of late rapier and dagger fencing, which was fast disappearing in favour of small-sword combat.

DATE	*c.*1640
ORIGIN	SPANISH
LENGTH	unknown

Southern Italian main-gauche dagger, *c.*1650

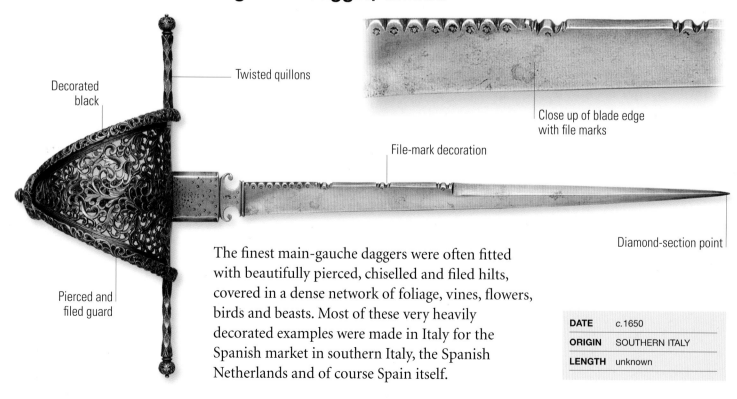

Decorated black

Twisted quillons

Close up of blade edge with file marks

File-mark decoration

Pierced and filed guard

Diamond-section point

The finest main-gauche daggers were often fitted with beautifully pierced, chiselled and filed hilts, covered in a dense network of foliage, vines, flowers, birds and beasts. Most of these very heavily decorated examples were made in Italy for the Spanish market in southern Italy, the Spanish Netherlands and of course Spain itself.

DATE	*c.*1650
ORIGIN	SOUTHERN ITALY
LENGTH	unknown

Italian main-gauche dagger, *c.*1650

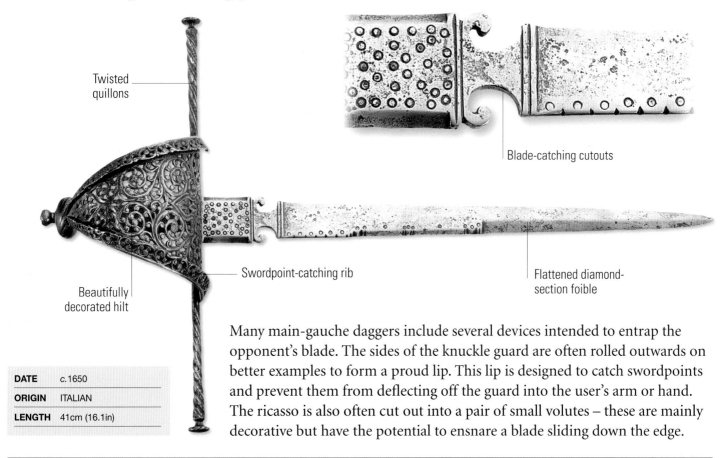

Twisted quillons

Blade-catching cutouts

Swordpoint-catching rib

Flattened diamond-section foible

Beautifully decorated hilt

DATE	*c.*1650
ORIGIN	ITALIAN
LENGTH	41cm (16.1in)

Many main-gauche daggers include several devices intended to entrap the opponent's blade. The sides of the knuckle guard are often rolled outwards on better examples to form a proud lip. This lip is designed to catch swordpoints and prevent them from deflecting off the guard into the user's arm or hand. The ricasso is also often cut out into a pair of small volutes – these are mainly decorative but have the potential to ensnare a blade sliding down the edge.

German main-gauche dagger, *c.*1660

This is an interesting German variation on the main-gauche theme. Rather than the usual triangular knuckle guard, this weapon is fitted with a rounded dish guard, acid-etched in the typical German manner, with additional bars at the edges. This piece was undoubtedly made as an en suite mate to a cup-hilt rapier with a guard having similar specific features, now lost. The blade is also typically German: very narrow with a deep central fuller along the lower half, in the trough of which is the maker's signature.

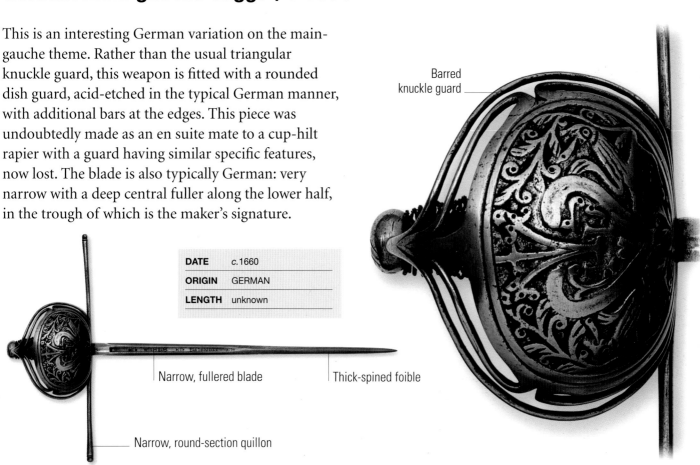

Barred knuckle guard

DATE	*c.*1660
ORIGIN	GERMAN
LENGTH	unknown

Narrow, fullered blade

Thick-spined foible

Narrow, round-section quillon

17th-century stilettos

The stiletto or stylet appeared late in the 16th century. Its development probably began with the production of miniature side-ring daggers. One of these little daggers would have been too small for fencing, but it nevertheless adhered to the fashion of the time.

Since it was useless as a fencing implement, this new form of dagger quickly lost its resemblance to the larger parrying dagger. At the height of its popularity in the mid-17th century, the all-metal stiletto was a weapon purely of last resort and of assassination.

Spanish stiletto, late 16th century

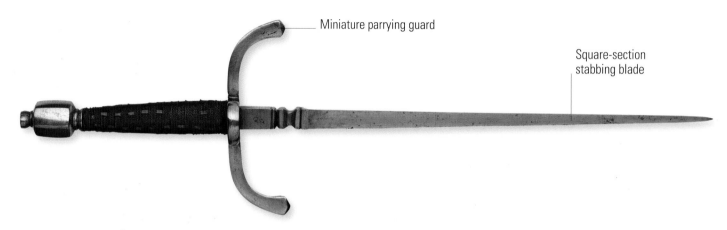

Miniature parrying guard

Square-section stabbing blade

This weapon could easily be mistaken for a typical late 16th-century parrying dagger, if not for its size and blade-type. It is perhaps three-quarters the size of a full-size parrying dagger, and thus is too small and delicate for sword-fighting. Its blade also has no sharp edges, being square in cross-section. The base or ricasso of the blade also exhibits a new decorative feature, a turned area just forward of the guard that emphasizes the delicate refinement of the weapon's lines. This "baluster-turning" quickly became a standard feature of 17th-century stilettos.

DATE	late 16th century
ORIGIN	SPANISH
LENGTH	unknown

Italian stiletto, late 16th century

Discoidal pommel

Long, triangular blade

Tapering baluster grip

Turned ricasso

This weapon is a superb demonstration of steel cutting, the hilt turned into a beautifully proportioned piece of architecture in miniature. The grip mutates skillfully from discoidal knobs into flowing tulip-like forms and continues seamlessly on to the strong needle-like blade. These all-metal weapons were accompanied by equally elegant scabbards, made entirely of steel or wood; three or four narrow lengths glued together to house the either triangular- or square-section blade and covered in paper-thin leather.

DATE	late 16th century
ORIGIN	ITALIAN
LENGTH	unknown

Italian stiletto, early 17th century

Cast copper-alloy hilt

Short, square-section blade

DATE	early 17th century
ORIGIN	ITALIAN
LENGTH	20cm (7.9in)

The hilt of this stiletto is quite different from the baluster-turned types. Instead of being cut out of a single piece of steel, the hilt of this weapon has been modelled in wax and then cast in copper alloy. The grip takes the form of an ape standing on its hind legs, and on its head stands a small animal, probably a dog.

Italian stiletto, *c.*1600

Baluster-turned hilt

Short blade

DATE	c.1600
ORIGIN	ITALIAN
LENGTH	unknown

Despite their overall smallness, most stilettos have a blade that makes up around three-quarters of their total length. This example is somewhat unusual in that its total length is divided nearly equally between blade and hilt. Such a small weapon would be especially easy to hide about one's person.

Italian stiletto, *c.*1600

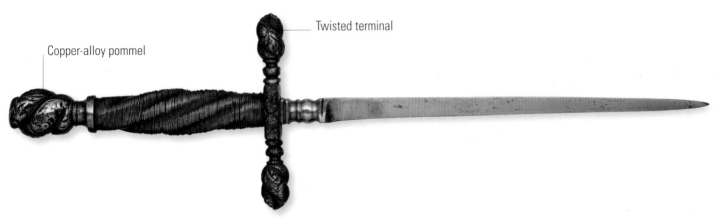

Twisted terminal

Copper-alloy pommel

DATE	c.1600
ORIGIN	POSSIBLY ITALIAN
LENGTH	unknown

This weapon shows a different construction to many other stilettos of the time. Here the pommel and guard are made in copper alloy, while the grip is wrapped in fine wire. The hilt seems out of proportion to the blade; it may be that the blade and hilt did not originally belong together.

Italian stiletto, *c.*1600

Baluster-turned ricasso

Triangular-section blade

While the blades of some stilettos are entirely plain, many of the finer examples display baluster-turnings on the base of the blade as well as the hilt. This produces an attractive unity between hilt and blade, a detail seen on very few forms of edged weapon. The grip of this example has been cut into a fluid, twisting form.

DATE	*c.*1600
ORIGIN	ITALIAN
LENGTH	unknown

Italian stiletto, *c.*1600

Spherical pommel

Swelling grip

Single cutting edge

Most all-metal stilettos with baluster-turned hilts have a spherical, discoidal or ovoid pommel, the size of which is carefully designed to balance the blade in the hand. When the perfect balance is achieved, the weapon seems almost weightless in the hand. The shape of the guard terminals usually matches that of the pommel, while the grip is usually twisted into graceful architectural forms.

DATE	*c.*1600
ORIGIN	ITALIAN
LENGTH	unknown

Italian gunner's stiletto, 1600

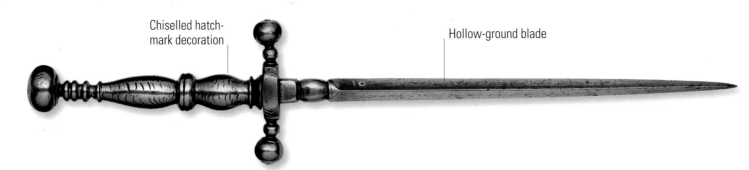

Chiselled hatch-mark decoration

Hollow-ground blade

Although the plainly smooth-surfaced stilettos are the most common, a number of examples show chiselled or punched decoration as well, such as the hatch-marks on the grip of this piece. The back of this blade is numbered, supposedly to enable the owner to determine the weight of a cannon ball so that he could range a shot effectively. However, the numbering is non-functional, and the blade is too short to be used as a measuring device.

DATE	1600
ORIGIN	ITALIAN
LENGTH	unknown

Italian stiletto, early to mid-17th century

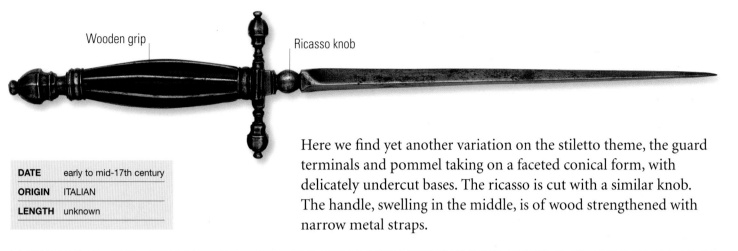

Wooden grip

Ricasso knob

DATE	early to mid-17th century
ORIGIN	ITALIAN
LENGTH	unknown

Here we find yet another variation on the stiletto theme, the guard terminals and pommel taking on a faceted conical form, with delicately undercut bases. The ricasso is cut with a similar knob. The handle, swelling in the middle, is of wood strengthened with narrow metal straps.

Spanish stiletto, late 17th century

Etched ricasso

Disk guard

Ribbed handle

DATE	late 17th century
ORIGIN	SPANISH
LENGTH	45.2cm (17.8in)

This later stiletto takes a very unusual form. While the grip flares towards the pommel, in a manner not unlike some earlier 16th-century daggers, the guard is really that of a small-sword in miniature; it is, however, too small to be an actual sword that has been broken and cut down.

Spanish stiletto dividers, *c.*1700–50

Splitting blade

Pivoting joint

Etched and gilt decoration

DATE	c.1700–50
ORIGIN	SPANISH
LENGTH	unknown

It was very popular in the Renaissance to draw parallels between the fighting arts and the sciences. Fight masters often saw themselves as scientists as well as martial artists, and they strove to communicate their skills in a learned, scientific way. This led to a fashionable association between weapons and scientific instruments, and thus noblemen often liked to collect both. The idea of combining the two into a single object, the stiletto that split apart to form a pair of architect's dividers, first occurred in the 16th century and was repeated many times.

17th-century plug bayonets

At some early date someone had the idea of whittling down the wooden haft of a knife and plugging it into the muzzle of a gun, turning it into a thrusting spear. This probably happened in Europe, and some believe the term "bayonet" is derived from the name of the French cutlery town, Bayonne. The gun was of course disabled, but if a spear was needed then the enemy were too close for the lack of a gun to be a problem.

British officer's or sporting bayonet, c.1660

Bone/ivory hilt

Decorative cross-guard finials (one missing)

Unusual curved blade

The elaborate and decorated bone or ivory hilt suggests this bayonet was for an officer or for sporting use. With such hard material, it is doubtful whether the hilt could have been secured in the muzzle and there are no marks to indicate its use in this way. The weapon was probably used merely as a knife.

DATE	c.1660
ORIGIN	BRITISH
LENGTH	41cm (16.1in)

British officer's or sporting bayonet, c.1660

Bone/ivory hilt

Dagger-type blade

Decorative cross-guard finials

This is another example of a decorated bone or ivory hilt but slightly less elaborate than the one above. While this weapon has a more conventional blade, both have a number of features that are almost identical, such as the tang buttons on the pommels and the cross guards, suggesting that they may be by the same maker.

DATE	c.1660
ORIGIN	BRITISH
LENGTH	45.1cm (17.8in)

British military bayonet, c.1680

Round hilt with pommel cap and cross guard (damaged)

Wide, thin, single-edged blade with false edge

Common to all plug bayonets is a slender, round, tapering handle with a bulbous swelling near where it joins the blade. The handle has to be resilient enough to allow it to be pushed into the muzzle and stay there, but not so tightly that it can't be removed. Most handles are therefore wooden as this material is slightly elastic.

DATE	c.1680
ORIGIN	BRITISH
LENGTH	45.8cm (18in)

British officer's bayonet, 1686

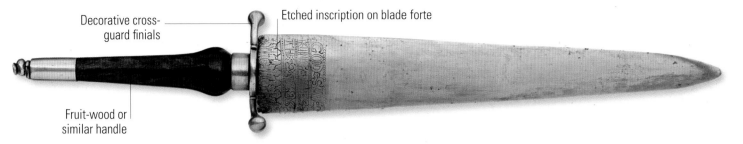

Decorative cross-guard finials

Etched inscription on blade forte

Fruit-wood or similar handle

DATE	1686
ORIGIN	BRITISH
LENGTH	46cm (18.1in)

This plug bayonet conforms more to the general type of serviceable military bayonet with its wooden handle, but it is of better quality than usual, suggesting that the weapon may have belonged to an officer. This is supported by the fact that the blade is inscribed "GOD SAVE KING JAMES THE 2 1686", which is an unusual feature on any type of bayonet and is useful for dating this general style.

British officer's bayonet, 1686

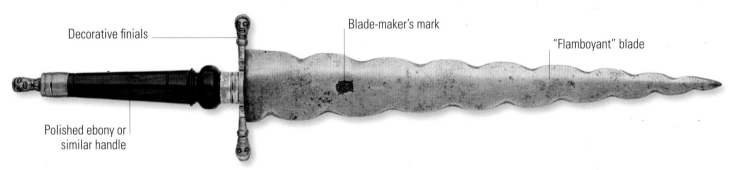

Decorative finials

Blade-maker's mark

"Flamboyant" blade

Polished ebony or similar handle

DATE	1686
ORIGIN	BRITISH
LENGTH	45.4cm (17.9in)

A bayonet as distinctive and of such quality as this one, with its highly polished grip of either ebony or other exotic wood and its gilded brass fittings, was undoubtedly used by an officer. The pommel, tang button and cross guard show close similarity to those of the two officer's bayonets on the previous page. The most distinctive feature is obviously the blade with its sinuous wavy edges, often referred to as "flamboyant" because of its likeness to a flickering flame.

Scandinavian officer's bayonet, 1700

Bulbous finials

Flattened diamond-section blade

Hilt with decorated gilt brass fittings

Blade-maker's mark

DATE	1700
ORIGIN	POSS. SCANDINAVIAN
LENGTH	48.7cm (19.1in)

A good-quality, possibly Scandinavian, bayonet. It has a wooden grip, painted possibly in imitation of tortoiseshell or an exotic wood, and gilded decorated brass hilt fittings. The cross guard with its downturned finials is more reminiscent of many 19th-century sword bayonets than of the typical English plug bayonet. Like others of this class, it shows few if any signs of having been thrust into a muzzle.

17th- and 18th-century civilian daggers

Walking-out and dress-type swords and daggers became a prominent feature among the rising classes in the period following the Reformation. Although such weapons were still very expensive, there was a larger class of people who could now afford them.

Daggers and knives that were primarily intended for functional use were often completed to a level of decoration that suggested the object might also be worn as an item of jewellery or statement of rank, as well as having a more practical day-to-day use.

English dagger, 1628

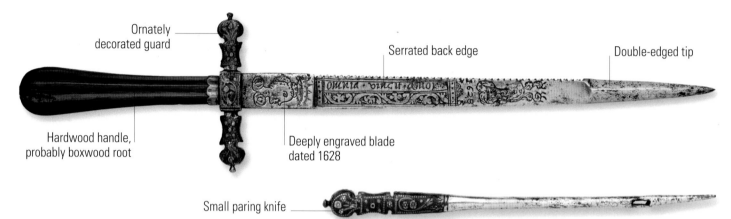

Ornately decorated guard

Serrated back edge

Double-edged tip

Hardwood handle, probably boxwood root

Deeply engraved blade dated 1628

Small paring knife

This very fine, high-quality combination set comprises a main dagger and matching paring knife, both of which fit together in the same scabbard. The blade of the main knife is beautifully decorated with deep engraving. The serrated edge had a practical application in that when cutting a joint of meat it could sever through the toughest parts; the paring knife was used to secure the treated item in position.

DATE	1628
ORIGIN	ENGLISH
LENGTH	32.7cm (12.9in)

The cutler's trade

In 17th- and 18th-century Europe, improved trade routes meant that raw materials such as iron were transported more easily to the main commercial towns and cities. Aided too by advances in industrial power, Solingen in Germany and Sheffield in England became important centres of blade production.

It took many craftsmen to produce a good-quality edged weapon. The manufacture of the blade was a highly skilled art and there were also specialist cross-guard and pommel makers, scalers (grip makers) and scabbard and sheath makers.

RIGHT A German bladesmith in his workshop. Many of Europe's best cutlers worked in Solingen, Germany and Sheffield, England.

English dagger, 1631

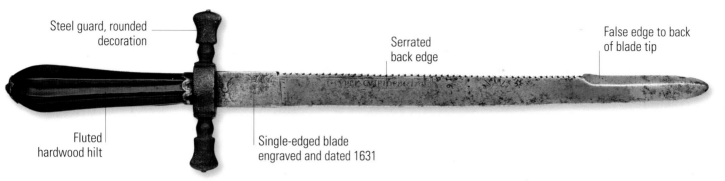

Steel guard, rounded decoration

Serrated back edge

False edge to back of blade tip

Fluted hardwood hilt

Single-edged blade engraved and dated 1631

DATE	1631
ORIGIN	ENGLISH
LENGTH	26.3cm (10.4in)

This is a fine example of a gentleman's utility knife, having a fluted wooden grip, and a steel ferrule and cross guard. The latter is simplistically decorated with rounded finials. The blade is flat and single-edged, yet has a sharpened false edge at the tip. The back edge of the blade is serrated. Engraved decoration on the blade indicates that it dates from 1631.

English dagger, mid-17th century

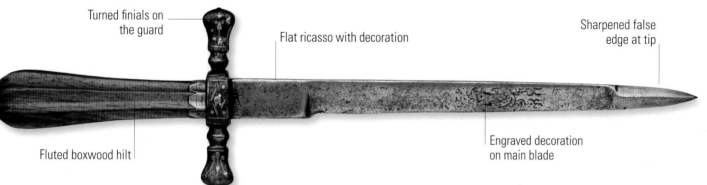

Turned finials on the guard

Flat ricasso with decoration

Sharpened false edge at tip

Fluted boxwood hilt

Engraved decoration on main blade

DATE	mid-17th century
ORIGIN	ENGLISH
LENGTH	31.4cm (12.4in)

This dagger has an interesting blade construction. The flat ricasso extends the back flat of the blade along almost the full length, effectively making this a single-edged knife with a double-edged tip. The steel guard is nicely formed with domed terminals and decoration on the quillon block. The fluted boxwood hilt is typical.

English quillon dagger, 1678

Slender quillons with rounded finials

Sharpened edge

Wooden haft, with wire-wrapped grip

Broad ricasso with dedication

DATE	1678
ORIGIN	ENGLISH
LENGTH	31.4cm (12.4in)

This English quillon dagger is inscribed on the blade "Memento Godfrey...1678". The long blade is single-edged for most of the length, and the ricasso area is broad and flat with the inscribed decoration. The tang of the blade is concealed by an ovoid-section wooden grip, which is covered with a twisted-wire wrapping.

Dutch or German quillon-form hunting dagger, *c.*1700

S-shaped guard with lion's-head finials

Single-edged blade, double-edged at tip

Carved wood grip

Inscribed decoration on blade

DATE	c.1700
ORIGIN	DUTCH/GERMAN
LENGTH	40.8cm (16.1in)

The structure and style of the grip on this weapon suggests that it is a hunting knife, and most probably Dutch or perhaps German in origin. It dates from the latter part of the 1600s or possibly the early 1700s. The ornate cross guard is brass, S-shaped and decorated with miniature lion's-head finials. The long, narrow, tapered blade has an inscribed decoration and is single-edged along most of its length, narrowing to a double-edged tip.

French or German stiletto, early to mid-18th century

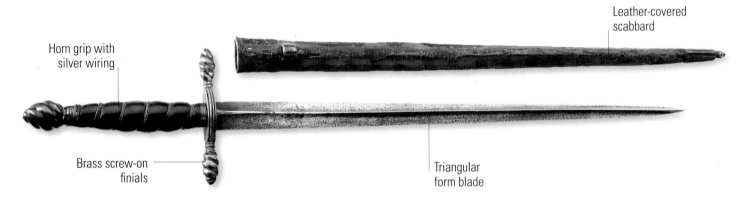

Leather-covered scabbard

Horn grip with silver wiring

Brass screw-on finials

Triangular form blade

This stiletto is French or possibly German. The triangular-section blade has a forte with remnants of decorative etching and gilding and the point has been lightly resharpened. Grooved finials are screwed onto quillons, the grip covered with silver-wire winding. The front of the brass scabbard has a leather cover; the rear is engraved with scrolling vine patterns.

DATE	early to mid-18th century
ORIGIN	FRENCH/GERMAN
LENGTH	48cm (18.9in)

Spanish or Italian short stiletto, mid-18th century

Blade double-edged towards tip

Horn grip

Decorated ricasso

This short thrusting stiletto is possibly the accompanying knife to a larger hunting weapon. It has an interesting horn, or narwhal, grip with decoration and wiring. The steel pommel cap has engraved decoration, and the steel ricasso of the blade a chiselled decoration. The blade has a long fore edge and a short false edge.

DATE	mid-18th century
ORIGIN	SPANISH/ITALIAN
LENGTH	24.9cm (9.8in)

Italian or Dalmatian Schiovona dagger, 1790

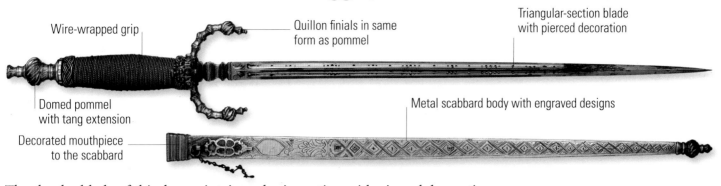

Wire-wrapped grip

Quillon finials in same form as pommel

Triangular-section blade with pierced decoration

Domed pommel with tang extension

Decorated mouthpiece to the scabbard

Metal scabbard body with engraved designs

The slender blade of this dagger is triangular in section with pierced decoration on the facings. The ricasso of the blade is decoratively segmented and may disguise a join where a new tang has been added. The pommel and cross-guard terminals are of matching design and the centre section of the guard is decorated with coloured, semi-precious stones. The grip is of wood with wire wrapping.

DATE	1790
ORIGIN	ITALIAN/DALMATIAN
LENGTH	45cm (17.8in)

Italian dagger, late 18th century

Decorated metal scabbard chape

Metal scabbard throat

Fluted wood grip

Double-edged tip

DATE	late 18th century
ORIGIN	ITALIAN
LENGTH	35cm (13.8in)

This late 18th-century knife is of a pattern popular around the Mediterranean. It has a distinctive blade with a double fuller, which converges towards the blade tip, and the ricasso features a relief-engraved emblem of a cockerel. The fluted wood grip has polished steel mounts, and the leather scabbard has steel mounts.

Italian utility knife, late 18th century

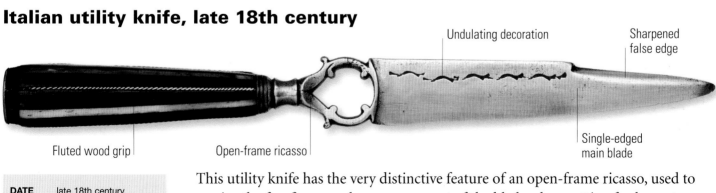

Undulating decoration

Sharpened false edge

Fluted wood grip

Open-frame ricasso

Single-edged main blade

DATE	late 18th century
ORIGIN	ITALIAN
LENGTH	24.5cm (9.6in)

This utility knife has the very distinctive feature of an open-frame ricasso, used to receive the forefinger and ease movement of the blade when cutting fresh meat on the bone. The blade shape is designed for both cutting and filleting. It is possibly the accompanying knife to a larger hunting knife set and probably Italian in origin.

18th- and 19th-century naval dirks

It was in the latter half of the 18th century that some short swords and dirks started to be carried by midshipmen and officers of the English Navy, and often these were conversions from other, broken weapons.

Such damaged weapons were far too valuable to be discarded, but instead could be resurrected as short swords, and the evolution into short dirks appears to have been influenced by this trend.

French long-bladed dirk (conversion), late 18th century

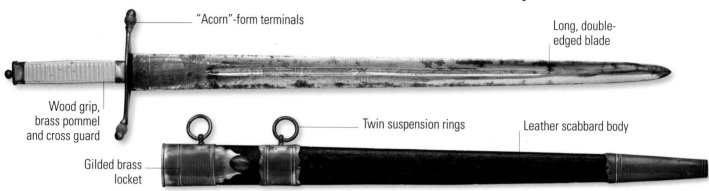

"Acorn"-form terminals

Long, double-edged blade

Wood grip, brass pommel and cross guard

Gilded brass locket

Twin suspension rings

Leather scabbard body

The blade of this conversion dirk appears to be from a hunting sword and it is engraved with scrolling designs. The grip's square form could be French and the leather scabbard appears to have gilded brass fittings. The "acorn" decoration on the cross guard doesn't seem to fit "naval traditions".

DATE	late 18th century
ORIGIN	FRENCH
LENGTH	58cm (23in)

British (?) long-bladed naval dirk (conversion), late 18th century

Shortened blade from a different sword

Bone hilt housing tang of blade

Unusual double guard

This interesting dirk is composed partially from a short sword, possibly a spadroon. The assembly of the blade, cross guard, grip and pommel is secured by drawing the tang of the blade through the pommel cap and peening (hammering) it into place.

DATE	late 18th century
ORIGIN	POSSIBLY BRITISH
LENGTH	61cm (24in)

British naval dirk (conversion), early 19th century

Downturned quillons with bulbous terminal

Blade from sword or bayonet

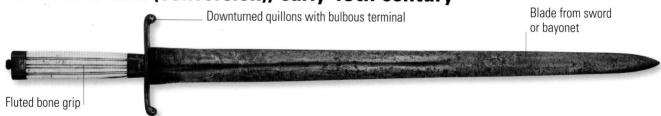

Fluted bone grip

This is quite a substantial item, and appears to be more similar to a short sword than a dirk. The blade is not dissimilar to some of the variations found on the bayonet for the English Baker rifle, although it is by no means certain that this is what this weapon has been converted from.

DATE	early 19th century
ORIGIN	BRITISH
LENGTH	58cm (23in)

American naval dirk, early 19th century

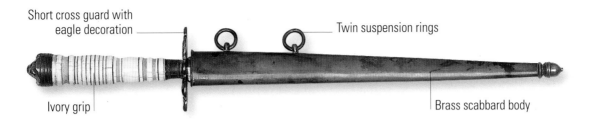

Short cross guard with eagle decoration

Twin suspension rings

Ivory grip

Brass scabbard body

DATE	early 19th century
ORIGIN	AMERICAN
LENGTH	19cm (7.5in)

This American Naval dirk has a brightly polished, slender, double-edged blade with a flattened diamond section. There are gilt-copper hilt fittings and a lion's-mask pommel, and an embossed cross guard with an eagle head holding a ball in its beak. The grip is turned ivory. The gilded brass scabbard has twin suspension rings.

Spanish naval officer's hanger sword, early 19th century

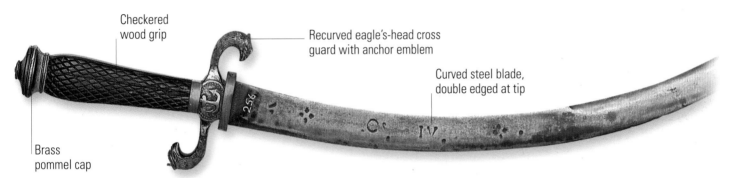

Checkered wood grip

Recurved eagle's-head cross guard with anchor emblem

Curved steel blade, double edged at tip

Brass pommel cap

DATE	early 19th century
ORIGIN	SPANISH
LENGTH	44.5cm (17.5in)

The curved blade of this Spanish naval officer's hanger sword from the early 1800s is single-edged with a double-edged tip. Stampings on the blade indicate "Cs IV" (Carlos IV, who died in 1819). The hilt fittings are brass, the pommel is in the form of a flattened urn, and the cross guard is decorated with eagle's-head terminals and an anchor emblem on the quillon block.

British long-bladed naval dirk, early 19th century

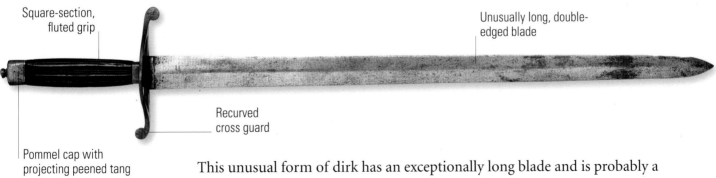

Square-section, fluted grip

Unusually long, double-edged blade

Recurved cross guard

Pommel cap with projecting peened tang

DATE	early 19th century
ORIGIN	BRITISH
LENGTH	60.7cm (24in)

This unusual form of dirk has an exceptionally long blade and is probably a conversion that has used the blade from some other weapon. The wood grip is square in cross-section, with grooved fluting on all sides. There is a copper or brass square-form pommel cap on the hilt, with the blade tang drawn through and peened. There is a metal ferrule at the base of the grip, and a cross guard with upturned and downturned quillons.

French boarding dagger, mid-19th century

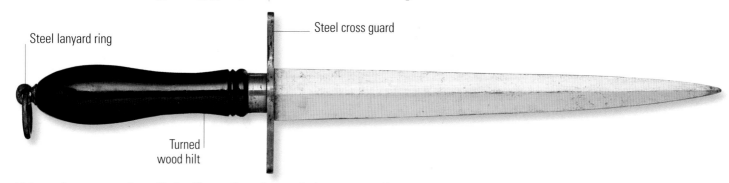

Steel lanyard ring

Steel cross guard

Turned wood hilt

Although commonly called a "boarding dagger", this is actually an "on-board" utility knife. Whereas knives were not normally carried on deck (for safety reasons), they were often required for work on the rigging. The lanyard ring was secured to a cord tied to the belt, as a prevention against loss if dropped.

DATE	mid-19th century
ORIGIN	FRENCH
LENGTH	35.6cm (14in)

British naval hanger, c.1850

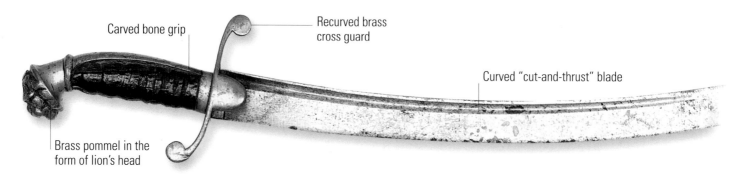

Carved bone grip

Recurved brass cross guard

Curved "cut-and-thrust" blade

Brass pommel in the form of lion's head

This naval hanger has a long, curved blade of the "cut-and-thrust" form, being mostly single-edged with a flat back and long fuller. The last third of the blade is double-edged. The pommel, backstrap, ferrule and cross guard are made of brass, the pommel decoration being that of a lion's head. There is no record of this pattern of hanger being issued to the English Navy; it is probable that they were sold to privateers, or even as export items to foreign naval powers.

DATE	c.1850
ORIGIN	BRITISH
LENGTH	45.7cm (18in)

Spanish naval dirk, 19th century

Double-edged blade with central spine

Plain steel cross guard

Turned steel hilt fittings

This is not strictly a naval dirk but more of a maritime knife used by sailors. The blade has a long, flat ricasso which tapers to a point to form the central spine of the blade. The cross guard is plain, flat and tapered, and the hilt is composed of an elongated ferrule and pommel cap connected by the central grip made of bone. The fluted grooves are not simply decoration but intended to improve the grip.

DATE	19th century
ORIGIN	SPANISH
LENGTH	32cm (12.6in)

Georgian dirks

The term "Georgian dirk" really embraces weapons from the mid-1700s to the start of Queen Victoria's reign. The Industrial Revolution had evolved, and more efficient means for the production of metal wares had come into being, as well as a growing middle class of people who could afford expensive items. The Georgian dirk offered a form of weapon that was also ornate enough to be considered a form of male jewellery.

British Georgian naval dirk, early 19th century

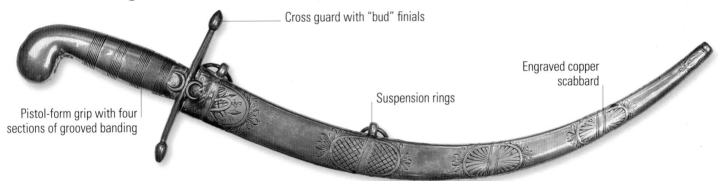

Cross guard with "bud" finials

Engraved copper scabbard

Suspension rings

Pistol-form grip with four sections of grooved banding

DATE	early 19th century
ORIGIN	BRITISH
LENGTH	22.8cm (9in)

The scabbard carrying the slender, curved, single-edged blade is engraved copper, with gilding featuring scrolling and checkering designs. Metal portions of the hilt are made of copper with gilding. The cross guard features "bud"-type finials and a double-crescent langet at the centre of the guard.

British Georgian dirk, early 19th century

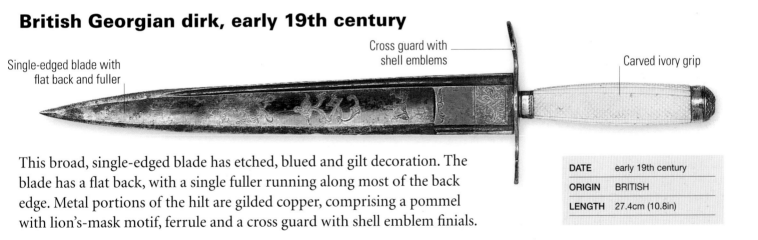

Cross guard with shell emblems

Carved ivory grip

Single-edged blade with flat back and fuller

This broad, single-edged blade has etched, blued and gilt decoration. The blade has a flat back, with a single fuller running along most of the back edge. Metal portions of the hilt are gilded copper, comprising a pommel with lion's-mask motif, ferrule and a cross guard with shell emblem finials.

DATE	early 19th century
ORIGIN	BRITISH
LENGTH	27.4cm (10.8in)

British Georgian naval dirk, early 19th century

Scrimshaw-engraved ivory grip

Suspension rings

Gilded metal scabbard

DATE	early 19th century
ORIGIN	BRITISH
LENGTH	18.4cm (7.25in)

This unusual Georgian naval dirk has a scrimshaw-decorated ivory grip depicting a rope and anchor. The blade is of shallow diamond section, etched with trophies, wreaths and flourishes. There are gilded copper fittings with a screw-on pommel and an unusual cross guard in the form of an elongated eight-pointed star.

British Georgian naval dirk, *c.*1820

Silver-decorated pommel

Suspension rings

Decorated brass scabbard

The blade of this unusual Georgian naval dirk has a plain, flattened diamond section. The turned ivory grip has a silver pique-work design of a fouled anchor in an oval, and the initials "RC" in scrolls. The small, rounded rectangular brass guard has a matching pommel embossed with tiny scales within a studded border. The brass scabbard is ornately engraved with a button chape and two suspension rings.

DATE	*c.*1820
ORIGIN	BRITISH
LENGTH	21.6cm (8.5in)

British Georgian naval dirk, *c.*1820

Turned ivory grip

Coiled snake-design pommel

Ornate buckles for former handling straps

Gilded metal scabbard, fully engraved

This Georgian naval dirk has a blade of shallow diamond section. The blade is etched with a crown, anchor and foliage designs. The grip is turned ivory, topped with a metal pommel bearing the unusual design of a coiled snake. The cross guard is formed as a small oval disc, engraved with the legend *Palmam Qui Meruit Feriat* ("Let him who merits bear the palm").

DATE	*c.*1820
ORIGIN	BRITISH
LENGTH	17.8cm (7in)

British Georgian dirk hanger, *c.*1820

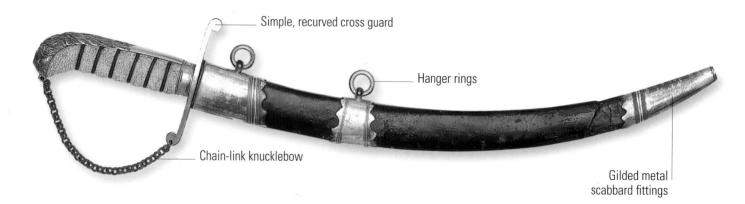

Simple, recurved cross guard

Hanger rings

Chain-link knucklebow

Gilded metal scabbard fittings

This dirk is like a small-sized hanger featuring a curved, single-edged blade etched with a decoration consisting of scrolled foliage, and a panel with the engraved initials "CLP" – presumably those of the former owner. The hilt comprises a brass backstrap in the form of a lion's head, with a segmented bone grip and gold wiring. The chain-link knucklebow appears to be a contemporary addition. The scabbard is made of black leather, with gilded metal fittings.

DATE	*c.*1820
ORIGIN	BRITISH
LENGTH	30.5cm (12in)

British Georgian naval officer's dirk, *c.*1820

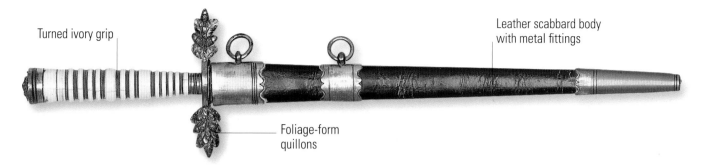

Turned ivory grip

Leather scabbard body with metal fittings

Foliage-form quillons

DATE	c.1820
ORIGIN	BRITISH
LENGTH	27.4cm (10.8in)

This extremely handsome naval dirk is reputed to have belonged to a member of the Suckling family. The blade is etched with the manufacturer's details: "Drury, sword cutler, 32 Strand, London". The blade is also etched with designs of a rope and fouled anchor, military trophies and scrolling foliage. There are gilded metal fittings to the hilt and to the black leather scabbard.

The Georgian Era

The period of British history known as the Georgian era spanned 1714–1830 and is named after its four monarchs, George I, George II, George III and George IV. It also included the nine-year Regency period presided over by the Prince Regent (later George IV). A time of huge social, political and economic change in Britain, it was an era that saw the agricultural revolution and the birth of the industrial age. Overseas, the battle for the American colonies was lost but the acquisition of foreign lands heralded an expanding empire.

The British throne had passed to the Hanoverian George I (1714–27) on the death of Queen Anne. His disinterest in ruling led to the appointment of the first Prime Minister. George II's reign (1727–60) saw territorial gains in America and Africa during the Seven Years War with France. Bouts of insanity rendered George III (1760–1820) unstable and in 1810 his son George became Prince Regent. A flamboyant figure famous for his extravagant lifestyle, his reign marked the start of social, legal and electoral reforms. His brother William IV succeeded him to the throne in 1830.

RIGHT A portrait of King George I painted by Sir Godfrey Kneller (1646–1723). The German-speaking king never learned English and preferred ministers to rule on his behalf.

Highland daggers and dirks

The distinctive Scottish dirk evolved from the early style "kidney dagger", which in turn had been developed from the "ballock knife". Two bulbous kidney-shaped lobes in the place where the quillons of the guard might exist were a characteristic feature. The knife was originally intended as an all-round survival and utility item, and some early examples had a serrated back edge. In later years, this feature became a symbolic series of indentations on the back of the blade, rather than being a serviceable sawtooth.

English or Scottish dudgeon-hilted dirk, 1603

Fluted dudgeon wood grip

Long, double-edged blade

This is a fine example of an early English, or probably Scottish, dirk having the characteristic "kidney-shaped" lobes covering the shoulders of the blade. The hilt is made of dudgeon, or boxwood root, with the tang of the blade drawn through and peened over. The blade is long, with a strong central spine running the entire length.

DATE	1603
ORIGIN	ENGLISH/SCOTTISH
LENGTH	46cm (18.1in)

Scottish dirk, c.1740

Carved wood grip | Heart-shaped escutcheon

Long, single-edged blade with flat back

This dirk, from the time of the Scottish Uprisings, has a long, single-edged blade, double-edged at the tip, and with a flat back and long fuller. The tang of the blade is drawn through the hilt and secured through a metal disc that protects the top of the wood grip. The grip itself is carved in a Celtic form of entwined design. The guard of the hilt forms an elliptical sleeve covering the shoulders of the blade.

DATE	c.1740
ORIGIN	SCOTTISH
LENGTH	41.5cm (16.3in)

Scottish dirk with ivory grip, mid-18th century

Carved bone or ivory hilt

Long, single-edged blade with flat back

This fine dirk has an ivory, or walrus tusk, hilt comprised of three sections. The pommel portion features a protective metal plate on the top, through which the tang of the blade has been drawn and secured. The grip is carved with a curved fluting, and the guard comprises an oval sleeve fitting over the shoulders of the blade.

DATE	mid-18th century
ORIGIN	SCOTTISH
LENGTH	50.3cm (19.8in)

Scottish military dress dirk, 1879

Single-edged blade with false edge tip, and etched decoration

Carved wood grip, balustrade form

Reinforced sleeve over blade shoulders

DATE	1879
ORIGIN	SCOTTISH
LENGTH	37cm (14.6in)

This dirk is the military form as adopted by the Highland regiments from the mid-1800s and is intended for parade and dress wear. The carved wood grip mimics the design of woven straps secured in place with steel pins. The base of the grip features a metal ferrule with the words "GORDON HIGHLANDERS".

Scottish full dress Highlander dirk, *c.*1900

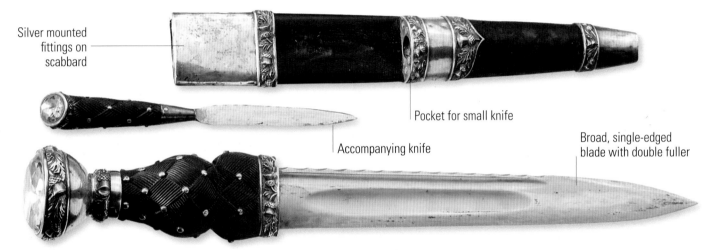

Silver mounted fittings on scabbard

Pocket for small knife

Accompanying knife

Broad, single-edged blade with double fuller

DATE	c.1900
ORIGIN	SCOTTISH
LENGTH	40cm (15.7in)

A full dress dirk with Cairngorm stones set in the pommel of both the dirk and the small knife. An interesting feature of the blade is the flat back with implied serration, and the two fullers – one thin and long close to the back, the other broader and shorter on the main body. Metal fittings are of finely chiselled silver.

Scottish Highland dirk with Cairngorm, *c.*1900

Decorated silver fittings and two pockets on scabbard

Faceted quartz stone set in pommel

Weave-design decorated grip

Single-edged blade with double-edged tip

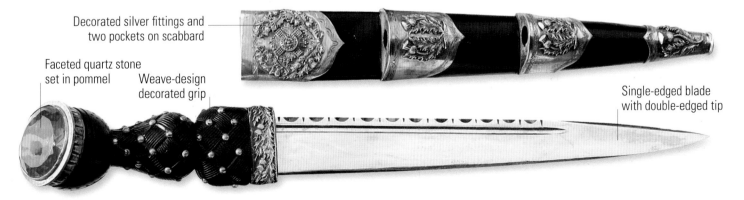

DATE	c.1900
ORIGIN	SCOTTISH
LENGTH	47cm (18.5in)

This is a full dress Highland dirk. The carved wood grip has silver mounts, the pommel mount featuring a faceted quartz stone (Cairngorm), and a basket-weave design to the grip with silver pins. The single-edged blade bears a scalloped design on the back (symbolic of a serrated edge). The scabbard pockets are for a knife and fork.

19th-century hunting and Bowie knives

The period from the end of the Napoleonic Wars in 1815 until the early 20th century heralded a boom period for European knife-makers. New markets were being established, primarily in the newly formed United States of America. In the aftermath of the American Civil War, economic development was fast expanding and the demand for commercial products was higher than could be supplied by the domestic economy. Europe took advantage of the new American market and exports of cutlery soared.

British knife by Wostenholm, Sheffield, mid-19th century

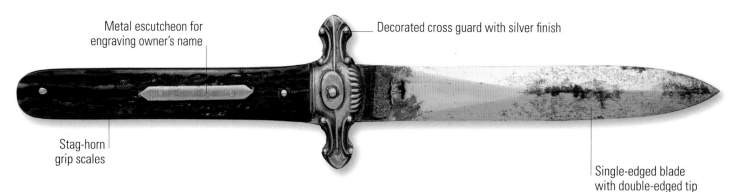

Metal escutcheon for engraving owner's name

Decorated cross guard with silver finish

Stag-horn grip scales

Single-edged blade with double-edged tip

A deluxe-quality British knife, manufactured by the firm of George Wostenholm – at one time the second-largest knife manufacturer in Sheffield. The blade and tang are constructed of a single piece of steel, the tang area (hilt) being faced with stag-horn scales secured by three rivets. The middle rivet is covered by a metal escutcheon (which could be engraved with an owner's name or initials). The steel guard is decorated with a scalloped design and is polished and nickel-plated. The straight, double-edged blade features an elongated ricasso which tapers into a central spine.

DATE	mid-19th century
ORIGIN	BRITISH
LENGTH	34cm (13.4in)

American CSA fighting knife, 19th century

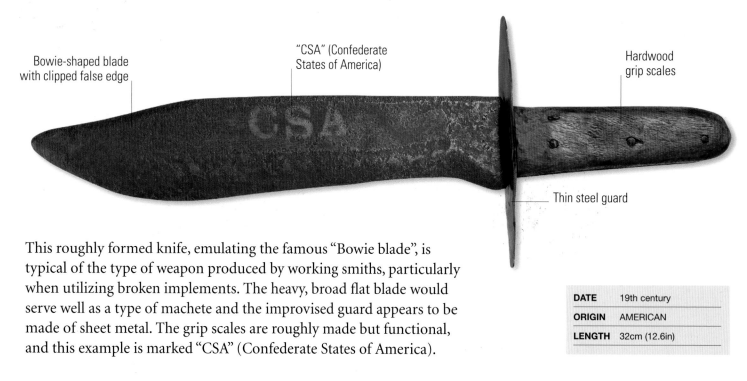

Bowie-shaped blade with clipped false edge

"CSA" (Confederate States of America)

Hardwood grip scales

Thin steel guard

This roughly formed knife, emulating the famous "Bowie blade", is typical of the type of weapon produced by working smiths, particularly when utilizing broken implements. The heavy, broad flat blade would serve well as a type of machete and the improvised guard appears to be made of sheet metal. The grip scales are roughly made but functional, and this example is marked "CSA" (Confederate States of America).

DATE	19th century
ORIGIN	AMERICAN
LENGTH	32cm (12.6in)

British coffin-handled hunting knife, mid-19th century

Stamped or etched brand name and trademark, and emblem of pyramids

Carved horn grip scales

Silver- or nickel-finished escutcheon

DATE	mid-19th century
ORIGIN	BRITISH
LENGTH	unknown

The "coffin-handle" knife was so named because of its superficial resemblance in shape to wooden coffins of the time. The design of this knife was particularly popular in the mid-19th century, and the British concern of George Nixon, etched on the blade, was an established knife-maker in this style. The Nixon name later changed to Nixon & Winterbottom.

British Bowie knife by Rodgers, mid- to late 19th century

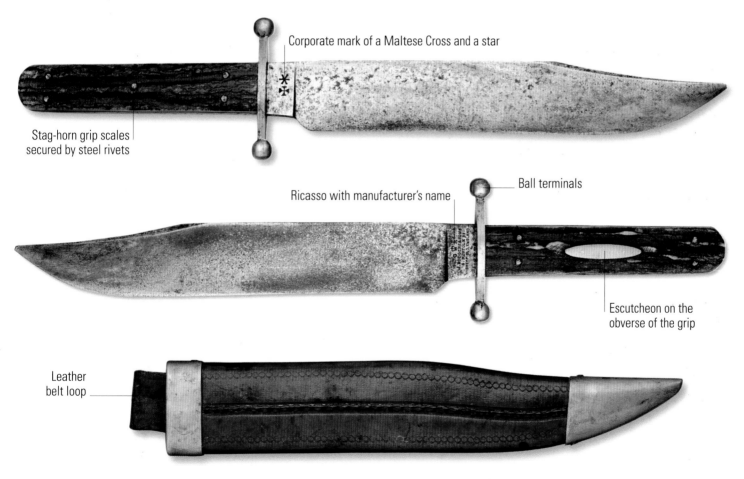

Corporate mark of a Maltese Cross and a star

Stag-horn grip scales secured by steel rivets

Ricasso with manufacturer's name

Ball terminals

Escutcheon on the obverse of the grip

Leather belt loop

DATE	mid- to late 19th century
ORIGIN	BRITISH
LENGTH	31.1cm (12.2in)

A fine example of a Bowie knife by Joseph Rodgers of Sheffield. The typical blade broadens slightly towards the tip, where the flattened back edge forms a sharpened false edge. The body of the blade is sharpened for the entire length, except at the ricasso where it narrows and thickens. The simple straight hilt has stag-horn grip scales. The cross guard is steel and nickel-plated with ball-end finials. The leather scabbard has a belt loop, and nickel-plated fittings to the locket and the chape.

British Sheffield-made Bowie knife, mid-19th century

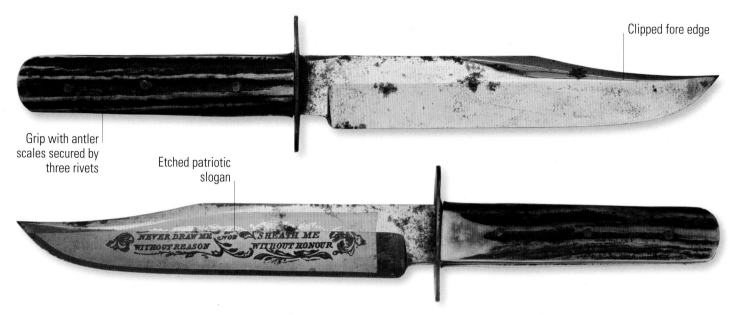

Clipped fore edge

Grip with antler scales secured by three rivets

Etched patriotic slogan

NEVER DRAW ME *nor* SHEATH ME WITHOUT REASON WITHOUT HONOUR

This knife pattern, made famous by the legend of James Bowie and the Alamo, is typical of the many pieces produced in Sheffield in the mid-19th century, and mainly intended for the American market. This specimen, manufactured by Edward Pierce and Co., is etched with the somewhat pious legend: "Never draw me without reason nor sheath me without honour".

DATE	mid-19th century
ORIGIN	BRITISH
LENGTH	32cm (12.6in)

British Raj personalized hunting knife, late 19th century

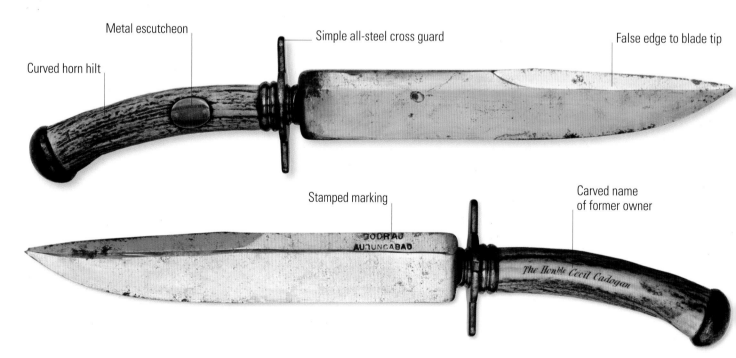

Metal escutcheon

Simple all-steel cross guard

False edge to blade tip

Curved horn hilt

Stamped marking

Carved name of former owner

BODRAU AURUNGABAD

The Honble Cecil Cadogan

This is a well-made hunting knife, but seemingly of a type produced in British India during the days of the Raj. The tang of the blade has been curved to fit the stag-horn grip, and secured firmly with a large metal cap at the pommel. The blade bears the stamped legend "Bodrau Aurungabad", presumably the arsenal in India where it was manufactured. The side face of the grip has been smoothed, and then engraved with the name: "The Honble [Honourable] Cecil Cadogan".

DATE	late 19th century
ORIGIN	BRITISH RAJ
LENGTH	30cm (11.8in)

British Raj double-edged hunting knife, late 19th century

Simple steel cross guard

Antler-horn grip secured with a steel end cap

Stamped name "BOPUT"

Double-edged blade with broad central fuller

DATE	late 19th century
ORIGIN	BRITISH RAJ
LENGTH	32cm (12.6in)

A stylishly manufactured hunting knife, apparently made under British rule in India. A wide fuller runs for most of the length of the substantial double-edged blade. The grip is made of horn and has a sturdy steel cross guard. The steel cap forming the pommel has the tang drawn through and peened over.

German single-edged hunting knife, late 19th century

Stag-horn grip scales secured by three rivets

Plain steel quillon

Single-edged blade with double-edged tip

DATE	late 19th century
ORIGIN	GERMAN
LENGTH	31cm (12.2in)

A typically styled hunting knife by Friedrich Neeff and Son, Solingen. The underside of the grip is contoured for the fingers, the steel cross guard is nickel-plated and the single-edged blade is double-edged at the tip. It was a form made in similar style by many of the German arms companies in the Ruhr Valley.

British Bowie-bladed knife, late 19th century

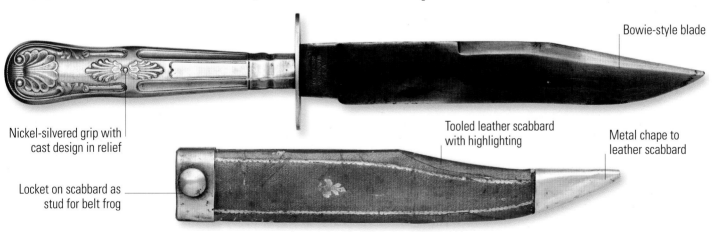

Bowie-style blade

Nickel-silvered grip with cast design in relief

Tooled leather scabbard with highlighting

Metal chape to leather scabbard

Locket on scabbard as stud for belt frog

DATE	late 19th century
ORIGIN	BRITISH
LENGTH	32cm (12.6in)

This is an unnamed example of a Bowie-bladed knife – not a true Bowie in the sense of being a workable hunting knife, but an example of a weapon designed as an ornament. The hilt style, with the classical decoration in relief, is reminiscent of the cutlery styles popular during the closing years of the 19th century.

19th-century folding knives

Folding knives, or clasp-knives, were one of the great innovations of the 19th century, for now it was possible to carry a knife where the blade was safely contained out of harm's way when not in use. Folding knives were very popular among the northern Mediterranean countries where they were known as navaja knives, the word *navaja* being Spanish for "clasp-knife". The usefulness of this design ultimately manifested itself in its most prolific form – the "pocket knife" or "penknife" as we know it today.

Italian or Corsican navaja knife, 19th century

Decorated metal hilt

Narrow, pointed single-edged blade

When opened, the blade of this 19th-century navaja knife is locked into position via a long spring on the back edge of the hilt. The clip of the spring can be released by pulling on a ring, which frees the blade for folding into the hilt. The above example has a metal hilt inset with silver inlay that features engraved decoration.

DATE	19th century
ORIGIN	ITALIAN/CORSICAN
LENGTH	35cm (13.8in)

Spanish (?) navaja folding knife, 19th century

Decorated metal hilt

Narrow, pointed, single-edged blade

Ring and spring locking mechanism

Knife blade closed

This navaja, possibly of Spanish origin, is shown with the blade both open and closed, and demonstrates that even a folding knife can have a blade as long as the hilt. Some examples of this knife pattern had a sliding tube at the top end of the hilt, which could be passed over the tip of the blade to firmly lock it in the closed position.

DATE	19th century
ORIGIN	POSSIBLY SPANISH
LENGTH	35cm (13.8in)

Spanish navaja knife, late 19th century

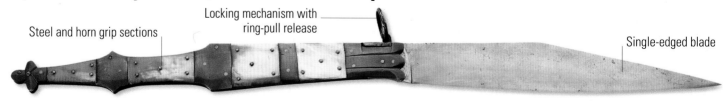

Steel and horn grip sections

Locking mechanism with ring-pull release

Single-edged blade

This mass-produced navaja knife bears the stamped marking "Navajas de Toledo", the city of Toledo being the main producer (and exporter) for the Spanish cutlery industry. The hilt portions are made of steel with horn scales pinned into recesses. The exposed blade, when opened, is just under 25.4cm (10in) in length.

DATE	late 19th century
ORIGIN	SPANISH
LENGTH	54.5cm (21.5in)

German large folding knife, late 19th century

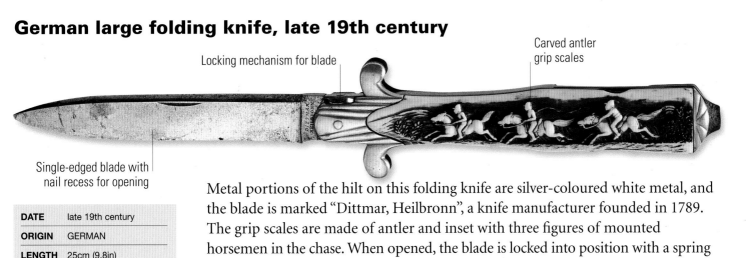

Locking mechanism for blade

Carved antler grip scales

Single-edged blade with nail recess for opening

DATE	late 19th century
ORIGIN	GERMAN
LENGTH	25cm (9.8in)

Metal portions of the hilt on this folding knife are silver-coloured white metal, and the blade is marked "Dittmar, Heilbronn", a knife manufacturer founded in 1789. The grip scales are made of antler and inset with three figures of mounted horsemen in the chase. When opened, the blade is locked into position with a spring clip. When closed, the same spring tension keeps the blade folded into the hilt.

Corsican navajas, late 19th century

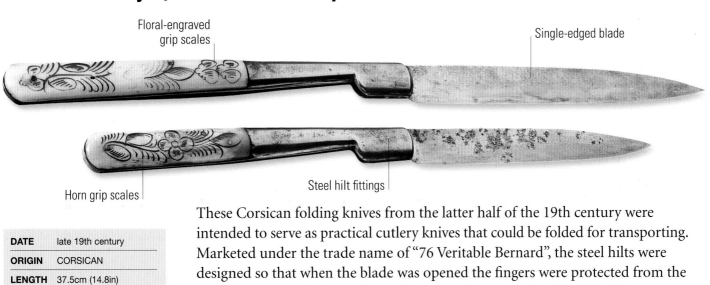

Floral-engraved grip scales

Single-edged blade

Horn grip scales

Steel hilt fittings

DATE	late 19th century
ORIGIN	CORSICAN
LENGTH	37.5cm (14.8in)

These Corsican folding knives from the latter half of the 19th century were intended to serve as practical cutlery knives that could be folded for transporting. Marketed under the trade name of "76 Veritable Bernard", the steel hilts were designed so that when the blade was opened the fingers were protected from the sharp edge by the bolster shape. The grip scales are made of polished horn.

Indian folding clasp-knife, 1875–1930

Clip to control locking spring

Knife in closed position

Brass hilt fittings with coloured inlay

This clasp-knife was one of many patterns mass-produced for the export markets of the British Raj during the late 19th and early 20th centuries. The short steel blade, with clipped point, folds out and is locked into position by a spring and clip that form the back section of the hilt. At the top end of the hilt is a hinged lever, which when raised depresses the spring and unlocks the blade, in readiness for closing.

DATE	1875–1930
ORIGIN	INDIAN
LENGTH	25cm (9.8in)

19th-century civilian fighting knives

The knife in its various forms has always found favour as a weapon of offence by the criminal and been used for self-defence by the citizen. Unlike a firearm, especially in the era of muzzle loading, a knife did not require special skills for loading, cleaning and maintenance. A knife was cheaper than a firearm. There was no ammunition supply to worry about. Except in the case of the switchblade, there was no risk of mechanical malfunction at a crucial moment. And, for those who might benefit, it was silent in use.

British daggerstick, *c.*1800

Ivory handle carved with dog's mask

Stiletto blade

Malacca cane body

Disguising a weapon always gave its user an advantage and the practice was not confined to the underworld. Most gentlemen in Georgian and Victorian England carried walking canes and were always at risk from attack on the badly lit streets. When not wearing a weapon, it made sense to carry one in the shaft of a cane.

DATE	c.1800
ORIGIN	BRITISH
LENGTH	25cm (9.8in)

African flywhisk dagger, 1870

The nature of this dagger suggests that it could have been used by a plantation owner, government official or military officer somewhere in the African colonies. Alternatively, it could have been used by a tribal chieftain, both to keep away flies and as a symbol of rank. In either case, one can imagine the need to have a weapon to hand.

DATE	1870
ORIGIN	AFRICAN
LENGTH	22cm (8.7in)

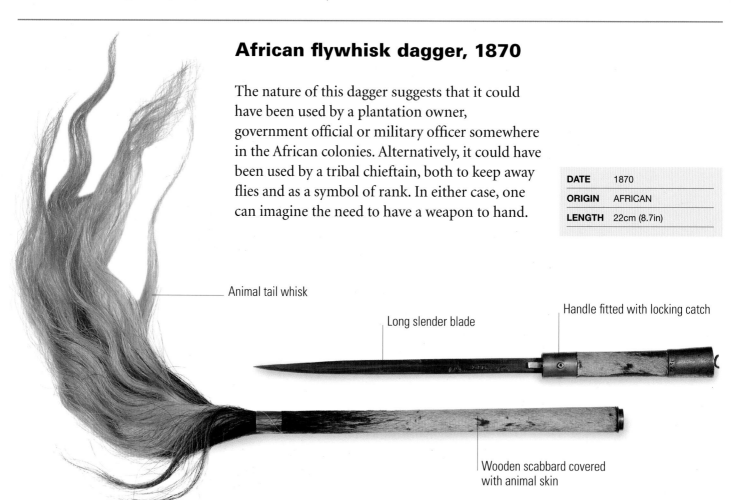

Animal tail whisk

Long slender blade

Handle fitted with locking catch

Wooden scabbard covered with animal skin

Spanish fighting knives, 19th century

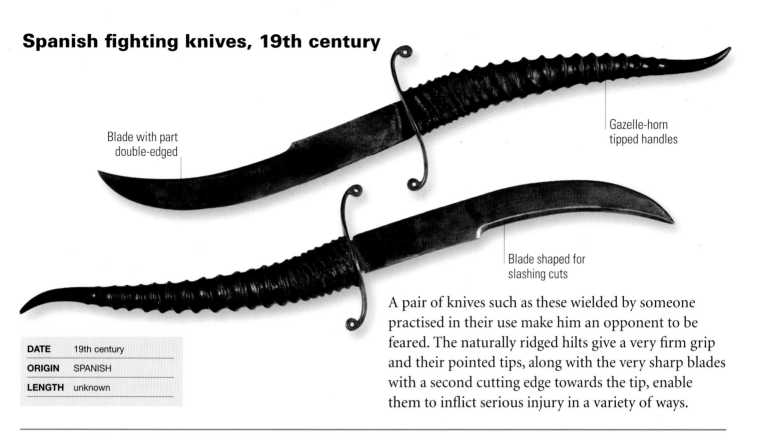

Blade with part double-edged

Gazelle-horn tipped handles

Blade shaped for slashing cuts

DATE	19th century
ORIGIN	SPANISH
LENGTH	unknown

A pair of knives such as these wielded by someone practised in their use make him an opponent to be feared. The naturally ridged hilts give a very firm grip and their pointed tips, along with the very sharp blades with a second cutting edge towards the tip, enable them to inflict serious injury in a variety of ways.

Italian knife with ivory grip, 19th century

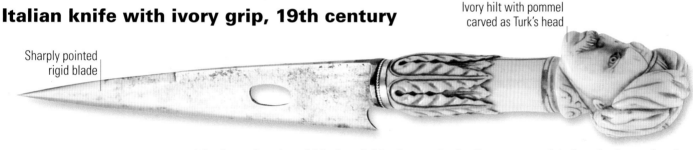

Ivory hilt with pommel carved as Turk's head

Sharply pointed rigid blade

DATE	19th century
ORIGIN	ITALIAN
LENGTH	28cm (11in)

The broad pointed blade of this dagger is similar to many kitchen knives of today but it leaves little doubt as to what its real purpose was. The plain functionality of the blade is made up for by a silver inlaid ivory hilt elaborately carved to represent acanthus leaves and with a pommel in the form of a Turk's head.

American push dagger, *c*.1870

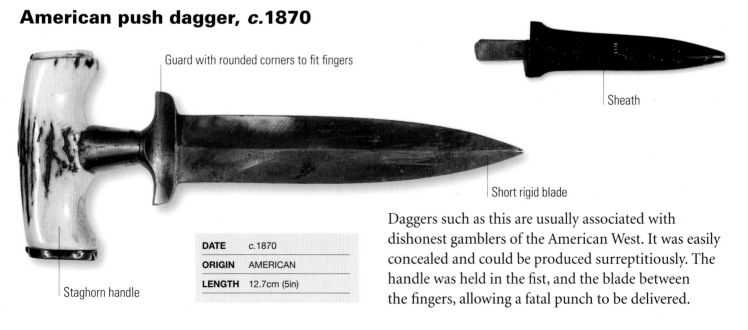

Guard with rounded corners to fit fingers

Sheath

Short rigid blade

Staghorn handle

DATE	c.1870
ORIGIN	AMERICAN
LENGTH	12.7cm (5in)

Daggers such as this are usually associated with dishonest gamblers of the American West. It was easily concealed and could be produced surreptitiously. The handle was held in the fist, and the blade between the fingers, allowing a fatal punch to be delivered.

19th-century combination knives

The combination of a gun with a knife was not a new concept. Military guns with bayonets, or civilian pocket pistols with folding bayonets, were commonplace to give an added degree of protection.

With the advances in gun technology during the 19th century, and the development of the self-contained cartridge, a new type of weapon with multi-shot capability evolved alongside traditional knife pistols.

French knife pistol, 19th century

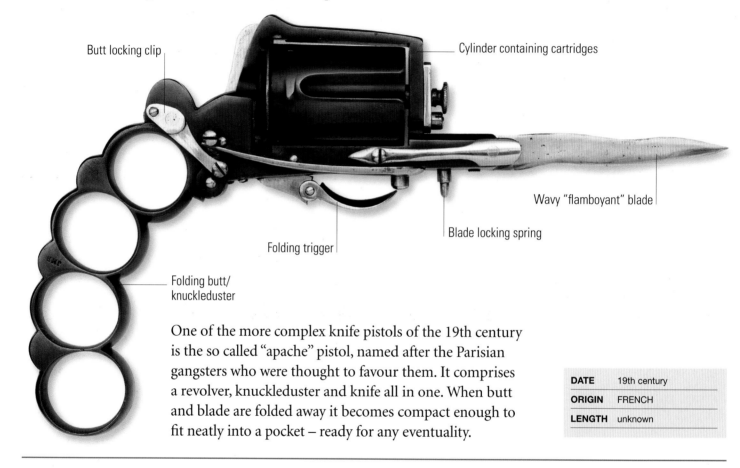

Butt locking clip

Cylinder containing cartridges

Wavy "flamboyant" blade

Blade locking spring

Folding trigger

Folding butt/ knuckleduster

One of the more complex knife pistols of the 19th century is the so called "apache" pistol, named after the Parisian gangsters who were thought to favour them. It comprises a revolver, knuckleduster and knife all in one. When butt and blade are folded away it becomes compact enough to fit neatly into a pocket – ready for any eventuality.

DATE	19th century
ORIGIN	FRENCH
LENGTH	unknown

Belgian pin-fire dirk pistol, *c.*1870

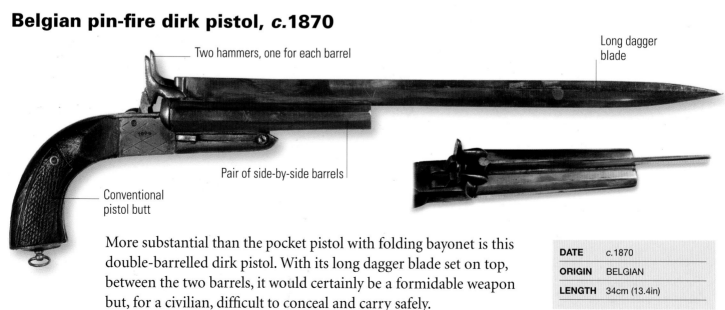

Two hammers, one for each barrel

Long dagger blade

Pair of side-by-side barrels

Conventional pistol butt

More substantial than the pocket pistol with folding bayonet is this double-barrelled dirk pistol. With its long dagger blade set on top, between the two barrels, it would certainly be a formidable weapon but, for a civilian, difficult to conceal and carry safely.

DATE	c.1870
ORIGIN	BELGIAN
LENGTH	34cm (13.4in)

Belgian knife pistol, *c.*1870

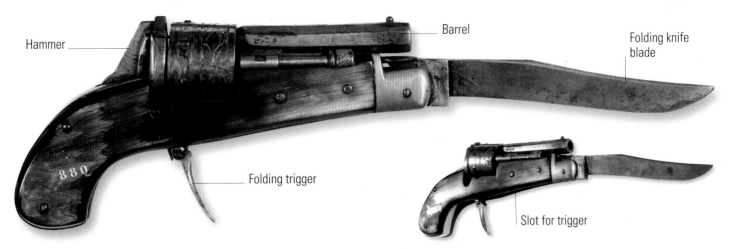

Hammer

Barrel

Folding knife blade

Folding trigger

Slot for trigger

DATE	c.1870
ORIGIN	BELGIAN
LENGTH	unknown

This combination weapon features a six-shot double-action cartridge revolver built in the form of a large pocket knife. Weapons like this do not offer a comfortable or secure grip for use as a revolver and are much less common than their single-shot counterparts. But perhaps it was sufficient to scare a victim or would-be attacker.

European knife-pistol-club, late 19th century

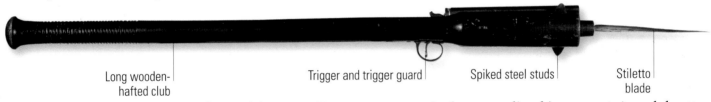

Long wooden-hafted club

Trigger and trigger guard

Spiked steel studs

Stiletto blade

DATE	late 19th century
ORIGIN	EUROPEAN
LENGTH	unknown

This multipurpose European weapon is almost medieval in concept. As a club, with spiked steel studs, it would be lethal in itself, but add a stiletto-like blade and a single-shot pistol and it becomes a formidable close-quarter weapon for either offence or defence. Similar devices without the pistol component were resurrected in the trenches of World War I.

The "apaches" of Paris

Every major city had its underworld members, whether engaged in petty theft or major crime. Victorian London had its "Bill Sykes" characters as portrayed by Dickens, the early 1900s United States had its immigrant Mafia and Paris was terrorised by gangs of "apaches", many wielding their unique revolver-knuckleduster-knives. Often lampooned for what is perceived as their characteristic dress of hooped shirt and black beret, these gangsters were notorious for their ruthlessness.

RIGHT The "apaches" were famous for their disregard of law and order as this illustration from a 1907 edition of *Le Petit Journal* clearly shows.

18th- and 19th-century socket bayonets

The problem with plug bayonets was that they literally plugged the muzzle, rendering the gun incapable of being fired. Nor were they really secure; a good wrench could pull them out of the muzzle, leaving the soldier at a disadvantage. The breakthrough was the socket bayonet – a blade fitted to a tube that slid over the muzzle and could be secured in place, allowing the gun to be fired.

British socket bayonet, *c.*1690

Dog-mask ornamentation

Clipped point

DATE	c.1690
ORIGIN	BRITISH
LENGTH	unknown

This unusual bayonet is an early example of a socket bayonet. With its elaborate design and decoration, however, it was more likely a sporting accessory than a battlefield weapon. A spring catch allows the pommel cap to be removed, opening up the tubular hilt and enabling it to fit on the muzzle of a gun.

British socket bayonet, *c.*1700

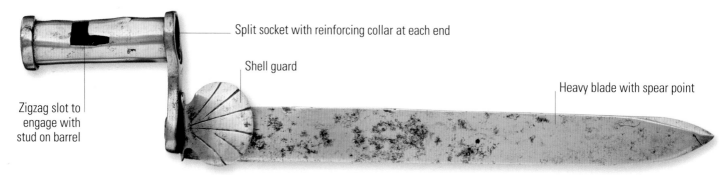

Split socket with reinforcing collar at each end

Shell guard

Heavy blade with spear point

Zigzag slot to engage with stud on barrel

At the time the socket bayonet was introduced, manufacture of gun barrels was not a precise art. To overcome this, sockets had reinforcing collars at each end and were split along their length so their diameters could be adjusted to fit the musket. This socket bayonet with its dagger-like shell guard is typical of its period.

DATE	c.1700
ORIGIN	BRITISH
LENGTH	44.3cm (17.4in)

British socket bayonet, East India Company, 1797

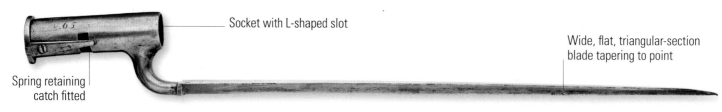

Socket with L-shaped slot

Wide, flat, triangular-section blade tapering to point

Spring retaining catch fitted

With a plain zigzag slot, the bayonet was not locked in place, and could easily be removed accidentally during use by pulling and twisting. The East India Company introduced this simple spring, possibly the design of Ezekiel Baker, which latches against the fixing stud once the bayonet is in place.

DATE	1797
ORIGIN	BRITISH
LENGTH	51.5cm (20.3in)

British bayonet for India Pattern musket, 1800

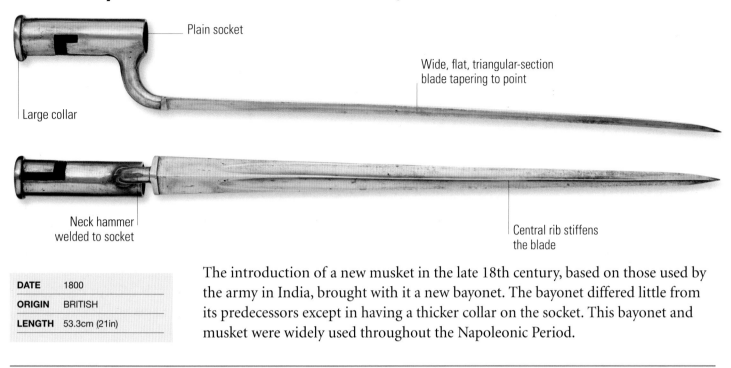

Plain socket

Wide, flat, triangular-section
blade tapering to point

Large collar

Neck hammer
welded to socket

Central rib stiffens
the blade

DATE	1800
ORIGIN	BRITISH
LENGTH	53.3cm (21in)

The introduction of a new musket in the late 18th century, based on those used by the army in India, brought with it a new bayonet. The bayonet differed little from its predecessors except in having a thicker collar on the socket. This bayonet and musket were widely used throughout the Napoleonic Period.

British bayonet with Gill's experimental locking system, *c.*1800

Tubular socket

Wide, shallow,
triangular-section blade

Pivoted lever

DATE	c.1800
ORIGIN	BRITISH
LENGTH	50.5cm (19.9in)

This standard service bayonet was modified by having a spring-loaded lever fitted to the socket collar. The nose of the lever is held in place behind the front sight when the bayonet is fitted, preventing its accidental removal. The old zigzag slot has been filled and a new one cut, bringing the bayonet below the barrel.

British bayonet for sea service musket, *c.*1805

Tubular socket

Flat, vertical blade
with short false edge

Zigzag slot
placed bayonet
on the right
when fixed

This bayonet is unusual in having a flat blade as opposed to the more usual flattened, triangular section. Although dated to the Napoleonic Period, the weapon may derive from the 18th century. Surviving records show that at that time the only bayonets that could fit this description were a number commissioned for naval use.

DATE	c.1805
ORIGIN	BRITISH
LENGTH	54cm (21.2in)

German or Swedish (?) bayonet, Model 1811, *c.*1811

Socket with
locking ring

Hollow-ground,
triangular-section blade

This bayonet is of unusual proportions and uncertain origin, though it closely resembles the Model 1811 for the Swedish infantry musket. The long, slender neck connects to an unusually long blade, offset much further from the socket than most other bayonets of this type. Its most interesting feature is the beautifully made locking ring, hinged at the bottom to facilitate assembly and replacement, and which is guided in its movement by a pin riding in a slot.

DATE	c.1811
ORIGIN	GERMAN/SWEDISH(?)
LENGTH	70cm (27.6in)

French bayonet, Model 1822, 1822

Socket with zigzag
slot on left

Hollow-ground,
T- section blade

Locking
ring

This bayonet is based on the model of 1777, introduced under General Gribeuval (1715–1789) as part of his programme to standardize French military equipment. It was the first to employ a locking ring placed in the centre of the socket to secure the bayonet. The Model 1822 bayonet differs only in being slightly longer and by having a slightly different pattern of locking ring which provides a more secure attachment.

DATE	1822
ORIGIN	FRENCH
LENGTH	53.1cm (21in)

Austrian bayonet, System Augustin rifle, Model 1842, 1842

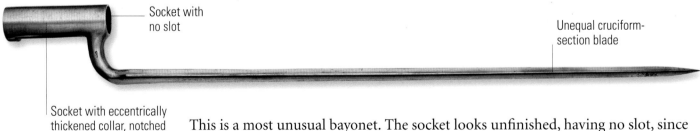

Socket with
no slot

Unequal cruciform-
section blade

Socket with eccentrically
thickened collar, notched
on opposite side

DATE	1842
ORIGIN	AUSTRIAN
LENGTH	56.5cm (22.2in)

This is a most unusual bayonet. The socket looks unfinished, having no slot, since the bayonet does not have to engage with the foresight of the musket or a stud beneath the muzzle. Instead, it has a collar thickened at one point in which a notch is cut. When the bayonet is fitted, it is slid over the muzzle to the forend, from which a spring clip projects, and then it is rotated. The thickened collar acts as a cam, lifting the spring catch which falls into the notch and secures the bayonet.

British bayonet for sappers and miners, 1st Pattern 1842, 1842

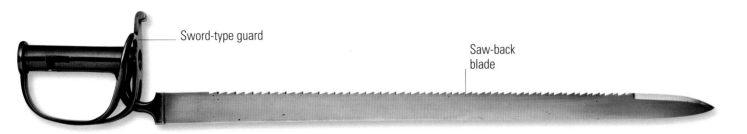

Sword-type guard

Saw-back blade

DATE	1842
ORIGIN	BRITISH
LENGTH	77.9cm (30.7in)

As can be seen, this bayonet has a very elaborate hilt, similar in style to many swords of the period, and a tubular socket which acted as the grip. It is equipped with a heavy blade, having a double row of saw-teeth along its wide back edge. This feature was intended to be used for cutting wood, though if used on anything other than shrubbery it must have been hard and exhausting work. These weapons never actually went into production and this one, probably the sample pattern, is thought to be the only one ever made.

British bayonet for sappers and miners carbine, 2nd Pattern 1842, 1842

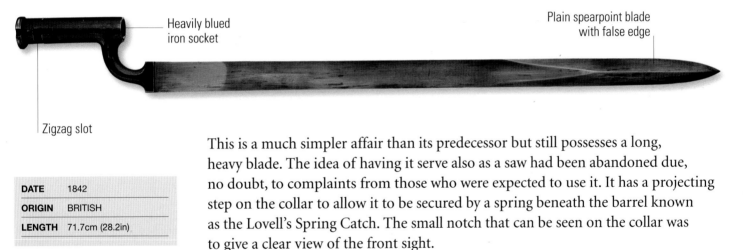

Heavily blued iron socket

Plain spearpoint blade with false edge

Zigzag slot

DATE	1842
ORIGIN	BRITISH
LENGTH	71.7cm (28.2in)

This is a much simpler affair than its predecessor but still possesses a long, heavy blade. The idea of having it serve also as a saw had been abandoned due, no doubt, to complaints from those who were expected to use it. It has a projecting step on the collar to allow it to be secured by a spring beneath the barrel known as the Lovell's Spring Catch. The small notch that can be seen on the collar was to give a clear view of the front sight.

British bayonet for Enfield rifle, Pattern 1853, 1853

Blued iron socket

Equilateral triangular-section blade cants outwards when fitted

Slot engages with front sight and locking ring closes behind it

A good wrought-iron socket fitted with a locking ring and a narrow, sharply pointed, triangular-section blade of the best Sheffield steel gave the Pattern 1853 bayonet a superb quality and singularity of purpose. It was by far the finest bayonet ever to enter British military service up to that time.

DATE	1853
ORIGIN	BRITISH
LENGTH	51.5cm (20.3in)

American bayonet, Winchester Model 1873 musket, 1873

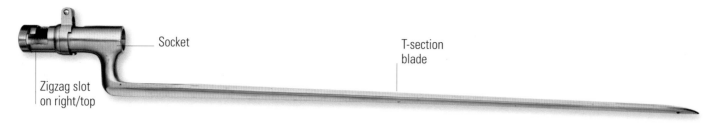

Socket

T-section blade

Zigzag slot on right/top

Unusually, these bayonets lack any markings. However, they are distinguished by being arranged to sit beneath the barrel when fitted, are finished bright all over, and have a long taper between the blade and the neck. They were not used in the US armed forces but were supplied with muskets to many South American countries.

DATE	1873
ORIGIN	AMERICAN
LENGTH	54.5cm (21.5in)

American bayonet, Springfield Model 1873 rifle, 1873

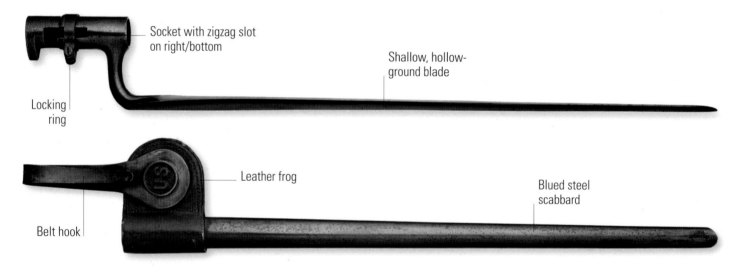

Socket with zigzag slot on right/bottom

Shallow, hollow-ground blade

Locking ring

Leather frog

Blued steel scabbard

Belt hook

The bayonet for the new Model 1873 Springfield "trapdoor" rifle so closely resembled the models of 1855 and 1870 that these were often converted by having the sockets resized to fit the smaller-diameter barrel of the 1873 rifle. It was the first American bayonet to be blued all over.

DATE	1873
ORIGIN	AMERICAN
LENGTH	54.1cm (21.3in)

British bayonet for Martini-Henry, Pattern 1876, 1876

Blued iron socket

Equilateral triangular-section blade

Zigzag slot to engage with front sight

The new Pattern 1876 bayonet was modelled on the Pattern 1853 but with some adjustments. The smaller-diameter barrel of the Martini-Henry rifle required a smaller diameter socket and, to compensate for it being a shorter rifle, the blade was made longer to maintain the "reach".

DATE	1876
ORIGIN	BRITISH
LENGTH	65.8cm (25.9in)

Dutch bayonet, Beaumont-Vitali rifle, Model 1871/88, 1888

Socket with zigzag on right/top

Cruciform-section blade

Collar with "hump" to bridge foresight

DATE	1888
ORIGIN	DUTCH
LENGTH	57.1cm (22.5in)

When the 1871 Beaumont rifle first entered into military service, the bayonet designed for it included a complex locking ring attachment with two adjusting screws. With the transition in 1888 from the single-shot rifle to magazine loading on the Vitali principle, the locking ring design was amended to a more conventional form with a single adjusting screw.

The 54th Massachusetts Volunteer Infantry

The Pattern 1853 Enfield rifle and bayonet was created for the British soldier using technology largely developed and perfected in the United States. Ironically, it played a significant role in the bloodiest war of the mid-19th century, the American Civil War. This was perhaps the first and last conflict in which this fine weapon was used in such large numbers – over 1 million were supplied in roughly equal numbers to both sides by British arms manufacturers. The 54th Massachusetts Volunteer Infantry was one of the more famous regiments to carry the rifles. It was the first military unit composed of African-American soldiers and it led one of the most legendary exploits of the Civil War, the assault on Fort Wagner. The heroism of one soldier, Sergeant William Carney, led to his becoming the first African-American to be awarded the Congressional Medal of Honor.

BELOW This lithograph by Currer & Ives, *The Gallant Charge of the 54th Regiment from Massachusetts*, depicts the assault by Union African-American troops on the Confederate-held Fort Wagner.

19th-century sword bayonets

The 19th century was a time of great innovation. It witnessed a complete transformation of the firearm, from the single-shot, muzzle-loading flintlock at its outset to the self-contained metallic cartridge and magazine-loading multi-shot rifles at its end. This innovation and diversity was not limited to the firearm itself but also found expression in a great diversity of bayonet designs.

British volunteer sword bayonet, *c.*1810

Iron "stirrup" hilt

Single-edged spearpoint blade

Muzzle ring with locking collar

The style of hilt on this bayonet is similar to the 1796 Pattern light cavalry sword, and was perhaps modelled on that since these bayonets were for use by mounted volunteers. They were not official issue and several varieties exist, some having brass hilts. They were generally used with rifles similar to the Baker rifle.

DATE	c.1810
ORIGIN	BRITISH
LENGTH	77.7cm (30.6in)

British Baker rifle sword bayonet, *c.*1815

Blade with fuller running the entire length

Pronounced S-shaped quillons

The S-shaped cross guard differs from any of the official military-issue varieties and suggests this might be a prototype or experimental bayonet, or even one for volunteers. Its blade with a fuller that runs to the tip is also an unusual feature since most Baker sword bayonets had plain blades.

DATE	c.1815
ORIGIN	BRITISH
LENGTH	75.2cm (29.6in)

British Baker rifle "hand" bayonet, *c.*1825

Catch release button

Thin sheet cross guard

Triangular-section blade

In 1825 the Rifle Brigade complained their "hand" or knife bayonets were too heavy. Their colonel submitted an alternative with a buckhorn handle which was much lighter. It was rejected by the Ordnance Board as being too fragile, and this one, with a smaller brass hilt, may have been created in its place for trial.

DATE	c.1825
ORIGIN	BRITISH
LENGTH	54.4cm (21.4in)

British Baker rifle sword bayonet with saw-back, *c*.1850

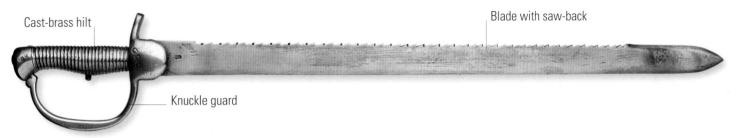

Cast-brass hilt

Blade with saw-back

Knuckle guard

In 1815 a sawback bayonet for the Baker rifle was suggested but seems not to have been developed. The one illustrated is probably a Second Pattern sword bayonet from around 1805 modified at a much later date, since it carries the royal monogram of Queen Victoria stamped on the pommel.

DATE	*c*.1850
ORIGIN	BRITISH
LENGTH	75.2cm (29.6in)

French Sabre-lance du Mosqueton des Cent Gardes, 1854

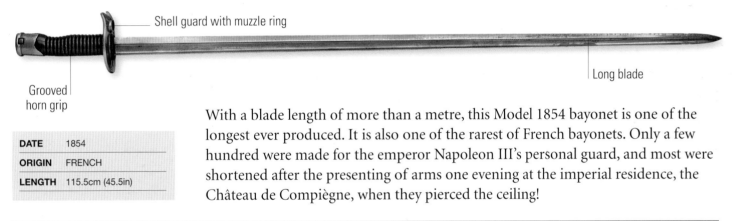

Shell guard with muzzle ring

Long blade

Grooved horn grip

DATE	1854
ORIGIN	FRENCH
LENGTH	115.5cm (45.5in)

With a blade length of more than a metre, this Model 1854 bayonet is one of the longest ever produced. It is also one of the rarest of French bayonets. Only a few hundred were made for the emperor Napoleon III's personal guard, and most were shortened after the presenting of arms one evening at the imperial residence, the Château de Compiègne, when they pierced the ceiling!

British Lancaster bayonet, Pattern 1855, 1855

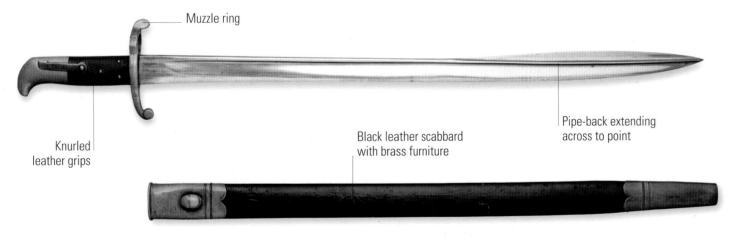

Muzzle ring

Pipe-back extending across to point

Black leather scabbard with brass furniture

Knurled leather grips

DATE	1855
ORIGIN	BRITISH
LENGTH	73.2cm (28.8in)

In 1855 the Corps of Sappers and Miners adopted Lancaster's oval-bored carbine and with it this very distinctive bayonet. Unlike most other British bayonets it has a brass pommel and cross guard, reminiscent of continental practice, and a so-called "pipe-back" blade. In this type of blade, the rounded back extends as a rib across the centre of the tip, creating a second or "false" edge. The bayonet was later adopted by the Royal Army Medical Corps as a sidearm.

American bayonet for Harper's Ferry rifle, 1855

One-piece cast-brass hilt

Straight cross guard with muzzle ring

Straight, single-edged blade turned upwards at point

This new service rifle with a calibre of .58 inches closely followed the British .577 inch Enfield Pattern 1853 rifle. The bayonet, representative of the early stages in the adoption of sword bayonets by the US military, also exhibits European influence with a brass hilt. It has a curious upturn at the point of the blade, rarely seen on bayonets of any nationality.

DATE	1855
ORIGIN	AMERICAN
LENGTH	67.3cm (26.5in)

British bayonet for Jacob's double-barrelled rifle, c.1859

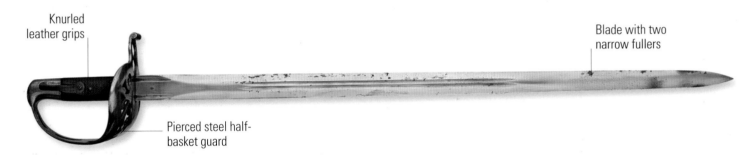

Knurled leather grips

Blade with two narrow fullers

Pierced steel half-basket guard

These bayonets were not official British military issue. They were designed by John Jacob for use with his double-barrelled rifle by the Indian Scinde Irregular Horse, which he commanded. Both rifle and bayonet were made by Swinburn and Son of Birmingham. With twin fullers and spear point, the blade resembles Scottish broadswords, and it has a heavy-gauge "half-basket" type of guard, making it weigh more. It would have made an ungainly weapon when fitted to the heavy rifle.

DATE	c.1859
ORIGIN	BRITISH
LENGTH	90.7cm (35.7in)

British naval cutlass bayonet, 1859

Knurled leather grips

Sheet-steel bowl guard

Plain blade with additional false edge

This is the second type of cutlass bayonet designed for use with the Pattern 1858 Naval Rifle. The first bayonet had ribbed wooden grips whereas this model has the more conventional checkered or "knurled" leather variety. It may have been successful as a cutlass but, as with the Jacob bayonet, when fitted to a rifle it must also have created a very unwieldy combination.

DATE	1859
ORIGIN	BRITISH
LENGTH	81.9cm (32.3in)

American sword bayonet for Navy rifle, Model 1861, 1861

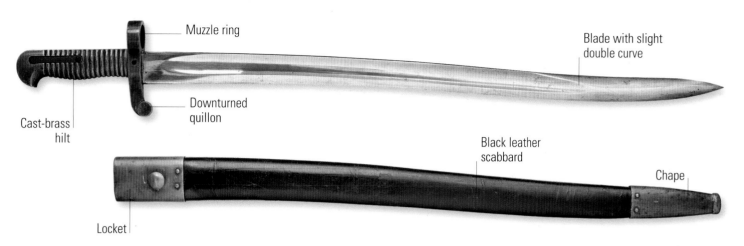

Muzzle ring

Blade with slight double curve

Cast-brass hilt

Downturned quillon

Black leather scabbard

Chape

Locket

DATE	1861
ORIGIN	AMERICAN
LENGTH	71cm (28in)

This bayonet was designed by Admiral John A. Dahlgren for use with the Plymouth/Whitneyville naval rifle. It was manufactured by the Collins Company of Hartford, Connecticut, who had a reputation for the great variety and high quality of axes they produced. With its heavy muzzle ring and cross guard with a slightly downturned quillon, it closely resembles the bayonets for the Spencer, Merrill and Zouave rifles. With their ribbed cast-brass grips and varying degrees of double curvature in their blades, these all reflect the trend in Europe, especially France, for "yataghan"-bladed sword bayonets. This bayonet was equipped with a heavy black leather scabbard fitted with a brass "top locket", or mouthpiece, a stud for securing it in a carrying "frog" and a brass tip or "chape".

French sword bayonet for Chassepot rifle, 1866

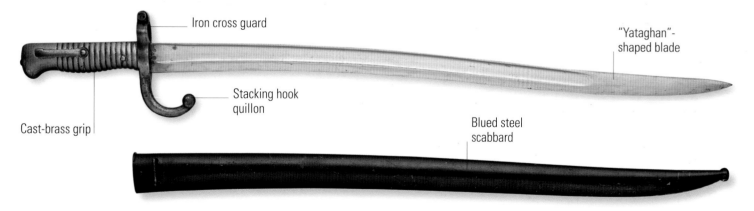

Iron cross guard

"Yataghan"-shaped blade

Stacking hook quillon

Cast-brass grip

Blued steel scabbard

DATE	1866
ORIGIN	FRENCH
LENGTH	70cm (27.6in)

Following the example set by Prussia in adopting Nicholas von Dreyse's new breech-loading needle-fire rifle with self-contained cartridge, the French responded by developing what was to become known as the Chassepot rifle. This rifle brought with it one of the world's most familiar bayonets. Their decorative hilts with cast-brass grips and polished-steel cross guard with a large hook quillon, combined with a stylish "yataghan" blade, heralded a new fashion in bayonet design which was copied almost worldwide. Add to that the allure of the name of the maker and date of manufacture engraved in script on the wide back edge of the blade, and it is easy to understand why they have adorned innumerable walls. But their true value lies in their representing the beginnings of a new era in firearms evolution.

British naval cutlass bayonet, 1872

Knurled leather grips

Reduced-diameter muzzle ring

Sheet-steel bowl guard

Straight, plain blade with additional false edge

The Pattern 1872 was the third and final cutlass bayonet to be put into service, differing from its predecessors with its narrower, straight blade. This certainly made it lighter but still created an unwieldy combination when fitted to a rifle. Few were newly manufactured, most being converted from the Pattern 1859 cutlass bayonet.

DATE	1872
ORIGIN	BRITISH
LENGTH	79.5cm (31.3in)

British Elcho bayonet for Martini-Henry, *c.*1872

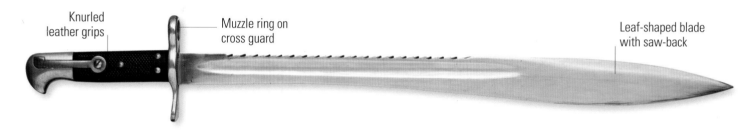

Knurled leather grips

Muzzle ring on cross guard

Leaf-shaped blade with saw-back

One of the most distinctive and unusual of British bayonets, designed by Lord Elcho, this seems to place greater emphasis on its effectiveness as a tool for sawing wood or hacking shrubbery than as a weapon. The leaf or spear shape of the blade perhaps inspired the German bayonet at the end of the century. This weapon was only partially successful as a tool and its function as a bayonet was questionable. Few were made and issued, and more conventional bayonets were used instead.

DATE	c.1872
ORIGIN	BRITISH
LENGTH	64.1cm (25.2in)

Austrian sword bayonet, Werndl rifle, 1873

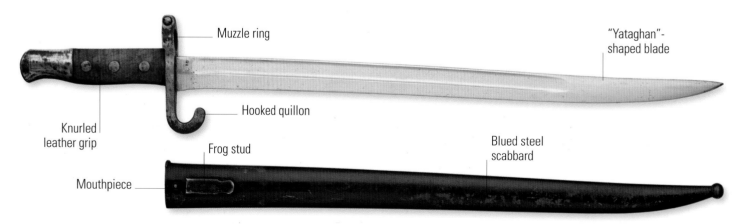

Muzzle ring

"Yataghan"-shaped blade

Hooked quillon

Knurled leather grip

Frog stud

Blued steel scabbard

Mouthpiece

This bayonet was used with various models of the Austrian Werndl military rifle and was basically a modification of its forerunner, the model of 1867. It used a coil spring in place of the leaf spring to operate the locking catch. Like the Chassepot of 1866, it has a distinctive "yataghan"-shaped blade.

DATE	1873
ORIGIN	AUSTRIAN
LENGTH	60.6cm (23.9in)

French bayonet, Gras rifle, Model 1874, 1874

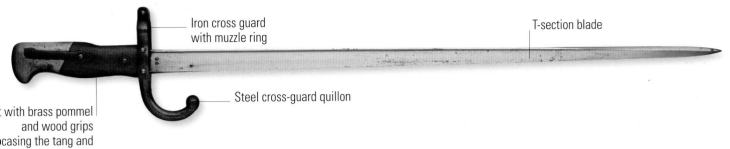

Iron cross guard
with muzzle ring

T-section blade

Steel cross-guard quillon

: with brass pommel
and wood grips
casing the tang and
secured by rivets

DATE	1874
ORIGIN	FRENCH
LENGTH	64.3cm (25.3in)

This bayonet marks the French departure from sword bayonets and the creation of the "epee" bayonet. Its most important feature is the T-section blade with its needle-like point, similar to the fencing epee. Its design makes it strong and light, an ideal combination for a bayonet. It was copied in the last of the British cavalry swords, the 1908 Pattern, and was the forerunner of the later Lebel bayonet.

British artillery sword bayonet, 1879 Pattern, 1879

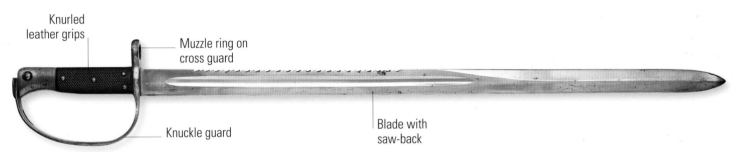

Knurled
leather grips

Muzzle ring on
cross guard

Knuckle guard

Blade with
saw-back

DATE	1879
ORIGIN	BRITISH
LENGTH	75.6cm (29.8in)

This was produced as one alternative to the Elcho bayonet. In view of its length and the nature of its hilt, the term "sword bayonet" is very apt. The knuckle guard made it easier to grip for use as a saw, and its longer blade made it more effective as a sword or as a bayonet when fitted to the short artillery carbine. However, its double row of teeth made its use as a saw very hard work, and like many dual-purpose bayonets it was never completely successful in either role.

Portuguese sword bayonet, Guedes rifle, Model 1885, 1885

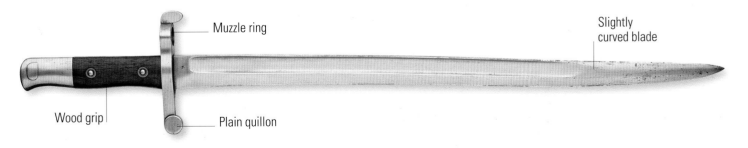

Muzzle ring

Slightly
curved blade

Wood grip

Plain quillon

DATE	1885
ORIGIN	PORTUGUESE
LENGTH	60.8cm (23.9in)

The "yataghan" shape of this bayonet is less pronounced, as the trend was now towards straight blades. Although for Portuguese use, these bayonets and their rifles were manufactured at the Steyr factory in Austria. The bayonets are usually marked with the place and date of manufacture on the back edge. The decorative hilt of an earlier era has been replaced with a more functional but finely engineered hilt.

British Lee-Metford bayonet Mk I, 1888

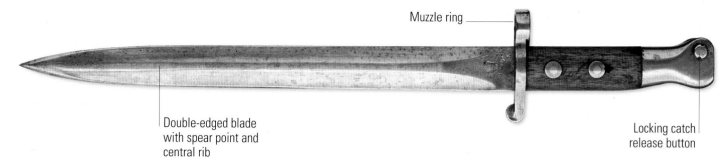

Muzzle ring

Double-edged blade
with spear point and
central rib

Locking catch
release button

This Model 1888 was the second pattern bayonet adopted for the Lee-Metford rifle, the first having the grips secured by three rivets. This rifle was fitted with a cleaning rod which projected from the bayonet mounting stud beneath the barrel. As a consequence, the hilt had a cavity within it to accommodate the end of the rod, and a drain hole at the bottom of this cavity was provided, adjacent to the upper grip rivet.

DATE	1888
ORIGIN	BRITISH
LENGTH	42.2cm (16.6in)

British sword bayonet Mk IV, 1887 Pattern, 1891

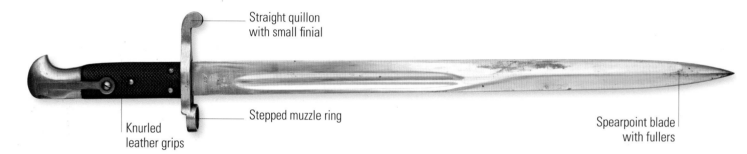

Straight quillon
with small finial

Knurled
leather grips

Stepped muzzle ring

Spearpoint blade
with fullers

The last of a series of bayonets developed for the Martini-Henry rifle, it evolved from experimental bayonets developed in 1886 for a proposed smaller-bore Martini-Henry rifle. This rifle was abandoned following the adoption of the Lee series of small-bore, bolt-action, magazine-loading rifles in 1888. The days of the Martini as a mainline weapon were numbered, but the experimental rifles were modified to standard Martini calibre, these 1887 Pattern bayonets being adapted to fit. As secondary arms, many of these rifles and bayonets were issued to the Navy.

DATE	1891
ORIGIN	BRITISH
LENGTH	60.3cm (23.7in)

German Mauser bayonet, 1884–1945

Fuller

Hilt with plain wood grips and flash guards

Blued spear
point blade

This bayonet, the third model, became the prototype for most bayonets used on Gewehr 98 and Kar 98 rifles until 1945. While following the same basic design, numerous variations occur. This example has plain wood grips secured by screw bolts, and on the back of the hilt a flash guard to protect the wood grips.

DATE	1884–1945
ORIGIN	GERMAN
LENGTH	39cm (15.4in)

19th-century knife bayonets

Many soldiers throughout the 19th century carried their own personal knives for use in a difficult situation, since none were officially issued. But the idea of combining the function of a bayonet with that of a knife is always a compromise. To make it handy enough to be used as a knife means the weapon has to be short. By making it short enough, the important element of "reach" is lost, which puts a soldier at a disadvantage when confronted by an enemy with a long bayonet fixed to his rifle.

Japanese bayonet for Murata rifle, Type 20, 1887

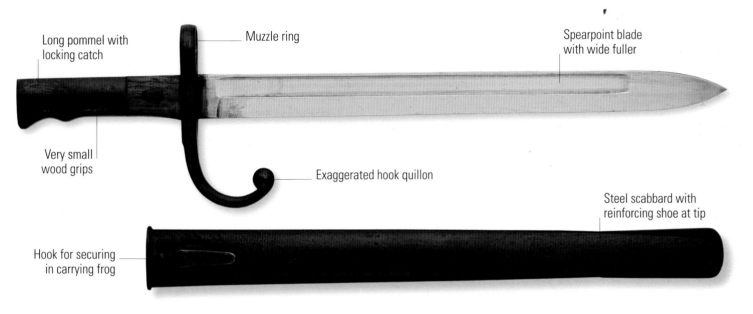

Long pommel with locking catch

Muzzle ring

Spearpoint blade with wide fuller

Very small wood grips

Exaggerated hook quillon

Steel scabbard with reinforcing shoe at tip

Hook for securing in carrying frog

DATE	1887
ORIGIN	JAPANESE
LENGTH	37cm (14.6in)

This bayonet was developed for the Murata Type 20 rifle and carbine, although it could also fit the Type 22 rifle. The whole hilt is very short, barely 90mm (3.5in), making it difficult to grasp despite the supposed shaping to fit the fingers, and giving the impression of an overly large hooked quillon.

Dutch Mannlicher carbine bayonet, 2nd type, 1895

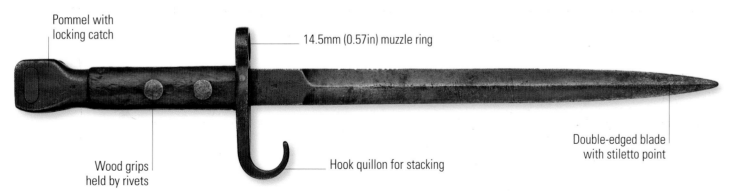

Pommel with locking catch

14.5mm (0.57in) muzzle ring

Wood grips held by rivets

Hook quillon for stacking

Double-edged blade with stiletto point

DATE	1895
ORIGIN	DUTCH
LENGTH	37.5cm (14.8in)

This bayonet was produced in two models for the Mannlicher cavalry carbine. The first had a short straight quillon, while this one, the Model 1895, has the stacking hook. Without the hook it is loosely reminiscent of the British 1888 Patterns. Its size and slender double-edged blade made it a useful fighting knife.

Presentation knives and daggers

Compared with the presentation of swords as marks of military achievement or personal respect, the presentation of knives of any form is a far more unusual occurrence. In the Third Reich in Germany, however, the reverse was true, and presentation of daggers based around the standard service patterns was widely practised. Even rarer are those knives presented to civilians to mark various occasions.

German presentation hunting hanger, mid-19th century

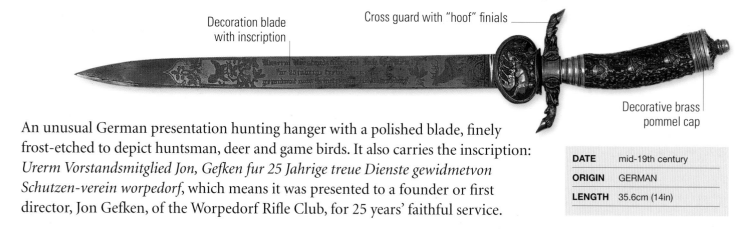

Decoration blade with inscription

Cross guard with "hoof" finials

Decorative brass pommel cap

An unusual German presentation hunting hanger with a polished blade, finely frost-etched to depict huntsman, deer and game birds. It also carries the inscription: *Urerm Vorstandsmitglied Jon, Gefken fur 25 Jahrige treue Dienste gewidmetvon Schutzen-verein worpedorf*, which means it was presented to a founder or first director, Jon Gefken, of the Worpedorf Rifle Club, for 25 years' faithful service.

DATE	mid-19th century
ORIGIN	GERMAN
LENGTH	35.6cm (14in)

South African presentation Bowie knife, 1885

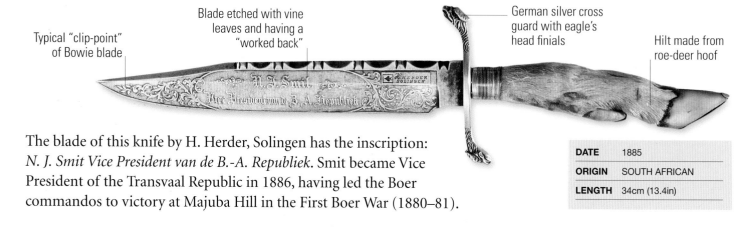

Typical "clip-point" of Bowie blade

Blade etched with vine leaves and having a "worked back"

German silver cross guard with eagle's head finials

Hilt made from roe-deer hoof

The blade of this knife by H. Herder, Solingen has the inscription: *N. J. Smit Vice President van de B.-A. Republiek*. Smit became Vice President of the Transvaal Republic in 1886, having led the Boer commandos to victory at Majuba Hill in the First Boer War (1880–81).

DATE	1885
ORIGIN	SOUTH AFRICAN
LENGTH	34cm (13.4in)

German Imperial dagger, 1900

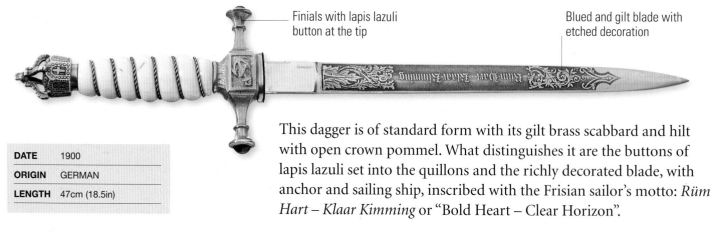

Finials with lapis lazuli button at the tip

Blued and gilt blade with etched decoration

DATE	1900
ORIGIN	GERMAN
LENGTH	47cm (18.5in)

This dagger is of standard form with its gilt brass scabbard and hilt with open crown pommel. What distinguishes it are the buttons of lapis lazuli set into the quillons and the richly decorated blade, with anchor and sailing ship, inscribed with the Frisian sailor's motto: *Rüm Hart – Klaar Kimming* or "Bold Heart – Clear Horizon".

British RN midshipman's presentation dirk, 1897 pattern, 1905

Suspension rings

Lion's-head pommel

Swept quillons with acorn finials

Royal Navy emblem

Wood grip covered with ray skin

DATE	1905
ORIGIN	BRITISH
LENGTH	37cm (14.6in)

This Royal Navy midshipman's presentation dirk, with blued and gilt blade, carries the inscription: "Chief Captain's Prize Awarded to R. C. R. Peploe HMS Britannia, December 1905". Although of standard overall pattern, such presentation dirks, especially from such a notable ship, are very rare. Supplied by J. R. Gaunt and Sons.

Saudi Arabian presentation jambiya, 20th century

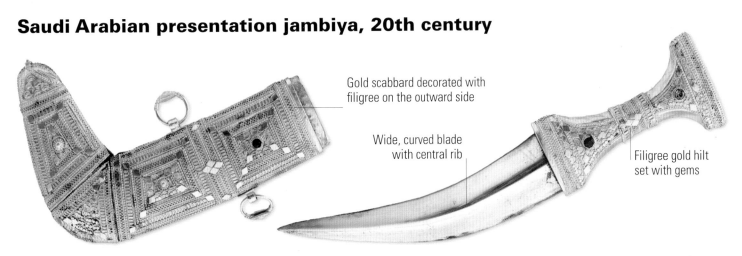

Gold scabbard decorated with filigree on the outward side

Wide, curved blade with central rib

Filigree gold hilt set with gems

DATE	20th century
ORIGIN	SAUDI ARABIAN
LENGTH	25.4cm (10in)

In style, this is a typical jambiya of Saudi Arabia with its boot-shaped scabbard and wide, curved and sharply pointed blade. What makes it unusual are its hilt and scabbard, each elaborately decorated with gold wire filigree. A jambiya such as this would only be worn by the highest-ranking members of society.

German Third Reich naval officer's dirk, 1933–45

Ivory grip with decorative wire binding

Blue and gilt blade with etched decoration

Elaborate globular finials

Eagle pommel with swastika

DATE	1933–45
ORIGIN	GERMAN
LENGTH	24.9cm (9.8in)

This is a rare presentation dagger to a Third Reich *Kriegsmarine* (Navy) officer. It differs from the standard-issue dagger in having blued and gilt panels of etched decoration on the blade depicting a warship and the eagle and swastika. Unfortunately, it has no presentation inscription so the recipient is unknown. Supplied by a well-known maker, E W Holler of Solingen.

Unusual bayonets

Most bayonets, though they may differ in details such as the shape and material of the hilt, the method of locking on to the gun, or the shape and length of the blade, still conform to a more or less conventional overall pattern. There are those, however, that differ widely from the conventions of their time. For example, some bayonets may have been developed for special purposes; some may be the first tentative steps into a new form ahead of their time; while others are just simply bizarre with no obvious explanation.

British socket bayonet, 1680

Plain split tube with zigzag slot to engage with stud on barrel

Semicircular hollow blade welded to socket

This is probably one of the simplest, though most likely experimental, bayonets developed at a time when the socket bayonet was first coming into existence. It consists of an iron-tube socket split along its full length, and locking slots that could fit over the muzzle and lock onto a rectangular stud. Attached to the socket is a tapered, hollow, pointed blade. The design was resurrected, again experimentally, by BSA in 1948 for use on submachine guns.

DATE	1680
ORIGIN	BRITISH
LENGTH	50.6cm (19.7in)

British plug bayonet, 1686

Flat blade thickened in the centre

Maker's mark

This is a most unusual plug bayonet by any standards and the reason behind its design can only be guessed at. With a blade 65mm (25.6in) wide, it could even function as a trowel, but entrenchment was not a feature of 17th-century warfare. The Rose and Crown mark suggests it was made by William Hoy about 1686.

DATE	1686
ORIGIN	BRITISH
LENGTH	29.4cm (11.6in)

British spear bayonet for Egg's carbine, 1784

Conventional socket
with zigzag slot

Spear point

One of the most unusual bayonets produced for British military service was this spear bayonet. It was designed for use with a new breech-loading flintlock cavalry carbine produced in 1784 by Durs Egg at the request of the Duke of Richmond, Master General of Ordnance. The bayonet's length made it impossible to carry it in the normal way of a scabbard attached to the belt. So it was designed to be reversed on the muzzle when not in use and, as a further refinement, the trigger guard had a shaped pocket at its forward end into which the tip of the spearhead could be lodged. It was not widely issued and was more experimental in nature.

DATE	1784
ORIGIN	BRITISH
LENGTH	84.5cm (33.3in)

American trowel bayonet, 1873

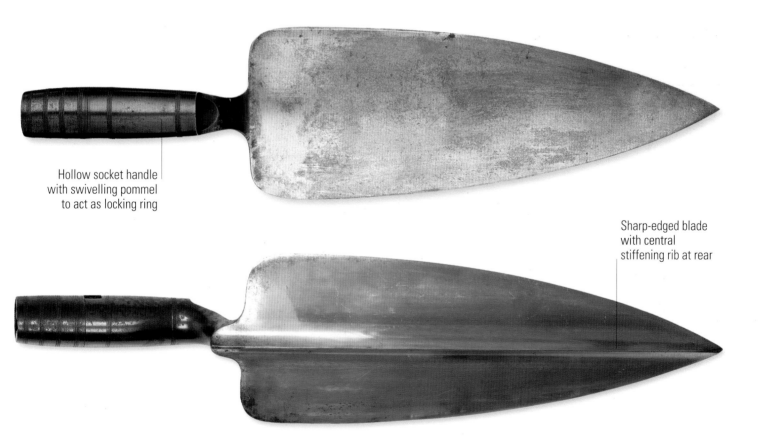

Hollow socket handle
with swivelling pommel
to act as locking ring

Sharp-edged blade
with central
stiffening rib at rear

DATE	1873
ORIGIN	AMERICAN
LENGTH	35.7cm (14.1in)

Viewed as a weapon, this Model 1873 bayonet could be considered barbaric. However, it was not a weapon. It was designed as a spade, or for use in the hand as a trowel. It was the third of its type used in American service, and it has the elegance of simplicity and good design.

18th- to 20th-century integral bayonets

The idea of a bayonet permanently attached to a firearm has been explored with varying success over two centuries. It is only practical if the bayonet can be stowed away when not in use but easily deployed as needed. It was used in the 18th and 19th centuries on civilian weapons like blunderbusses and pistols, where the blade was folded away and held against a spring, and could be opened by a trigger. It was tried on some military firearms but never extensively. It has regained popularity in some military circles more recently.

British flintlock blunderbuss by Grice with spring bayonet, *c.*1780

Ramrod pipes offset to allow bayonet to lie beneath barrel

Pivot for bayonet mounted on barrel

Muzzle fitted with retaining catch for bayonet on underside

Triangular hollow-ground blade

The blunderbuss, a muzzle-loading firearm, was a popular means of self-defence in the homes of the gentry. Being a single-shot weapon, the fitting of a spring-loaded bayonet that could be brought into use simply by moving a catch gave the user a second line of defence if a shot failed to achieve its purpose.

DATE	c.1780
ORIGIN	BRITISH
LENGTH	24.9cm (9.8in)

British Elliott's carbine with folding bayonet, 1785

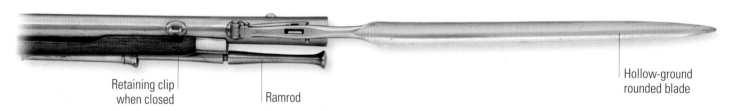

Retaining clip when closed

Ramrod

Hollow-ground rounded blade

The folding bayonet was also experimented with by the military authorities in Britain for use by cavalry, but it was never adopted. In comparison with a socket bayonet mounted on the muzzle, the mountings of a folding bayonet were flimsy and would hardly stand up to the rigours of extended use in battle.

DATE	1785
ORIGIN	BRITISH
LENGTH	39.9cm (15.5in)

American ramrod bayonet, Springfield rifle, Model 1884, 1884

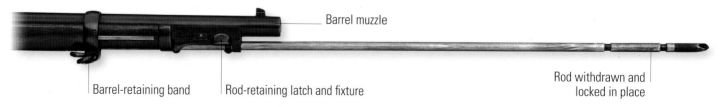

Barrel muzzle

Barrel-retaining band

Rod-retaining latch and fixture

Rod withdrawn and locked in place

A clearing rod that could double as a bayonet had been used on the North-Hall musket in 1833 but was resurrected for use on this Springfield rifle. A notch cut in the sharpened rod, combined with a catch beneath the barrel of the gun, allowed the bayonet to be pulled forward and locked firmly in position.

DATE	1884
ORIGIN	AMERICAN
LENGTH	59.2cm (23.3in)

Japanese military carbine, Arisaka Type 44, 1911

Bayonet assembly slides over
muzzle and is fixed in place

Cruciform-section blade
with chisel point

Pivot pin extended to
form stacking hook

DATE	1911
ORIGIN	JAPANESE
LENGTH	43.9cm (17.2in)

This Japanese bayonet was developed for the Arisaka Type 44 carbine used by mounted troops. It could be locked in the open or closed position by a simple catch, and when not in use was folded away beneath the barrel. Carbines with these bayonets saw service until the end of World War II.

Chinese AK47 assault rifle, Type 56, 1980

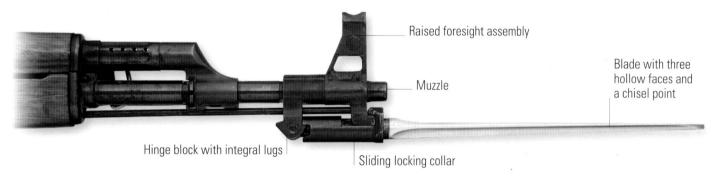

Raised foresight assembly

Blade with three
hollow faces and
a chisel point

Muzzle

Hinge block with integral lugs

Sliding locking collar

DATE	1980
ORIGIN	CHINESE
LENGTH	36.2cm (14.3in)

The simple, reliable and rugged AK47 has become ubiquitous, continuing to find many adherents more than 60 years after it was developed by Mikhail Kalashnikov in 1947. This one, made in China, was used by Iraqi forces during the Gulf War of 1990–91. It is fitted with a short folding bayonet.

Italian Fascist Youth (*Balilla*) Carbine with folding bayonet

The Italian Fascist Youth organization was created shortly after the rise to power of Benito Mussolini. It replaced the traditional boy scout movement for boys between the ages of 8 and 14 years. The age range was later extended up to 18 years. Like the later Hitler Youth movement, its main objective was to indoctrinate young Italians in the principles of fascism. But it was also intended to provide basic military training and to this end, the older boys were issued with rifles. Only 750mm (29.5in) long and complete with a 250mm (9.8in) folding bayonet, blunted at the tip to avoid accident, these rifles were fully functional miniature versions of the Mannlicher Carcano cavalry carbines.

ABOVE The Italian Fascist Youth organization shared many of the same ideals as the later Hitler Youth movement. During military exercises, older boys were armed with bayonet rifles.

Fighting knives of World War I

When Europe went to war in 1914, it was not foreseen that a new form of combat would emerge – trench warfare. The dilemma experienced by all sides when overrunning an enemy position was that the long length of a rifle with fixed bayonet quickly became a dangerous hindrance. To fight and survive in a narrow trench, a soldier needed a more compact fighting knife: the trench dagger was about to evolve.

German fighting knife, 1914

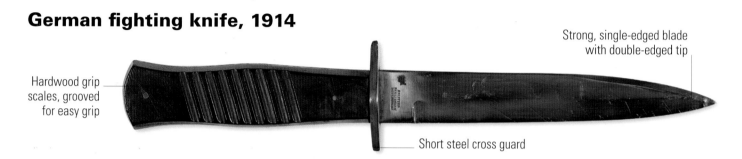

Hardwood grip scales, grooved for easy grip

Strong, single-edged blade with double-edged tip

Short steel cross guard

Known by the Germans as the *Nahkampfmesser* ("Close-combat knife"), a wide range of patterns was created for the German war effort. This example is a style that was widely reproduced by many companies, such as Gottlieb Hammesfahr and Erfurt Gewehrfabrik, although many examples are unmarked.

DATE	1914
ORIGIN	GERMAN
LENGTH	28cm (11in)

German fighting knife, 1914

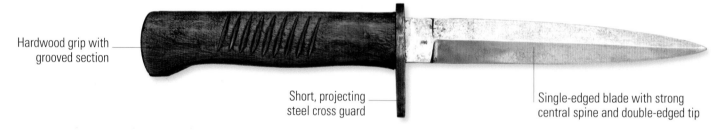

Hardwood grip with grooved section

Short, projecting steel cross guard

Single-edged blade with strong central spine and double-edged tip

A variation pattern of the close-combat knife, with a wooden grip. This specimen was possibly made by the company of Ernst Busch, Solingen, which is known to have manufactured an identical specimen with a solid-steel hilt. Both patterns are considered to be quite uncommon variations.

DATE	1914
ORIGIN	GERMAN
LENGTH	28.6cm (11.3in)

British push dagger, by Robbins of Dudley, 1916

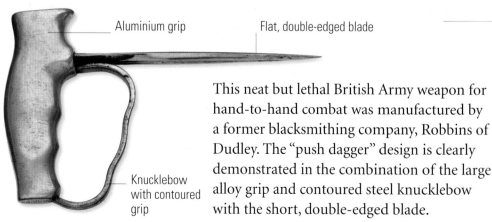

Aluminium grip

Flat, double-edged blade

Knucklebow with contoured grip

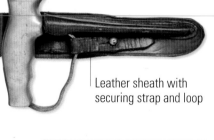

Leather sheath with securing strap and loop

This neat but lethal British Army weapon for hand-to-hand combat was manufactured by a former blacksmithing company, Robbins of Dudley. The "push dagger" design is clearly demonstrated in the combination of the large alloy grip and contoured steel knucklebow with the short, double-edged blade.

DATE	1916
ORIGIN	BRITISH
LENGTH	17.5cm (6.8in)

French fighting knife, 1916

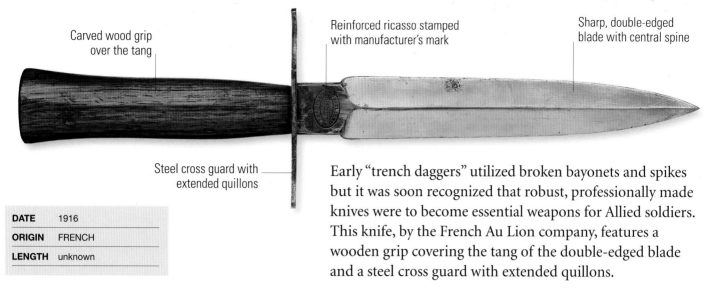

Carved wood grip over the tang

Reinforced ricasso stamped with manufacturer's mark

Sharp, double-edged blade with central spine

Steel cross guard with extended quillons

DATE	1916
ORIGIN	FRENCH
LENGTH	unknown

Early "trench daggers" utilized broken bayonets and spikes but it was soon recognized that robust, professionally made knives were to become essential weapons for Allied soldiers. This knife, by the French Au Lion company, features a wooden grip covering the tang of the double-edged blade and a steel cross guard with extended quillons.

American Model 1917 knucklebow knife, 1917

Leather scabbard body with steel mounts

Hardwood grip

Triangular-section blade

Steel knucklebow with pyramidal projections

DATE	1917
ORIGIN	AMERICAN
LENGTH	37cm (14.6in)

This close-quarter fighting knife was issued to US troops when they joined the European campaign. It is distinguished by a bayonet-style blade and knucklebow guard.

American knuckle knife, Model 1918, 1918

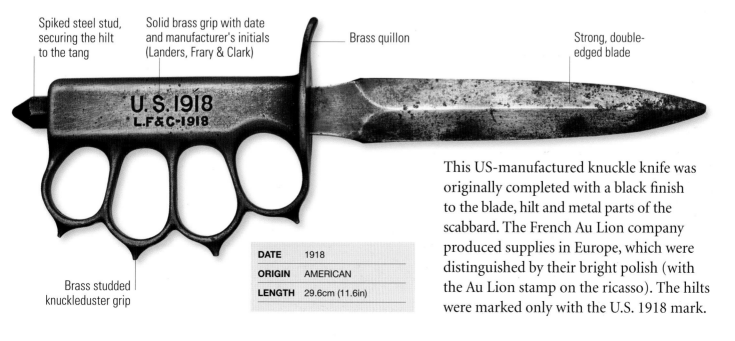

Spiked steel stud, securing the hilt to the tang

Solid brass grip with date and manufacturer's initials (Landers, Frary & Clark)

Brass quillon

Strong, double-edged blade

Brass studded knuckleduster grip

DATE	1918
ORIGIN	AMERICAN
LENGTH	29.6cm (11.6in)

This US-manufactured knuckle knife was originally completed with a black finish to the blade, hilt and metal parts of the scabbard. The French Au Lion company produced supplies in Europe, which were distinguished by their bright polish (with the Au Lion stamp on the ricasso). The hilts were marked only with the U.S. 1918 mark.

Bayonets of World War I

At the outbreak of World War I, military thinking had changed little since the mid-19th century, despite the advent of vastly improved firepower. It was still thought that troops could be deployed in massed ranks and engage in bayonet charges. But this was a war of entrenchment and little mobility, and the fields of Flanders showed the deadly futility of the fixed-bayonet charge across No Man's Land against a barely visible dug-in enemy defended by barbed wire, machine guns, mortars and artillery.

French Lebel epee bayonet, 1886

Muzzle ring

Hook quillon

Cupro-nickel or brass grip

Long, slender and sharply pointed blade

The Lebel bayonet with its long, slender, cruciform blade, resembling the fencing sword, or epee, is probably one of the most distinctive bayonets from its era. It was first introduced in 1886 for use with the new Lebel rifle, the world's first small-calibre, high-velocity rifle utilizing a smokeless propellant.

DATE	1886
ORIGIN	FRENCH
LENGTH	64cm (25.2in)

American Springfield bayonet, 1905

Ribbed wooden grips

Muzzle ring

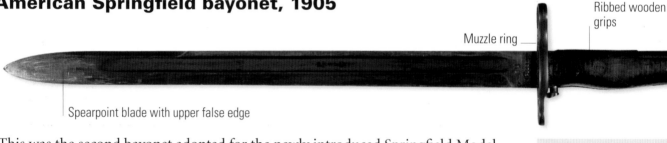

Spearpoint blade with upper false edge

This was the second bayonet adopted for the newly introduced Springfield Model 1903 rifle, which initially used the bayonet of its predecessor, the Krag. However, President Theodore Roosevelt insisted a new bayonet with a longer blade be designed to compensate for the shorter length of the rifle.

DATE	1905
ORIGIN	AMERICAN
LENGTH	52.6cm (20.7in)

British SMLE bayonet, Pattern 1907, 1907

Muzzle ring

Fuller

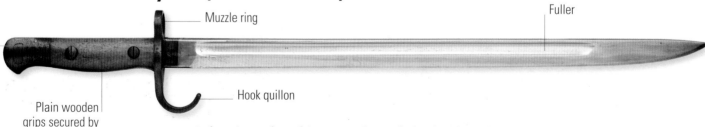

Hook quillon

Plain wooden grips secured by screw bolts

DATE	1907
ORIGIN	BRITISH
LENGTH	55.3cm (21.8in)

When introduced in 1903, this rifle had a short bayonet modelled on the 1888 pattern. However, this was felt to be too short for use with a shortened rifle so a longer pattern, inspired by the Arisaka Type 30, was introduced. The hooked quillon was eventually deemed to be too cumbersome and was abandoned in 1913, but many of this pattern saw service during World War I. Unusually, the muzzle ring does not actually fit on the muzzle but on a stud mounted beneath it.

British bayonet Pattern 1913, 1914

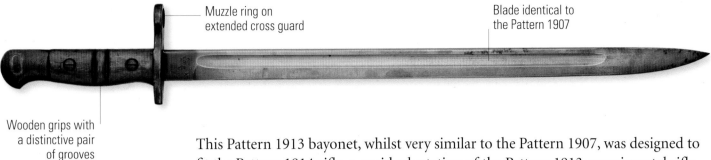

Muzzle ring on extended cross guard

Blade identical to the Pattern 1907

Wooden grips with a distinctive pair of grooves

DATE	1914
ORIGIN	BRITISH
LENGTH	55.6cm (21.9in)

This Pattern 1913 bayonet, whilst very similar to the Pattern 1907, was designed to fit the Pattern 1914 rifle, a rapid adaptation of the Pattern 1913 experimental rifle discontinued at the outbreak of war and modified to .303in calibre. Unlike the SMLE, this rifle had a muzzle projecting beyond the end of the stock, and so this bayonet was designed so that the muzzle ring actually fits on the muzzle. It therefore has an extended cross guard to enable it to do that.

American bayonet for American Enfield rifle Model 1917, 1914

Wooden grips with distinctive pair of grooves

Muzzle ring on extended cross guard

Blade identical to Patterns 1907 and 1913

Drain hole

The British Pattern 1914 rifle and bayonet were already being manufactured under contract in America when it entered the war. Adapted to .30-06 calibre, the Pattern 1914 rifle became the Model 1917. Both rifle bayonets are identical, except for the US ownership marks and date on the American blade.

DATE	1914
ORIGIN	AMERICAN
LENGTH	54.4cm (21.4in)

German Mauser bayonet Model 98/05, 1915

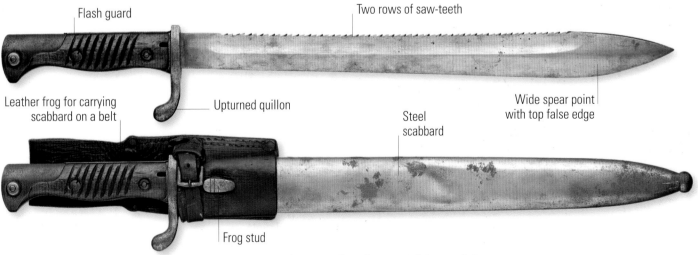

Flash guard

Two rows of saw-teeth

Leather frog for carrying scabbard on a belt

Upturned quillon

Steel scabbard

Wide spear point with top false edge

Frog stud

Numerous bayonets exist for the German Gewehr 98 rifle of 1898. This model with saw-teeth originated in 1905 for issue to infantry NCOs. The more durable scabbard dates from 1914. Saw-teeth were provided for cutting brushwood, not for inflicting more severe wounds, a popular misconception at the time.

DATE	1915
ORIGIN	GERMAN
LENGTH	50.8cm (20in)

American Model 1915 bayonet, 1915

Stub quillon

Plain wooden grips

Metal sheath with leather frog

Spearpoint blade with upper false edge

Muzzle ring

A Russian contract for 300,000 Model 1895 rifles and bayonets was placed with the Winchester company in 1915, and in Russia this bayonet is referred to as the Model 1915. The steel parts are polished bright and the Winchester name appears on the blade side of the cross guard.

DATE	1915
ORIGIN	AMERICAN
LENGTH	51.7cm (20.4in)

Canadian Ross rifle bayonet, 1915

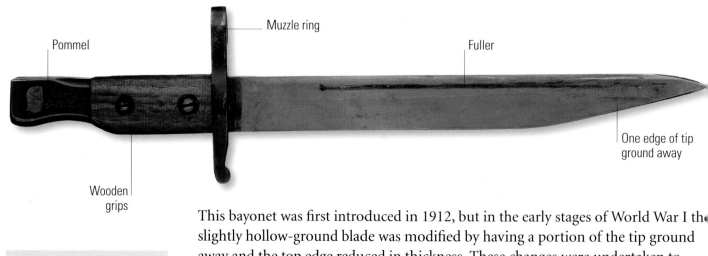

Muzzle ring

Pommel

Fuller

One edge of tip ground away

Wooden grips

DATE	1915
ORIGIN	CANADIAN
LENGTH	38.5cm (15.2in)

This bayonet was first introduced in 1912, but in the early stages of World War I the slightly hollow-ground blade was modified by having a portion of the tip ground away and the top edge reduced in thickness. These changes were undertaken to enable the blade to penetrate its target more easily. In addition, the once polished bright blades gave way to a dull matt finish. Whether this was done simply to ease manufacture or to reduce reflection is open to question.

German Mauser ersatz bayonet, 1916

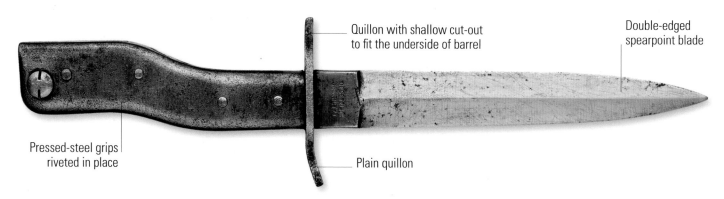

Quillon with shallow cut-out to fit the underside of barrel

Double-edged spearpoint blade

Pressed-steel grips riveted in place

Plain quillon

The term "ersatz" means a substitute or makeshift, in this case indicating that it was constructed using metal grips riveted together, on the grounds of speed and convenience. The hilt was usually painted field grey and the blade polished bright. This bayonet also functioned as a convenient trench knife.

DATE	1916
ORIGIN	GERMAN
LENGTH	26.1cm (10.3in)

German Mauser ersatz bayonet, 1916

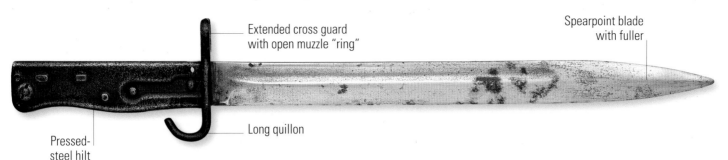

Extended cross guard with open muzzle "ring"

Spearpoint blade with fuller

Long quillon

Pressed-steel hilt

DATE	1916
ORIGIN	GERMAN
LENGTH	43cm (17in)

This is another example of the many ersatz bayonets produced, again for use with the Model 88 and 98 Gewehr rifles or captured French Lebel and Russian Mosin-Nagant rifles. The pressed-steel hilt is a little more elaborately formed, although on this example the quillon has been bent further backwards subsequent to manufacture. Like the other bayonets, this would have had a hilt and scabbard painted field grey, and a polished blade.

British mountable revolver bayonet for Webley Mk VI, 1916

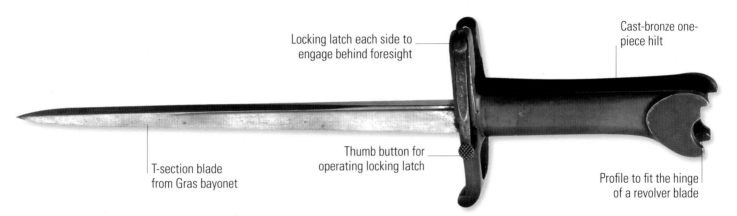

Locking latch each side to engage behind foresight

Cast-bronze one-piece hilt

T-section blade from Gras bayonet

Thumb button for operating locking latch

Profile to fit the hinge of a revolver blade

DATE	1916
ORIGIN	BRITISH
LENGTH	32.4cm (12.8in)

This bayonet was the brainchild of Lieutenant Arthur Pritchard. Made by Greener of Birmingham, it used a Gras bayonet blade and was only for private purchase. The pommel sits tightly up against the revolver frame. The muzzle ring slides over the foresight and is locked in place by two sprung levers on the cross guard.

German Mauser ersatz bayonet, 1917

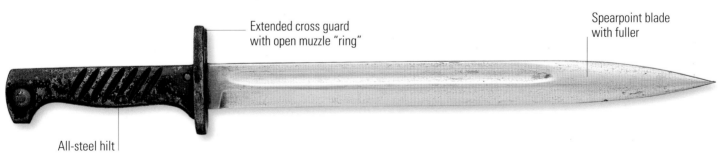

Extended cross guard with open muzzle "ring"

Spearpoint blade with fuller

All-steel hilt

DATE	1917
ORIGIN	GERMAN
LENGTH	43.9cm (17.3in)

These ersatz versions of the Model 88/98 bayonets were designed to fit the Model 88 and 98 rifles and, by using adapters, captured Russian Mosin-Nagant and French Lebel rifles too. The all-steel hilt reflects the grooved wooden grips of the standard bayonet and was originally painted field grey. It has the open muzzle "ring" common on many ersatz bayonets.

Survival weapons of World War II and after

As the world went to war in 1939, fighting knives and other survival weapons were redesigned to fill a variety of purposes, depending upon the conditions under which they would be used. Some pieces were designed solely as assassination items, while others were intended to double as working tools for building shelter or finding food. Part of the early training for British Commandos was for each man to take his turn locating food – namely, to find an animal or bird, kill it, butcher it, cook it and supply it to his colleagues.

American Carlson's Raiders machete (Collins Pattern No 18), 1934 onward

Black/green horn grip secured by five rivets

Steel cross guard, upturned on both sides

Broad falchion-shaped blade, with prominent false edge

Scabbard decorated with leather tooling and the Collins' company logo

Brown leather scabbard with belt loop

Issued to the 2nd Marine Raider Battalion during the Guadalcanal Campaign in the Pacific, this knife's "machete-style" hilt is common to a number of Collins' weapons; its distinctive "beaked" pommel ensures a firm grip. The single-edged blade, with false edge tip, makes it an excellent all-round tool as well as a weapon.

DATE	1934 onward
ORIGIN	AMERICAN
LENGTH	36cm (14.2in)

German flight utility knife, 1936 onward

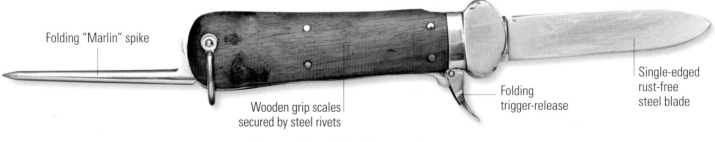

Folding "Marlin" spike

Wooden grip scales secured by steel rivets

Folding trigger-release

Single-edged rust-free steel blade

DATE	1936 onward
ORIGIN	GERMAN
LENGTH	35.2cm (13.9in)

Originally introduced for the army parachute units, the knife was subsequently adopted by all Luftwaffe parachute units. The knife blade was normally retracted, to keep it out of the way and prevent accidental injury to the wearer; it could be released by one hand. By holding the knife down and pushing the trigger, the blade drops into position, useful if a parachutist is trapped in a tree.

Soviet fighting knife, Armenian pattern, 1940 onward

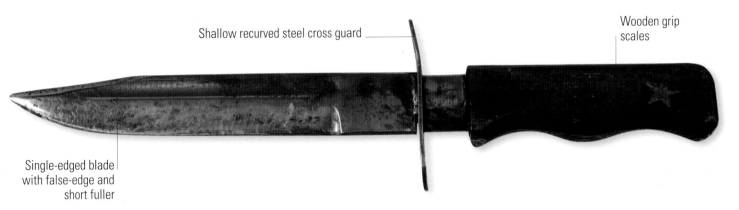

Shallow recurved steel cross guard

Wooden grip scales

Single-edged blade with false-edge and short fuller

DATE	1940 onward
ORIGIN	ARMENIAN
LENGTH	26cm (10.2in)

Manufactured in Armenia for the Soviet Armenian troops fighting alongside the Red Army, this weapon was intended as a general service knife, although its usefulness as a close-combat weapon was not overlooked. The blade is single-edged, with a double-edged tip and a fuller close to the back of the blade. This specimen has a ferrule between the main grip and the guard. In post-war years, the Armenian contingents continued to equip their troops with a similar dagger, although the main Russian troops preferred to have dual-purpose knife-bayonets.

English Fairbairn-Sykes commando knife, 2nd pattern, 1941 onward

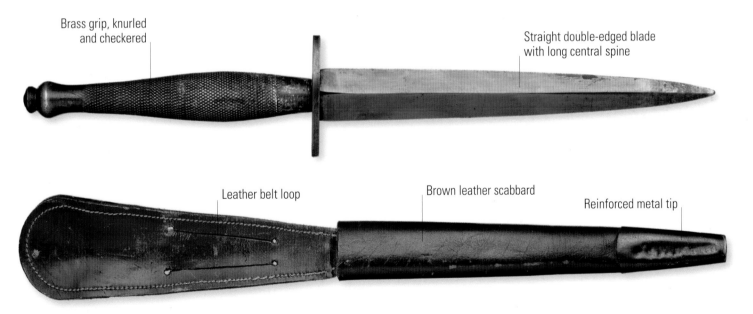

Brass grip, knurled and checkered

Straight double-edged blade with long central spine

Leather belt loop

Brown leather scabbard

Reinforced metal tip

DATE	1941 onward
ORIGIN	ENGLISH
LENGTH	30cm (11.8in)

The classic fighting knife of the Commando, the Fairbairn-Sykes knife is perhaps the most identifiable commando knife in the world, and its design features were copied by many other nations for their own special troops. The blade is a straight stiletto form, double-edged with a central spine, and the tang of the blade projects through the hilt and is secured at the other end with a locking button. The finely checkered grip is made of turned brass, while the guard is made of steel and rounded at the end of the quillons. This specimen is an example of the Fairbairn-Sykes 2nd pattern (the 1st pattern had a recurved cross guard and a more acutely pointed blade with flat ricasso). It appears to be a private purchase example, as the scabbard is shown without the usual leather side tags.

American USMC KA-BAR (USN Mk 2) fighting-utility knife, 1941 onward

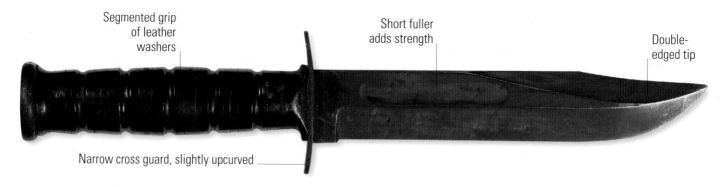

Segmented grip
of leather
washers

Short fuller
adds strength

Double-
edged tip

Narrow cross guard, slightly upcurved

One of the most successful fighting-utility knives ever made, the KA-BAR was created by the Union Cutlery Company of Olean, New York State. Designed as an all-purpose survival tool, it is equally effective as a hammer, can opener or defensive weapon. Initial manufacture was exclusive to Government Order, and the knife was adopted by the US Marine Corps and the Navy.

DATE	1941 onward
ORIGIN	AMERICAN
LENGTH	32cm (12.6in)

British and American OSS/SOE dart and wrist dagger, 1942 onward

Triangle-section
blade with
deep fuller

Cylindrical dart, fired
from small crossbow

Smooth rounded hilt and pommel

Specially manufactured out of surgical steel, these weapons were designed for dispatching an opponent quietly. The dart could be fired from a folding, pistol-sized crossbow, while the wrist dagger was carried in a leather sheath with arm or leg straps for concealment. The weapons were mainly deployed behind enemy lines.

DATE	1942 onward
ORIGIN	BRITISH & AMERICAN
LENGTH	17.5cm (6.8in)

English Fairbairn-Sykes commando knife, 3rd pattern, 1942 onward

Turned and ribbed grip

Straight double-edged blade

The 3rd pattern Fairbairn-Sykes knife was the version that was most widely manufactured, both during World War II and well into the postwar years. Following the production of the original pattern by Wilkinson Sword, the design was modified and improved in the following models, and then contracted out to other manufacturers. The ringed grip is the distinguishing feature of the the 3rd pattern dagger, more than 1 million of which are thought to have been produced.

DATE	1942 onward
ORIGIN	ENGLISH
LENGTH	29.6cm (11.7in)

American Mk 3 trench knife with M8 scabbard, 1943 onward

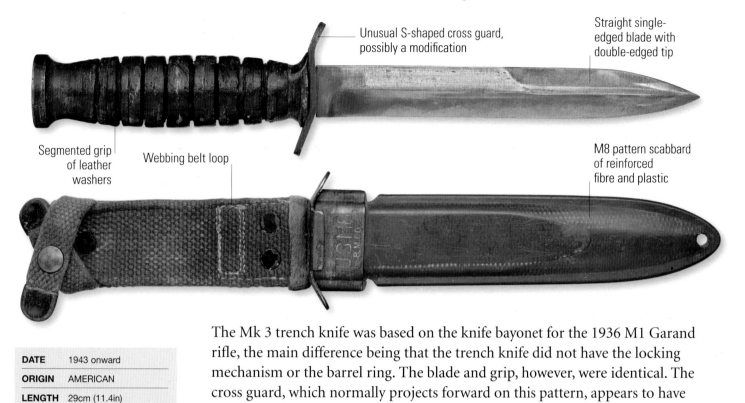

Unusual S-shaped cross guard, possibly a modification

Straight single-edged blade with double-edged tip

Segmented grip of leather washers

Webbing belt loop

M8 pattern scabbard of reinforced fibre and plastic

DATE	1943 onward
ORIGIN	AMERICAN
LENGTH	29cm (11.4in)

The Mk 3 trench knife was based on the knife bayonet for the 1936 M1 Garand rifle, the main difference being that the trench knife did not have the locking mechanism or the barrel ring. The blade and grip, however, were identical. The cross guard, which normally projects forward on this pattern, appears to have been modified with an upsweep on the underside.

German utility-fighting knife for the Bundeswehr, *c.*1970s

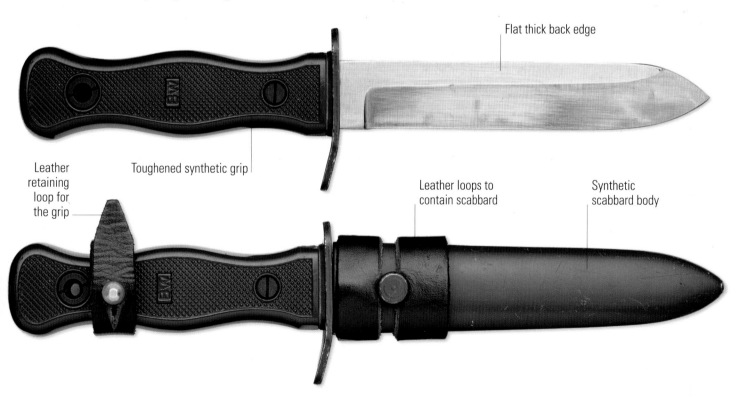

Flat thick back edge

Leather retaining loop for the grip

Toughened synthetic grip

Leather loops to contain scabbard

Synthetic scabbard body

DATE	c.1970s
ORIGIN	GERMAN
LENGTH	26cm (10.2in)

Although the role of the fighting knife in modern armies has diminished, military thinking still holds that a neat general-purpose knife is a useful tool. Advances in materials now mean that non-rusting and non-degrading components can be used to assemble knives capable of lasting for years without any visible deterioration.

German Third Reich edged weapons

The city of Solingen, in the Ruhr Valley, has been recognized as a centre of excellence in the production of edged weapons for over 700 years. Following the German surrender and disarmament after World War I, its edged-weapons industry experienced a period of steep decline. Swords and daggers, which had been prevalent in the Imperial Period, had always been viewed as symbols of authority and officialdom, particularly in Prussian culture. The emergence of the National Socialist Government (NSDAP) in 1933 created an opportunity to develop weapons of a new design to reflect the culture of the Third Reich.

German Hitler Youth knife, *c.*1933

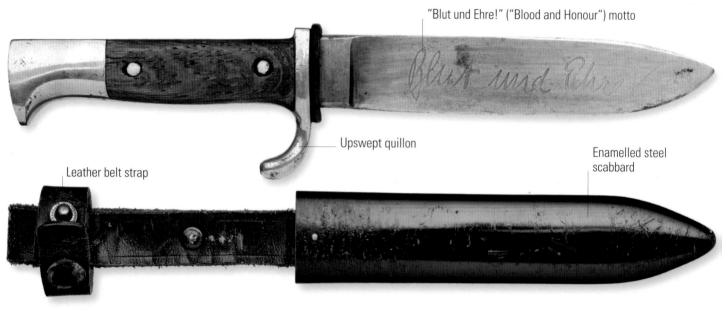

"Blut und Ehre!" ("Blood and Honour") motto

Upswept quillon

Leather belt strap

Enamelled steel scabbard

The Hitler Youth knife (HJ Fahrtenmesser, "Hiking Knife") was put into production in 1933. The blade is short and single-edged (examples made before 1938 featured the *Blut und Ehre!* motto) and the hilt is steel with a nickel plate finish. The knife would usually feature the Hitler Youth swastika emblem.

DATE	*c.*1933
ORIGIN	GERMAN
LENGTH	24.8cm (9.8in)

German SA service dagger, *c.*1933

"Alles für Deutschland" ("Everything for Germany") motto

National Socialist emblem

Steel blade

SA emblem

The SA, or *Sturm Abteilung* ("Storm Detachment"), were the militia who kept order at Nazi Party meetings. This service dagger was introduced in 1933 and based on a south German medieval design. The wood-and-steel hilt is emblazoned with National Socialist and SA emblems. The accompanying brown metal scabbard would have been ornamented with nickel trimmings.

DATE	*c.*1933
ORIGIN	GERMAN
LENGTH	35.4cm (14in)

German SS officer's dagger, 1936

"Meine Ehre heißt Treue"
("My Honour is named Loyalty") motto

Silver eagle and
swastika emblem

Steel blade, unsharpened

SS runic badge in grip

DATE	1936
ORIGIN	GERMAN
LENGTH	37cm (14.6in)

Introduced in December 1933, the SS dagger was based on the same design as the SA dagger, but with minor differences. The grip is made of hardwood which is stained black and has silver finish insignia, including the SS runic symbol at the top of the grip. The cross guards are finished in a nickel silver plating.

German RAD hewer, *c.*1934

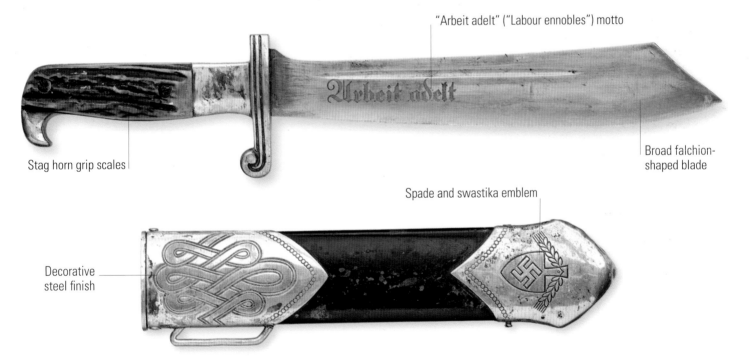

"Arbeit adelt" ("Labour ennobles") motto

Stag horn grip scales

Broad falchion-
shaped blade

Spade and swastika emblem

Decorative
steel finish

DATE	c.1934
ORIGIN	GERMAN
LENGTH	37.7cm (14.8in)

The RAD (*Reichs Arbeit Dienst*, "Reich's Labour Service") aimed to give young people experience of manual labour in the community. The design of this heavy-duty hewer, which was carried by full-time personnel only, was based on a traditional German hatchet. A heavily ornamented black metal scabbard carried the broad steel blade, which was falchion shaped with a short fuller close to the back edge. The organizational motto, *Arbeit adelt*, is etched on the blade. The hilt is made of iron, with nickel plating and stag horn grip scales. The steel scabbard has decorated steel fittings: the upper one bears a scroll design, while the lower one features a version of the national emblem of the RAD service – a spade head with swastika and corn stalks.

German Luftwaffe Flying Officer's dagger, 1934

Disc pommel with
"sun-wheel" swastika

Cross guard quillons in
form of stylized wings

Long slender blade

Maker's trademark

Leather and
silver wire wrapping

DATE	1934
ORIGIN	GERMAN
LENGTH	50.5cm (20in)

This dagger design was originally created for the *Deutsche Luftsportverband*, or "German Airsports Organization", which was a secret means of training air personnel while Germany was forbidden to operate a military air force under the terms of the Treaty of Versailles of 1919. In March 1935, the Luftwaffe came into existence and Germany declared its intention to begin rapid military expansion. This dagger would have been carried in a blue leather-wrapped scabbard with chain suspension.

The restoration of German pride

Uniforms and edged weapons had long been regarded as symbols of rank and status in Germany. The German love of order and discipline seemed to have come to the fore at around the time of Bismarck and the creation of the Second Reich (1871–1918). In this period of industrial growth and new prosperity, virtually every organization and service within Germany wore a uniform and carried a sword or dagger. This kind of adornment extended beyond the navy and army to hunters, postal workers, railway officials and so on.

In the years following World War I, most of this was swept away with the austerity of the new Weimar Republic and the heavy reparations imposed upon the defeated Germany. One of the key promises made by Hitler, sensing the people's resentment at the outcome of the war, was that he would restore German pride. The adoption of dress weapons for the Nazis' militarist formations was one aspect of this. New Nazi-inspired uniforms and daggers were created for other services, too, such as the German Red Cross and the Civil Service. The psychological effect was palpable. People started to feel important again; they were being given recognition and status.

ABOVE Adolf Hitler taking the salute at the 1938 Party Rally in Nuremberg. In the foreground is Reichs Labour Service leader Konstantin Hierl, wearing his own special RAD hewer. Another officer wears the 1937 Pattern RAD officers' hewer.

German army officer's dagger, 1935

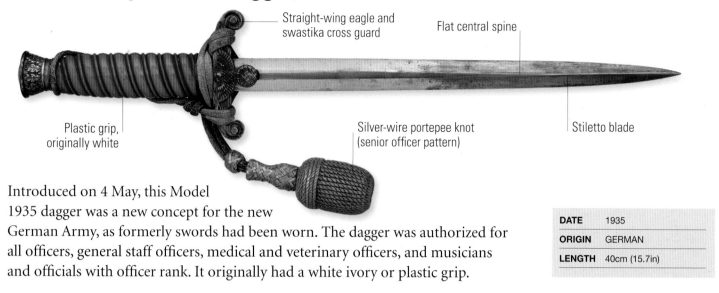

Straight-wing eagle and swastika cross guard

Flat central spine

Plastic grip, originally white

Silver-wire portepee knot (senior officer pattern)

Stiletto blade

Introduced on 4 May, this Model 1935 dagger was a new concept for the new German Army, as formerly swords had been worn. The dagger was authorized for all officers, general staff officers, medical and veterinary officers, and musicians and officials with officer rank. It originally had a white ivory or plastic grip.

DATE	1935
ORIGIN	GERMAN
LENGTH	40cm (15.7in)

German Luftwaffe dagger, 1937

White, plastic grip over wood base, with silver-wire wrap

Stiletto blade with flat central spine

Globe-form pommel

Cross guard in the form of an eagle clutching the swastika

DATE	1937
ORIGIN	GERMAN
LENGTH	40cm (15.7in)

Introduced in 1937 for Luftwaffe officers, this stylish new dagger features a cross guard in the form of the Luftwaffe eagle. The thin stiletto blade is unsharpened and is secured to the hilt with the tang passing through the grip and screw-locked with a globe pommel. The pommel is decorated with oak leaf motifs and a swastika. Some deluxe examples of this dagger had an ivory grip with a Damascus steel blade.

German state official dagger, 1938

White mother-of-pearl grip scales

Unsharpened stiletto blade

Silver-plated hilt in the form of a stylized eagle head

Cross guard in the form of a political pattern eagle and swastika

DATE	1938
ORIGIN	GERMAN
LENGTH	40cm (15.7in)

Introduced in March 1938 for all State and Civil Service Leaders, this dagger is very stylish, having an elegant hilt in the form of an eagle's head, with mother-of-pearl grip scales. All the hilt metal parts are made of brass, with a silver plate finish. The cross guard is very distinctive, featuring a political form spread-wing eagle, with upturned tips to the wings and a wreath with a swastika emblem clutched at the talons.

Bayonets of World War II

By the time World War II erupted, warfare had become much more mechanized. Soldiers were also more mobile and the widespread adoption of the submachine gun and automatic rifle meant that troops had greater individual firepower. But the need for close-quarter engagement still arose, in street fighting or commando operations, where the bayonet, especially the shorter versions, came into its own.

German or Belgian Mauser export bayonet, 1920s–30s

Plain wooden grip

Full muzzle ring

Single-edged blade with fullers

This is a typical Mauser "export" bayonet, manufactured in vast quantities in both Germany and Belgium and exported around the world during the interwar years. Unlike the majority of German service bayonets at this time, the export bayonets often had a complete muzzle ring and were either deeply blued or polished all over.

DATE	1920s–30s
ORIGIN	GERMAN/BELGIAN
LENGTH	38.5cm (15.2in)

Japanese Arisaka bayonet, 1939

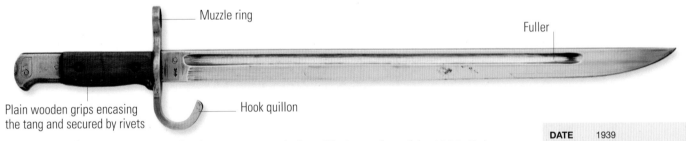

Muzzle ring

Fuller

Plain wooden grips encasing the tang and secured by rivets

Hook quillon

This bayonet was created to fit the Type 99 Arisaka rifle introduced in 1939. It is almost identical to the original Arisaka bayonet, the Type 30 of 1897, and at the time of production had a heavily blued hilt and either a bright or blued blade.

DATE	1939
ORIGIN	JAPANESE
LENGTH	73.5cm (28.9in)

British entrenching tool/bayonet, 1939–45

This was not designed as a weapon. As a wartime expedient, the helve of the entrenching tool was adapted to accept the No. 4 bayonet so it could be used as a probe for detecting landmines. The spade portion could easily be removed for this type of work and to simplify carrying.

DATE	1939–45
ORIGIN	BRITISH
LENGTH	unknown

No. 4 spike bayonet

Wooden haft

Spade

British bayonet for the No 4 rifle, No 4, Mk II, *c.*1940

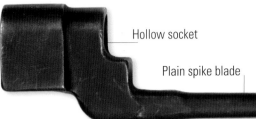

Hollow socket

Plain spike blade

The No 4 rifle and bayonet were urgently introduced at the start of the war. This rifle was a simplified version of the SMLE (Short, Magazine, Lee-Enfield).

DATE	c.1940
ORIGIN	BRITISH
LENGTH	25.4cm (10in)

British Sten machine carbine bayonet, Mk I, 1942

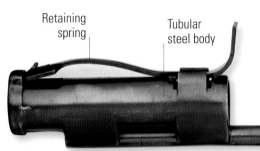

Retaining spring

Tubular steel body

Originating with Captain White of the Glasgow Home Guard, it reappeared in 1942 as the redesigned Mk I. The 20cm (8in) steel spike is welded to a steel body and uses a leaf spring clip attachment.

DATE	1942
ORIGIN	BRITISH
LENGTH	30cm (11.8in)

American bayonet for Garand M1 rifle, Model M1, 1943

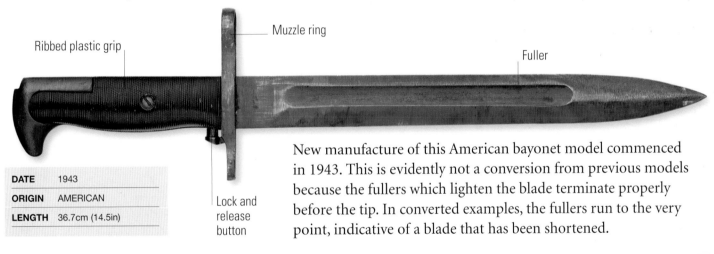

Ribbed plastic grip

Muzzle ring

Fuller

DATE	1943
ORIGIN	AMERICAN
LENGTH	36.7cm (14.5in)

Lock and release button

New manufacture of this American bayonet model commenced in 1943. This is evidently not a conversion from previous models because the fullers which lighten the blade terminate properly before the tip. In converted examples, the fullers run to the very point, indicative of a blade that has been shortened.

American bayonet for M1 carbine, Model M4, 1944

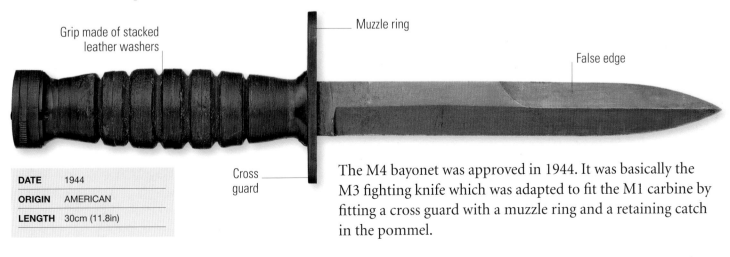

Grip made of stacked leather washers

Muzzle ring

False edge

DATE	1944
ORIGIN	AMERICAN
LENGTH	30cm (11.8in)

Cross guard

The M4 bayonet was approved in 1944. It was basically the M3 fighting knife which was adapted to fit the M1 carbine by fitting a cross guard with a muzzle ring and a retaining catch in the pommel.

Bayonets up to the present day

Despite the increasingly hi-tech nature of warfare, reliance still has to be ultimately placed on the soldier at the battlefront. When all else fails, the bayonet, used in its traditional role on the rifle, or used with stealth as a fighting knife, or used as a combination tool, is probably more an essential piece of equipment than it was in the past. Even now, a soldier on parade would be incomplete without one.

Czech VZ/24 knife bayonet, *c.*1926

Full muzzle ring

Spearpoint blade

Introduced around 1926 for the VZ/24 rifle, this is a shortened version of the VZ/23, and several variants exist. Unusually, the cutting edge of the blade is on the upper side. It was widely exported to Europe, the Middle East and South America.

DATE	c.1926
ORIGIN	CZECH
LENGTH	43.3cm (17in)

British knife bayonet, No 7, Mk I, 1945

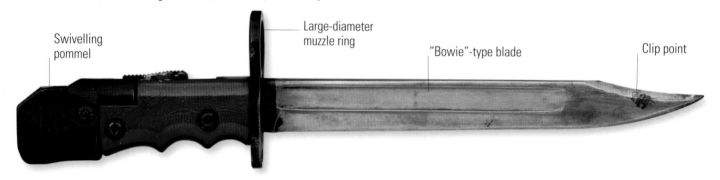

Swivelling pommel

Large-diameter muzzle ring

"Bowie"-type blade

Clip point

Designed for the No 4 rifle, this knife bayonet was first used on the Sten gun Mk V. After limited use, around 1947 the Guards began to use it for parade duty and this continued until the 1970s. The unusual swivelling pommel allowed the weapon to be used as a bayonet or, in the position shown, as a fighting knife.

DATE	1945
ORIGIN	BRITISH
LENGTH	32.3cm (12.7in)

Russian knife bayonet for AK47 assault rifle, 1947

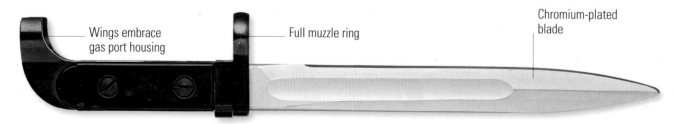

Wings embrace gas port housing

Full muzzle ring

Chromium-plated blade

DATE	1947
ORIGIN	RUSSIAN
LENGTH	32.6cm (12.8in)

This is a bayonet of very distinctive appearance. The pommel has two projections that partially wrap around the barrel, and slide along it when fitted, to give extra support. The cross guard has a traditional muzzle ring; immediately to the rear of this are the two locking catches that engage in recesses on the barrel.

British L1A3 bayonet for L1A1 SLR, 1957

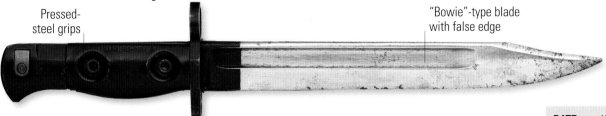

Pressed-steel grips

"Bowie"-type blade with false edge

DATE	1957
ORIGIN	BRITISH
LENGTH	30.5cm (12in)

One of a series of bayonets for this rifle, all with minor differences and all evolving from the No 5 bayonet. This one has a recessed lock-release button on the other side of the pommel and a fuller which terminates close to the hilt. All have blackened hilts.

South African pattern No 9 socket bayonet, c.1960

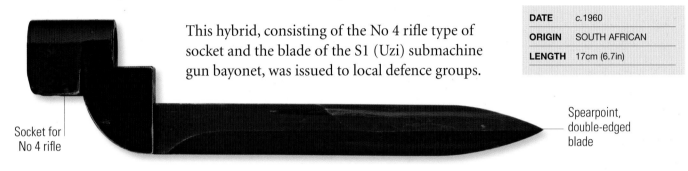

This hybrid, consisting of the No 4 rifle type of socket and the blade of the S1 (Uzi) submachine gun bayonet, was issued to local defence groups.

DATE	c.1960
ORIGIN	SOUTH AFRICAN
LENGTH	17cm (6.7in)

Socket for No 4 rifle

Spearpoint, double-edged blade

British knife bayonet L3A1 for SA80 (L85A1) rifle, 1985

Slot for stud on scabbard

Tubular handle

Clip point and part-serrated edge

DATE	1985
ORIGIN	BRITISH
LENGTH	28.6cm (11.3in)

This bayonet, a stainless-steel investment casting with tubular hilt, departs widely from earlier concepts. The blade is serrated like a kitchen knife and has a hole to engage with a stud on the scabbard, for use as a wire-cutter. Later, a bottle-opener was built into the hilt.

French knife bayonet for SIG 540/542 rifle, 1985

Plano-convex blade

DATE	1985
ORIGIN	FRENCH
LENGTH	unknown

Plastic-sheathed steel hilt

This is an elegantly simple but purposeful bayonet of Swiss design for the SIG rifle used by the Foreign Legion. It has a tubular steel hilt, partly encased in plastic with a catch built into the pommel, and a slender blade that is flat on one face and convex on the other.

Civilian knives to the present day

From the 19th century to the 21st century, the development of the modern knife has seen many novel interpretations. Revised and modified variations of some ancient knife styles came into being, together with "automatic" knives which flick open mechanically. Today, the classic Bowie knife endures in numerous updated forms alongside expressive, free-flowing styles that make the most of modern technology, such as the extravagant designs of Spanish knife-maker Martinez Albainox.

British bichwa double-bladed parrying knife, late 20th century

Wood grip scales mounted on central tang, secured by rivets

Short, double-edged blade either side of main grip

Short, double-edged blade either side of main grip

Smooth knucklebow

The bichwa (sometimes spelled bich'hwa) originated in India and usually had slightly curved, or wavy, blades. Some examples had two blades either side of the central grip. It was designed as a parrying knife, used in the left hand to thwart an opponent's blade, while the right hand retained a longer offensive weapon (sword or long dagger). This example appears to be a privately manufactured item, European and of modern construction.

DATE	late 20th century
ORIGIN	BRITISH
LENGTH	36.4cm (14.3in)

German flick knife, late 20th century

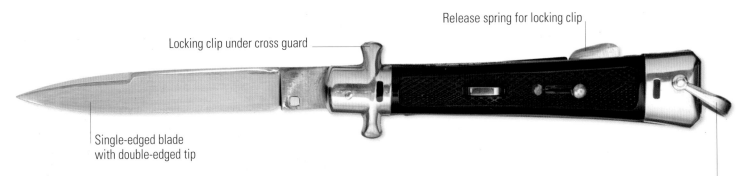

Release spring for locking clip

Locking clip under cross guard

Single-edged blade with double-edged tip

Lanyard ring

The flick-knife is, in reality, a spring-operated lock-back knife. The design has been known since the latter part of the 19th century, although its widespread popularity (and notoriety) seems to be encapsulated in the "Teddy boy" era of the early 1950s. The blade is folded into a hilt like a regular clasp-knife, and locked into position – under spring tension – with a clip. Depression of the button on the face of the grip releases the blade which swings out and into the open position, locked there by a spring clip inside the cross guard. Depressing a release spring on the side of the grip allows the blade to be folded back into a safe, closed position.

DATE	late 20th century
ORIGIN	GERMAN
LENGTH	24cm (9.4in)

West German Bundeswehr gravity knife, 1970s onward

Dark green toughened plastic grip mounted on aluminium body

Release trigger for blade

Short, single-edged blade of rust-free material

Connector ring for lanyard

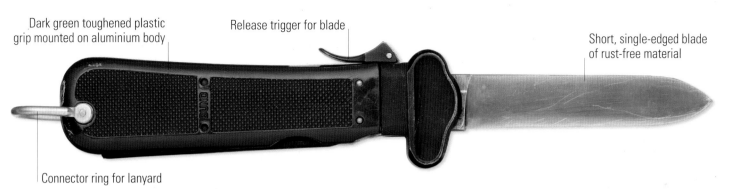

DATE	1970s onward
ORIGIN	WEST GERMAN
LENGTH	25.7cm (10.1in)

The design of this item has been clearly influenced by the World War II flight utility knife for the *Fallschirmjäger* (Paratroopers). Construction features have been improved, and the knife is lighter than the original wartime version. It is also designed to be stripped down for easy maintenance and repair work. The original examples were not designed to strip down, and were prone to fracturing on the spring.

West German spring-operated switchblade knife, 1970s onward

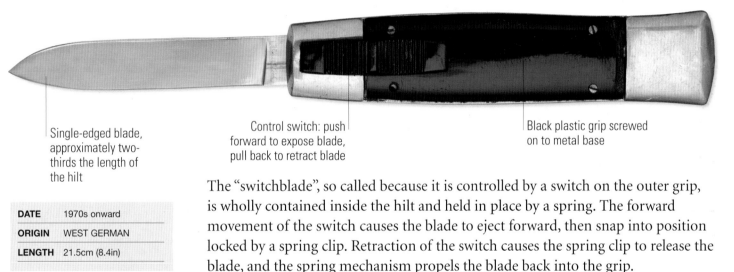

Single-edged blade, approximately two-thirds the length of the hilt

Control switch: push forward to expose blade, pull back to retract blade

Black plastic grip screwed on to metal base

DATE	1970s onward
ORIGIN	WEST GERMAN
LENGTH	21.5cm (8.4in)

The "switchblade", so called because it is controlled by a switch on the outer grip, is wholly contained inside the hilt and held in place by a spring. The forward movement of the switch causes the blade to eject forward, then snap into position locked by a spring clip. Retraction of the switch causes the spring clip to release the blade, and the spring mechanism propels the blade back into the grip.

American Applegate-Fairbairn knife, 1980s

Short double-edged blade with engraved facsimile signatures

Steel cross guard with short, downswept quillons

Grooved grip scale of tough synthetic secured to the tang with a single screw

DATE	1980s
ORIGIN	AMERICAN
LENGTH	28cm (11in)

This knife was a joint venture by Rex Applegate, America's leading exponent of military close-combat knife-fighting, and W. Fairbairn, of the famous Fairbairn and Sykes design team. It appears that only commemorative copies were produced, for collectors interested in the historical association.

American keyring punch dagger and sheath, late 20th century

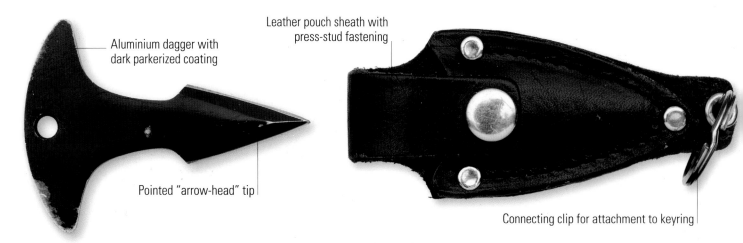

Aluminium dagger with dark parkerized coating

Leather pouch sheath with press-stud fastening

Pointed "arrow-head" tip

Connecting clip for attachment to keyring

Intended as a personal self-defence item, this punch dagger is an evolutionary development of the punch daggers designed in the United States in the mid-1800s. Although not designed to create a knife-like slash wound, it is a formidable item when held in the clenched fist – capable of breaking a bone with a direct hit.

DATE	late 20th century
ORIGIN	AMERICAN
LENGTH	7.2cm (2.8in)

Taiwanese butterfly knife, late 20th century

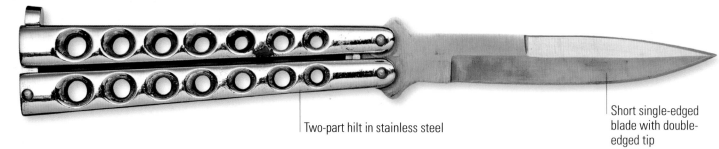

Two-part hilt in stainless steel

Short single-edged blade with double-edged tip

This folding knife does not have a tang. The blade is riveted to the two halves of the grip, each rivet acting as a hinge. Separating the halves of the grip at the base causes one half and the blade to swing around so that the blade faces down and insets into the grip. The second part of the grip follows round and covers the rest of the blade – now totally enclosed within the two halves of the grip.

DATE	late 20th century
ORIGIN	TAIWANESE
LENGTH	23.4cm (9.2in)

American Damascus steel knife, present day

Handle scales made from mammoth tooth

Curved Damascus steel blade

This vibrantly coloured fixed-blade knife, by the California knife-maker P. J. Ernest, is made from Damascus steel in the ladder pattern. Both the knife and bolsters were heat-coloured to bring out the intricate pattern of the steel. The handle scales are made from Siberian mammoth tooth.

DATE	present day
ORIGIN	AMERICAN
LENGTH	17.5cm (6.8in)

American bodyguard knuckleduster knife, present day

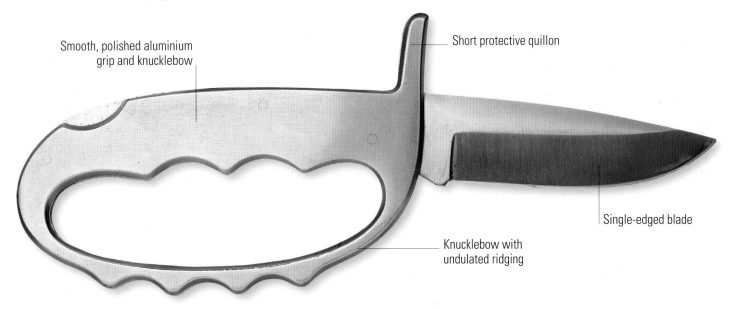

Smooth, polished aluminium grip and knucklebow

Short protective quillon

Single-edged blade

Knucklebow with undulated ridging

DATE	present day
ORIGIN	AMERICAN
LENGTH	23cm (9.1in)

The interpretation of what is permissible to carry as an item of self-defence is quite different in the United States compared to Europe. The above item is clearly of very modern manufacture, and is a very clean, 20th-century style. Designed as a "bodyguard" item, the intended market is unclear. Trained personnel, licensed as bodyguards, would be permitted to carry such a defensive weapon. If carried by an unlicensed person it carries the risk of being presumed to be a weapon of assault rather than defence.

Spanish Martinez Albainox knife, present day

Curved grip

Sharply curved blade

Pommel

Notched lower edge

Secondary blade

DATE	present day
ORIGIN	SPANISH
LENGTH	28.5cm (11.2in)

There is a school of modern knife-making that promotes the concept of knives of somewhat fantastical form – seemingly more rooted in the world of science-fiction than practical knife design. The above specimen by the Spanish company Martinez Albainox is clearly an impressive example. Intended purely as a collector's piece, the artistic sweep of the blade and the flow of the metal present a surreal appearance when compared to the utter simplicity of design of the Applegate-Fairbairn knife, for example. There are so many exposed points and edges on the item that any bearer might be advised to wear a suit of chain mail before unsheathing this weapon!

African knives and daggers

It is not surprising that the forms of knives and daggers found in Africa are almost infinitely diverse, given the size of the continent, the tribal nature of the people, and pervasive influences from the ancient Egyptians, Romans and other invader/trader nations.

Although the workmanship cannot compare with that of other continents, the artistic style with which African smiths have designed their weapons is unsurpassed. The abstract nature of African art, its originality and vitality, attract worldwide admiration.

Yakoma or Ngbandi knife, mid-19th century

Incised chevrons and cross-hatching

Copper strip binding

The tribal knives of the Yakoma and Ngbandi are similar and difficult to tell apart. In addition to their formal function, they were also used as currency, in particular to pay a "bride price". This blade has some nicely incised decoration; the hilt is bound with copper and it is made with a leather-covered pommel.

DATE	mid-19th century
ORIGIN	ZAIREAN
LENGTH	48.3cm (19in)

Mangbetu knife, mid-19th century

Wooden hilt with cylindrical pommel

Sickle-shaped blade sharpened on both edges

The Mangbetu of northeastern Zaire called this weapon a "trumbash", and its very particular shape is said to derive from ancient Egypt. In fact, a contemporary illustration of Rameses III (king of Egypt 1184–1156BC) shows him using a very similar "sickle-sword" when in the act of executing his enemies.

DATE	mid-19th century
ORIGIN	ZAIREAN
LENGTH	22.9cm (9in)

Konda shortsword, mid-19th century

Wooden sheath covered with brass nail heads

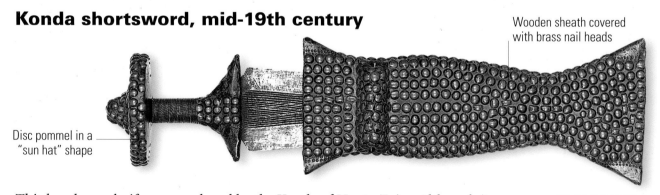

Disc pommel in a "sun hat" shape

This handsome knife was produced by the Konda of Haute-Zaire. Although its general shape commends it to close fighting, there is no doubt that in peaceful times it would have doubled as a particularly useful general-purpose knife. The wooden hilt and sheath are studded with brass nail heads forming a dense covering.

DATE	mid-19th century
ORIGIN	ZAIREAN
LENGTH	31.2cm (12.25in)

Ngala knife, late 19th century

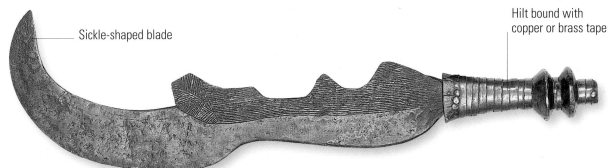

Sickle-shaped blade

Hilt bound with copper or brass tape

DATE	late 19th century
ORIGIN	ZAIREAN
LENGTH	43.2cm (17in)

These Ngala swords from Zaire, with their unique form of sickle-shaped blade, were sometimes used for a particularly gruesome form of execution. The victim was secured to the ground with his head tied to a supple tree bent over for the purpose. At the moment of decapitation the head was catapulted into the distance.

Sudanese dagger, late 19th century

Blade swells out slightly towards the tip

Handle made from a lightweight, dense boxwood-type timber

DATE	late 19th century
ORIGIN	SUDANESE
LENGTH	26.7cm (10.5in)

This dagger from Sudan is typical of those carried by followers of the Mahdi during the last quarter of the 19th century. It was intended primarily for stabbing, and the blade swells out towards the tip, which is slightly thickened in section. The blade is sharp on both edges and is contained in a leather sheath lined with cotton.

Sudanese double dagger, late 19th century

Blades etched with inscriptions in Thuluth script

Coloured-glass beadwork

DATE	late 19th century
ORIGIN	SUDANESE
LENGTH	56cm (22in)

This double dagger comes from Sudan and is associated with followers of the Mahdi during the 1880s. The blades are etched with inscriptions in Thuluth script, which derives from that used by the Mamluks for monumental inscriptions. The wooden grip and sheaths are covered with multicoloured beadwork.

Hadendoa dagger, late 19th century

Carved with flutes

Blade of shallow diamond section

Hilt made of ebony

DATE	late 19th century
ORIGIN	NORTHEAST AFRICAN
LENGTH	19.5cm (7.7in)

The Hadendoa are a Nilotic people from Sudan, Egypt and Eritrea. Their unique style of dagger has an H-shaped ebony hilt, sometimes with silver-wire binding and fittings; it was carried in a leather sheath. It was extensively used when fighting against the British in support of the Mahdi in Sudan at the end of the 19th century, and was sometimes used to "hamstring" British horses.

Nubian arm dagger, *c.*1900

Flat blade sometimes inscribed

Ebony hilt

Nubia is a region of Sudan close to the River Nile. These daggers are found in leather sheaths which have woven leather straps to bind them to the wearer's arm. The circular pommel is lathe-turned and looks very similar to the counter used in the game of draughts. Often the dagger hilts have a pommel made of ivory.

DATE	c.1900
ORIGIN	NUBIAN
LENGTH	27.4cm (10.8in)

Somali "Billa" knife, *c.*1900

Silver pommel

Ivory hilt

Thin, broad blade

This Somali knife was produced by Arab cutlers who imported the skills of silversmithing from Oman. Arab interaction with Africa's east coast occurred through trade and traders; indeed, Zanzibar was ruled by Oman and Muscat during the 18th and 19th centuries. Only the finest of these knives have hilts of ivory and silver; others are made from horn or wood.

DATE	c.1900
ORIGIN	SOMALI
LENGTH	43.4cm (17.1in)

Sudanese throwing knife, *c.*1900

Projecting blades

Leather-bound
cotton-covered grip

These multi-bladed throwing knives do not seem to have been produced for use, and may have had a ceremonial function or even have been made purely for the souvenir market. Sometimes stamped with geometric ornament, they have grips often bound with leather over cotton cloth.

DATE	*c.*1900
ORIGIN	SUDANESE
LENGTH	unknown

Moroccan jambya or koummya, early 20th century

Wooden grip

Sharp inside cutting edge

Metal pommel

These daggers are among the most numerous ever to have been produced in Africa, and their design conforms very closely. However, the grips can be made from wood, bone or ivory, while the mounts are of brass, silver and even gold. The blades are mostly plain or undecorated.

DATE	early 20th century
ORIGIN	MOROCCAN
LENGTH	31cm (12.2in)

Central African arm knife, 20th century

Very shallow diamond-section blade

Iron pommel integral
with the blade

These parts are made
from woven leather

This type of arm dagger is commonly encountered all over Central and North Africa, from Nigeria to Sudan, and from the Sahara Desert to Cameroon. They are distinguished by the woven leather bindings to the hilt and by the protruding flattened iron pommel. They were and still are made by a large variety of tribes and craftsmen, perhaps the finest being Mandingo leatherworkers.

DATE	20th century
ORIGIN	CENTRAL AFRICAN
LENGTH	unknown

Persia, Middle East and Turkey

This geographic area has been home to a multitude of peoples and dynasties possessing fabulous wealth and artistry, and this is reflected in their weapons. The best knives and daggers came from the court workshops set up to reflect the majesty, wealth and reputation of their patrons. The quality of production would tend to diminish with distance from court, where function and cost were critical considerations.

Venetian or Turkish khanjar dagger, *c.*1520

Brightly gilt

Ivory grip with incised design filled with black substance

This most unusual dagger was made in Venice for the Turkish market. The blade shape is found on daggers from the Mediterranean to Scotland. Venetian craftsmen specialized in the manufacture of weapons and armour for export to Turkey, and they were very accomplished at interpreting Turkish ornament.

DATE	c.1520
ORIGIN	VENETIAN/TURKISH
LENGTH	38.6cm (15.2in)

Ottoman Turkish knife, 17th century

Blade made from watered steel

Jade hilt inlaid with gold and stones

The blade of this dagger comes from Persia or India, and is made from watered steel. The jade hilt is only inlaid with gold at the top and the rest of the hilt is plain to enable the dagger to slide down deep into its sheath, with only the decorated pommel showing. The hilt is Turkish and dates from the 17th century.

DATE	17th century
ORIGIN	OTTOMAN TURKISH
LENGTH	19cm (7.5in)

Persian khanjar, *c.*1800

This fine Persian khanjar has a walrus-ivory hilt of the best quality. It is beautifully carved with a naked couple standing between two trees; at their feet are three naked children. It was made during the Qajar Dynasty, *c.*1800. The depiction of naked human figures is unusual in Persian art, but other daggers with similar subjects are known. It is possible they were made for the prurient, or for non-Muslims. The blade is made from finely watered steel.

Central reinforcing rib

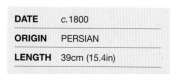

DATE	c.1800
ORIGIN	PERSIAN
LENGTH	39cm (15.4in)

Finely carved walrus-ivory hilt

Ottoman Turkish khanjar with nephrite grips, early 18th century

Jade grip inlaid with gold

Twin fullers lined with brass

Three garnets on pommel

DATE	early 18th century
ORIGIN	OTTOMAN TURKISH
LENGTH	34cm (13.4in)

The two-piece grips are made of jade. There are two different types of jade called nephrite and jadeite respectively; the former is slightly harder than the latter. This classic Ottoman dagger dates from the early 18th century, although the shape of the hilt is more commonly found on daggers of the 17th century.

Ottoman Turkish silver-mounted khanjar dagger, *c.*1740

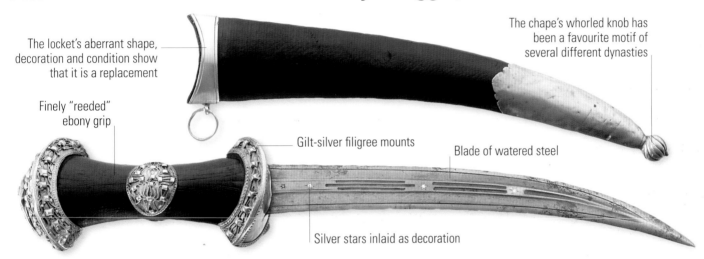

The locket's aberrant shape, decoration and condition show that it is a replacement

The chape's whorled knob has been a favourite motif of several different dynasties

Finely "reeded" ebony grip

Gilt-silver filigree mounts

Blade of watered steel

Silver stars inlaid as decoration

DATE	*c.*1740
ORIGIN	OTTOMAN TURKISH
LENGTH	42cm (16.5in)

Silver stars are found inlaid into Turkish blades from the 17th to the 19th centuries. This dagger, dating from *c.*1740, has a "reeded" ebony grip and is fitted with fine-quality filigree mounts made from gilt silver. This is a large dagger, and the original owner would have worn it in a prominent position.

Ottoman Turkish bichaq knife with agate grip, early 19th century

Agate hilt

Silver sheath mounts

DATE	early 19th century
ORIGIN	OTTOMAN TURKISH
LENGTH	33cm (13in)

The bichaq serves principally as a knife, although it could be called into service as a dagger. This Ottoman example has an agate hilt with a gold-set jewel inlaid into the pommel. The blade has a false-damascened inscription, and it retains its original silver-mounted sheath. It dates from the early 19th century.

Ottoman Turkish khanjar, early 19th century

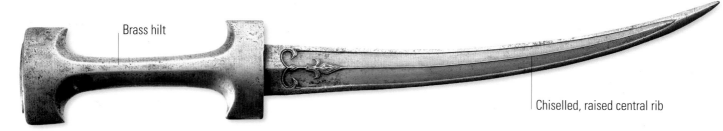

Brass hilt

Chiselled, raised central rib

The shape of this dagger was found across Ottoman Turkey during the 18th and
19th centuries, but it is particularly associated with the Kurds. The grip is made
from brass, and the double-edged blade is carved with a central rib and forms two
shallow "fullers" between it and the slightly raised edges.

DATE	early 19th century
ORIGIN	OTTOMAN TURKISH
LENGTH	40.5cm (15.9in)

Uzbek kard, early 19th century

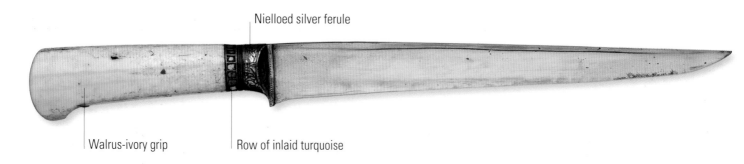

Nielloed silver ferule

Walrus-ivory grip

Row of inlaid turquoise

This dagger comes from Bukhara in Uzbekistan (formerly Turkestan), which was
an important city on the Silk Road. Their weapons production famously employed
the use of turquoise, either cut or polished, or as polished chips. The silver ferrule is
decorated with niello (a shiny black alloy) and the grip is made from walrus tusk.

DATE	early 19th century
ORIGIN	UZBEK
LENGTH	unknown

Ottoman Turkish stiletto, early to mid-19th century

Gilt brass
mounts

Blade as slender as possible, yet sufficiently
strong so as not to bend or break

This unusual dagger dates from the period during the 19th century when Turkey
was intensely influenced by Western Europe (especially France). It is Turkish-made,
but this particular type of dagger is known as a stiletto in Europe. The hilt and
sheath mounts are made from gilt brass, whilst the blade is a simple, slender but
strong spike designed for maximum penetration.

DATE	early to mid-19th century
ORIGIN	OTTOMAN TURKISH
LENGTH	33.5cm (13.1in)

Persian khanjar, early to mid-19th-century

An attractive Qajar khanjar built to create an impression, this dagger is fitted with a dark-coloured watered blade that has been chiselled and false damascened with an allegorical scene of a lion attacking an antelope. The hilt features two cabochon turquoises in gold mounts; the use of gold on the black blade combines with the light-coloured walrus-ivory hilt to produce a rich effect.

Walrus-ivory hilt

Dark watered blade
(Qara Khorasan)

Allegorical scene of
strength victorious

DATE	early to mid-19th century
ORIGIN	PERSIAN
LENGTH	37cm (14.6in)

Lawrence of Arabia

T.E. Lawrence ("Lawrence of Arabia") famously led an army of Arab tribes to victory against the Turks during World War I. Many depictions of Lawrence, such as this portrait, show him wearing Arab dress and a dagger. One particular dagger owned by Lawrence has an interesting history. In 1917, he was in Jidda for talks with Sharif Husain – head of the Arab nationalists – when he made his way illegally to Mecca. There he ordered a dagger with a gold hilt and sheath, probably supplying his own gold sovereigns to be melted down. "I did it because I wanted to choose my own gold dagger … (it was made) … in the third little turning to the left off the main bazaar, by an old Najd goldsmith." Lawrence sold the dagger in 1923 for £125 to his friend Lionel Curtis, who presented it to All Souls College, Oxford, where it remains. He used the money to refurbish Clouds Hill, his Dorset home close to where he was killed riding his motorcycle on 19 May 1935.

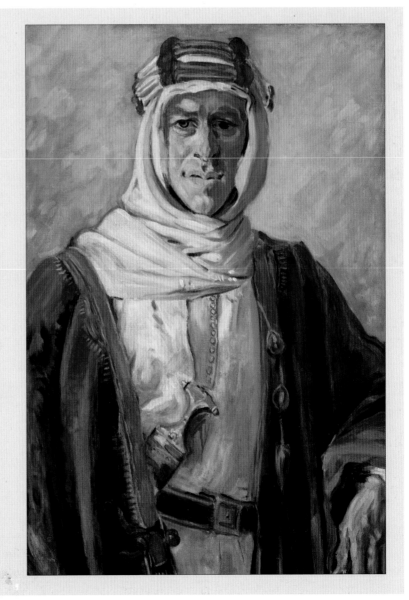

RIGHT Portrait of T.E. Lawrence wearing the silver-gilt Meccan dagger presented to him by Sharif Nasir in 1917.

Balkan Ottoman bichaq, mid-19th century

Suspension loop to attach the belt

Zoomorphic finial with a hole in the mouth to allow for drainage

A silver-mounted Ottoman knife, or bichaq, from the Balkans. The scrolling foliate ornament covers the hilt as well as the sheath, whilst the pommel is in the form of a stylized animal's head, as is the finial of the sheath. The blade of the knife is thin and probably intended to function mostly as a utility knife.

DATE	mid-19th century
ORIGIN	TURKISH (BALKANS)
LENGTH	27cm (10.6in)

Saudi Arabian janbiyya/khanjar, mid-19th century

This silver-mounted Arabian janbiyya is from the Hijaz-Asir region. The double-edged blade is almost flat and has a simple chiselled device. The hilt and sheath are covered with silver, which is decorated with engraved decoration, granulation and filigree. Colloidal hard soldering is the process whereby tiny silver balls (granulation) or decorative silver wire (filigree) are applied decoratively to a silver ground with an organic compound. The work is then covered with silver salt and heated until the organic compound is driven off, and the salt turns to metal and fuses the decoration to the ground.

DATE	mid-19th century
ORIGIN	SAUDI ARABIAN
LENGTH	56cm (22in)

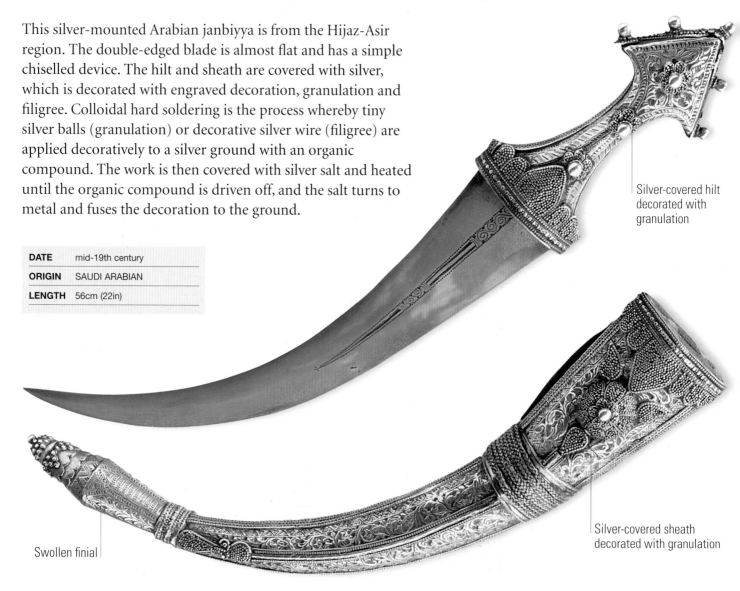

Silver-covered hilt decorated with granulation

Silver-covered sheath decorated with granulation

Swollen finial

Omani janbiyya/khanjar, mid-19th century

The hilt of this Omani janbiyya, or dagger, is made from horn, probably from a rhinoceros, and was presumably believed to possess magical properties or to confer virility to its owner. Subsequent to the decline in the supply of rhinoceros horn, the giraffe horn and hoof became a popular material for use on grips. Now that conservation has become of great concern, the grips are usually made from plastic.

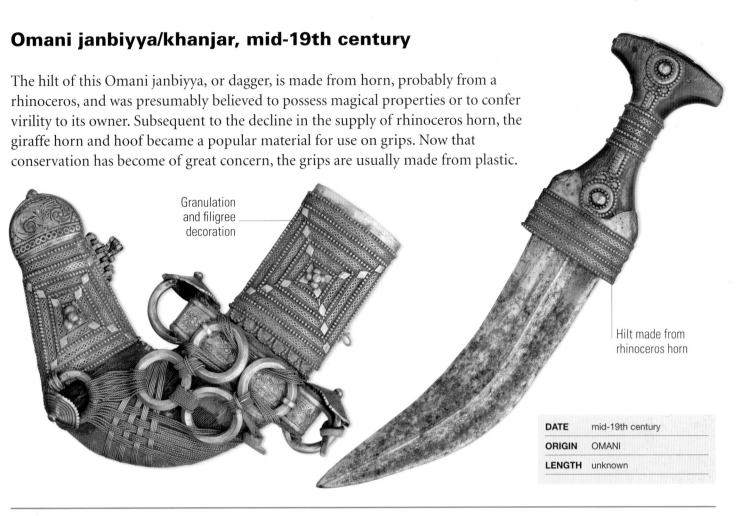

Granulation and filigree decoration

Hilt made from rhinoceros horn

DATE	mid-19th century
ORIGIN	OMANI
LENGTH	unknown

Saudi Arabian janbiyya/khanjar, late 19th century

These janbiyyas with their distinctive long, curved blades are particularly associated with the conservative Wahabi sect of Sunni Muslims. The grip is made from horn, and reinforced with steel, copper and brass; the front has extensive silver ornamentation. The blade is noticeably thin and flat. The sheath, from a later date, is covered with multicoloured leatherwork.

DATE	late 19th century
ORIGIN	SAUDI ARABIAN
LENGTH	63cm (24.8in)

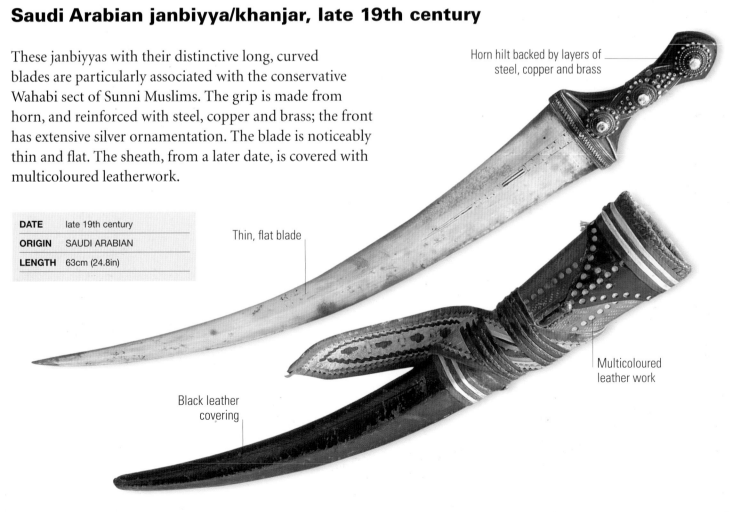

Horn hilt backed by layers of steel, copper and brass

Thin, flat blade

Multicoloured leather work

Black leather covering

Yemeni khanjar and sheath, late 19th century

This is the classic form of Arabian khanjar and probably comes from Yemen. The horn is decorated with gold-foil imitations of the Venetian ducat (coin). The gold ducat was clearly held in esteem long after the Venetians ceased to be actively involved in trade in the area. The blades are burnished bright and the Indian-made sheath is fitted with a pierced silver chape.

DATE	late 19th century
ORIGIN	YEMENI
LENGTH	28cm (11in)

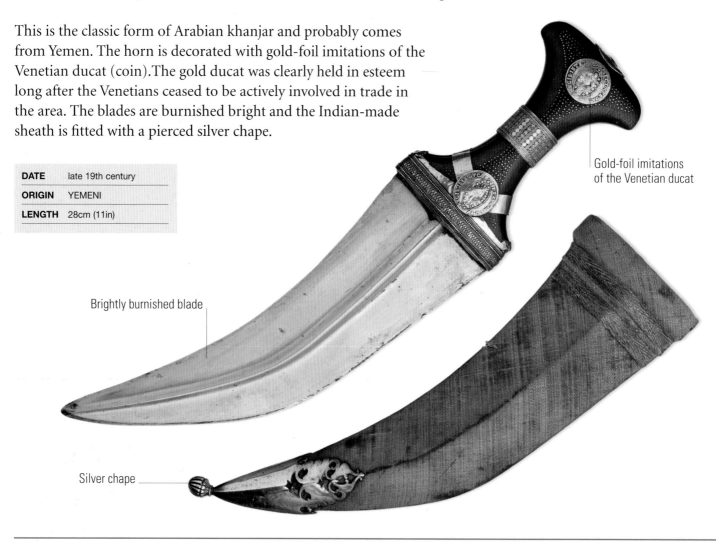

Gold-foil imitations of the Venetian ducat

Brightly burnished blade

Silver chape

Saudi Arabian janbiyya/khanjar, late 19th century

This massive dagger from Hijaz or Asir, western Saudi Arabia, is easily amongst the longest ever produced. The polished blade is stoutly reinforced by the raised central rib, and the hilt is secured by large and prominent silver-headed rivets. It seems likely that this weapon would also have been employed for various everyday purposes.

Large silver-headed rivets secure the grips

Stout reinforcing rib

Sheath covered in brown leather

DATE	late 19th century
ORIGIN	SAUDI ARABIAN
LENGTH	65cm (25.6in)

Persian khanjar, 19th century

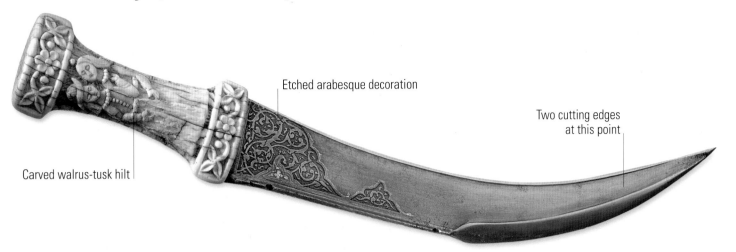

Etched arabesque decoration

Two cutting edges
at this point

Carved walrus-tusk hilt

DATE	19th century
ORIGIN	PERSIAN
LENGTH	41cm (16.1in)

The hilt of this 19th-century Persian khanjar is carved from a single section of walrus tusk and depicts a fashionably dressed couple carved in relief. The curved blade is T-section for half the length of the back edge, and is etched at the forte with an arabesque design. The blade is also etched with a pattern intended to imitate the watering of "Damascus" steel.

Omani janbiyya/khanjar, *c.*1900

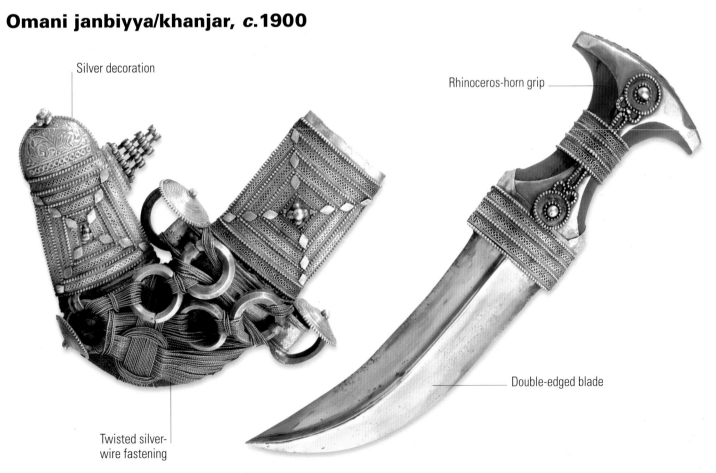

Silver decoration

Rhinoceros-horn grip

Double-edged blade

Twisted silver-
wire fastening

DATE	c.1900
ORIGIN	OMANI
LENGTH	32cm (12.6in)

The silversmiths of Oman are renowned for their skills, particularly in the use of granulation. The back of the chape is embossed by the maker '*amal Abdullah Al-Beham* ("the work of Abdullah Al-Beham"), and the front of the sheath sports seven thick rings of silver. These are secured with twisted-silver wire, and the largest outside rings are used to fasten the sheath to a broad belt.

Saudi Arabian (probably Meccan) janbiyya/khanjar, *c.*1900

Both the hilt and the sheath are entirely covered with sheet silver on this dagger which probably comes from Mecca. The decorative silver ornaments applied to the hilt help provide a decent grip, whilst the sheath has engraved borders and an upturned finial, or *thum* (literally, "garlic bulb" in Arabic).

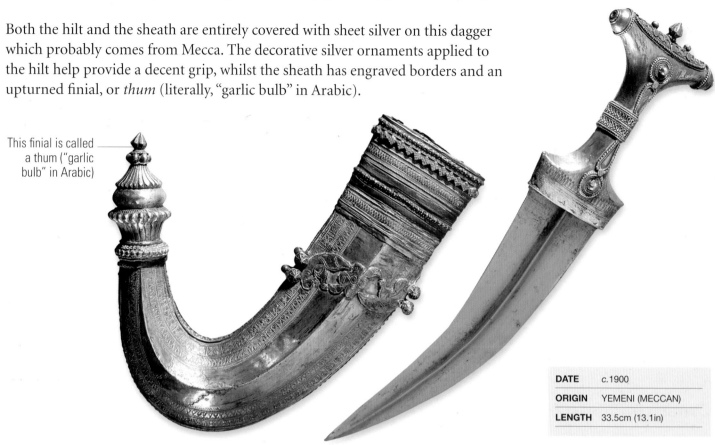

This finial is called a thum ("garlic bulb" in Arabic)

DATE	c.1900
ORIGIN	YEMENI (MECCAN)
LENGTH	33.5cm (13.1in)

Saudi Arabian janbiyya/khanjar, early 20th century

Few Arabian daggers are quite so distinctive as this example from Asir or Tehama in Saudi Arabia. The silver hilt and sheath display granulation as a decorative technique that also helps provide a firm grip. These elaborate daggers are still produced by Arab silversmiths for the tourist market today.

DATE	early 20th century
ORIGIN	SAUDI ARABIAN
LENGTH	46.5cm (18.3in)

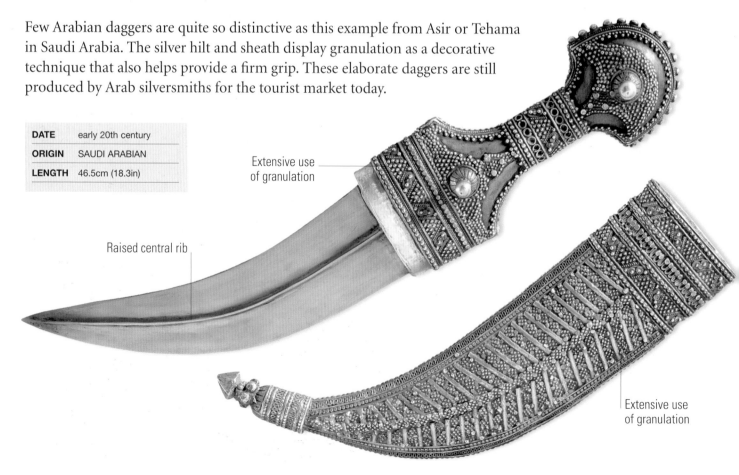

Extensive use of granulation

Raised central rib

Extensive use of granulation

Omani janbiyya/khanjar, mid-20th century

Perhaps the most common dagger from the Arabian Peninsula, this example comes from Oman. The wooden hilt is faced with an undecorated sheet of silver, whilst the silver band at the bottom is embossed with foliage, and is designed to fit over the top of the sheath to prevent the ingress of sand and water.

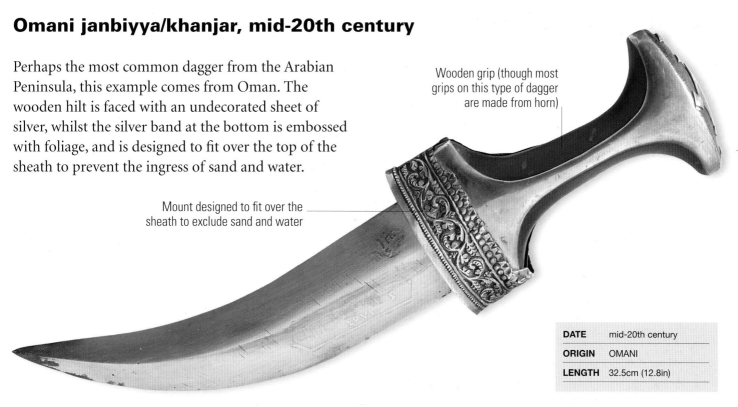

Wooden grip (though most grips on this type of dagger are made from horn)

Mount designed to fit over the sheath to exclude sand and water

DATE	mid-20th century
ORIGIN	OMANI
LENGTH	32.5cm (12.8in)

Omani janbiyya/khanjar, *c.*1975

This late 20th-century Omani janbiyya is of poor quality. These types of daggers were produced not only for the tourist industry but also to fulfil a domestic Omani convention that the janbiyya (or khanjar) is an integral part of the national dress. It is unlikely that such a weapon would ever be required to see service.

DATE	c.1975
ORIGIN	OMANI
LENGTH	99cm (39in)

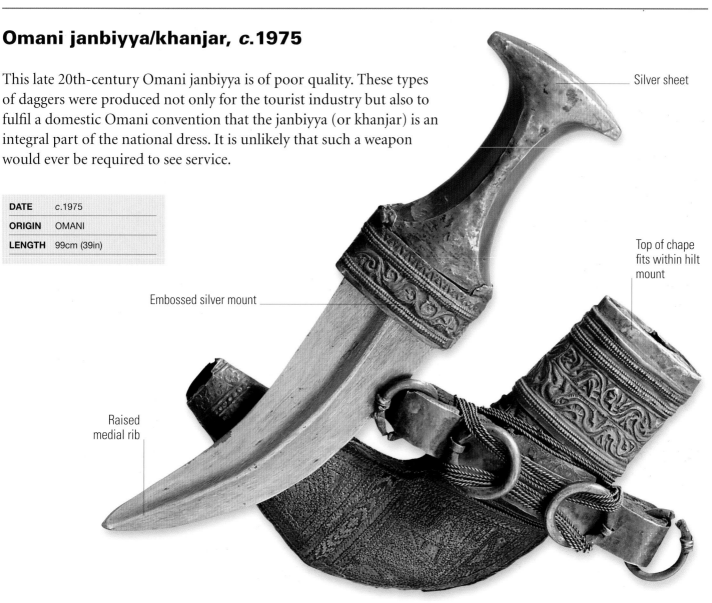

Silver sheet

Top of chape fits within hilt mount

Embossed silver mount

Raised medial rib

Indo-Persian khanjars

The expression "Indo-Persian" covers both the vast subcontinent of India itself and the lands occupied or ruled over by Persia when its empire was at its apogee. *Khanjar* is the general Arabic word for dagger.

Often, however, the term is used by collectors to describe a body of daggers with curved, double-edged blades from India, mostly with jade hilts, and from Persia, frequently with walrus-ivory or steel hilts.

Indian khanjar with Mughal hilt, late 17th century

Gold koftgari decoration

Shallow fullers

Carved jade hilt

The hilt is made from dark green nephrite (jade), the supply of which is supposed to have been exhausted before the end of the 17th century. The classic Mughal "pistol"-shaped hilt is carved with flowers and foliage in relief. The blade, which is probably of later date, is decorated with a repeated interlaced geometric pattern in gold koftgari.

DATE	late 17th century
ORIGIN	INDIAN
LENGTH	unknown

Indian khanjar, c.1700

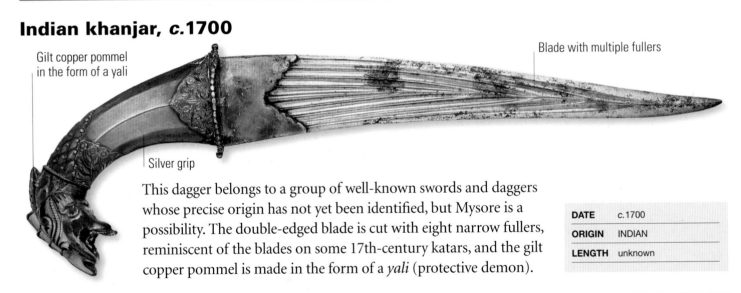

Gilt copper pommel in the form of a yali

Blade with multiple fullers

Silver grip

This dagger belongs to a group of well-known swords and daggers whose precise origin has not yet been identified, but Mysore is a possibility. The double-edged blade is cut with eight narrow fullers, reminiscent of the blades on some 17th-century katars, and the gilt copper pommel is made in the form of a *yali* (protective demon).

DATE	c.1700
ORIGIN	INDIAN
LENGTH	unknown

Indo-Persian khanjar and scabbard, early 19th century

A good-quality Persian dagger, the blade is of watered steel and is chiselled with the image of a lion attacking a gazelle (an allegorical scene). The ivory hilt is carved from a single piece of walrus tusk with figures and an inscription meaning "The shining blade of this amazing khanjar is so sharp it can split a thorn".

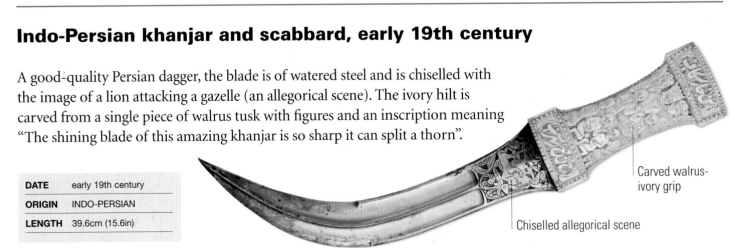

DATE	early 19th century
ORIGIN	INDO-PERSIAN
LENGTH	39.6cm (15.6in)

Carved walrus-ivory grip

Chiselled allegorical scene

Indian khanjar, *c.*1900

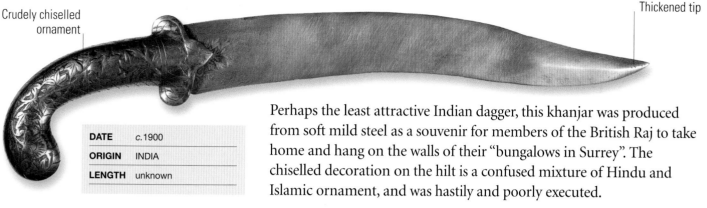

Crudely chiselled ornament

Thickened tip

DATE	c.1900
ORIGIN	INDIA
LENGTH	unknown

Perhaps the least attractive Indian dagger, this khanjar was produced from soft mild steel as a souvenir for members of the British Raj to take home and hang on the walls of their "bungalows in Surrey". The chiselled decoration on the hilt is a confused mixture of Hindu and Islamic ornament, and was hastily and poorly executed.

Indo-Persian five-bladed khanjar, mid-19th century

Etched cartouches

These all-steel daggers were produced in considerable quantities in Persia (now Iran) during the Qajar Dynasty (1779–1925). The earliest examples use watered steel and have decoration chiselled in relief and emphasized by details in thick gold koftgari.

Five sprung-blade tips

DATE	mid-19th century
ORIGIN	INDO-PERSIAN
LENGTH	unknown

Indo-Persian five-bladed khanjar, mid-19th century

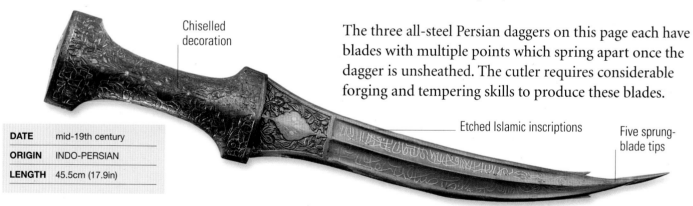

Chiselled decoration

The three all-steel Persian daggers on this page each have blades with multiple points which spring apart once the dagger is unsheathed. The cutler requires considerable forging and tempering skills to produce these blades.

Etched Islamic inscriptions

Five sprung-blade tips

DATE	mid-19th century
ORIGIN	INDO-PERSIAN
LENGTH	45.5cm (17.9in)

Indo-Persian triple-bladed khanjar, late 19th century

Three sprung-blade tips

DATE	late 19th century
ORIGIN	INDO-PERSIAN
LENGTH	49cm (19.3in)

The steel grip of this triple-bladed dagger is filled with a plaster-like substance which swells when moisture is absorbed. When this happens, the braised seam will begin to split open, as is the case here. Cartouches filled with Islamic inscriptions can clearly be seen decorating the hilt.

Indo-Persian kards

Kard is Farsi (the most widely spoken Persian language) and refers to a dagger with a straight, single-edged blade where the hilt is without a guard. Collectors apply the term to similar daggers from India and the Middle East. They may be fitted with delicately worked hilts of exotic materials, with blades of fine watered steel, but each will be of the same form as those made from more common materials.

Persian gold-inlaid kard, *c.*1800

Single-edged blade | Gold-inlaid decoration | Walrus-ivory grip

A classical Persian dagger of *c.*1800, this kard has a fine watered-steel single-edged blade which is decorated with gold-inlaid foliage in relief at the forte. This decoration continues around the grip strap. The grips are made from two pieces of walrus ivory. It seems ironic that these beautiful daggers were intended to be entirely covered by their sheath, with the exception of the last inch of the hilt.

DATE	*c.*1800
ORIGIN	PERSIAN
LENGTH	37.5cm (14.7in)

Uzbek kard with lapis lazuli hilt, *c.*1800

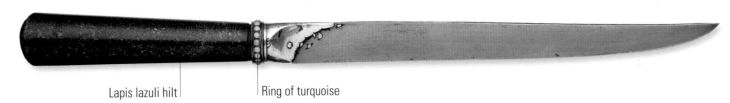

Lapis lazuli hilt | Ring of turquoise

Lapis lazuli from Afghanistan is one of the most attractive stones with an intense blue colour. The ring at the base of the grip is decorated with polished turquoise, and this is almost a signature of production from Bukhara in Uzbekistan (formerly Turkestan). The small metal ferrule at the forte of the blade is also a feature of edged weapons from the Balkans.

DATE	*c.*1800
ORIGIN	UZBEK
LENGTH	34.7cm (13.6in)

Indian kard with stone handle, *c.*1800

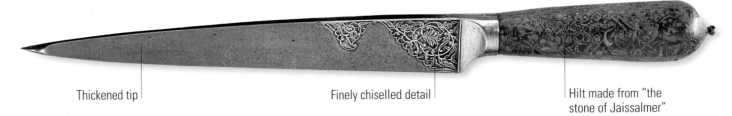

Thickened tip | Finely chiselled detail | Hilt made from "the stone of Jaissalmer"

This high-quality Indian kard has a watered steel blade and is chiselled with foliage at the forte, while the tip is thickened to add strength at the point of impact. The hilt is made from "the stone of Jaissalmer", a yellow- and orange-coloured conglomerate which is highly attractive due to its clearly visible constituent parts.

DATE	*c.*1800
ORIGIN	INDIAN
LENGTH	44cm (17.3in)

Persian chiselled kard, *c.*1800

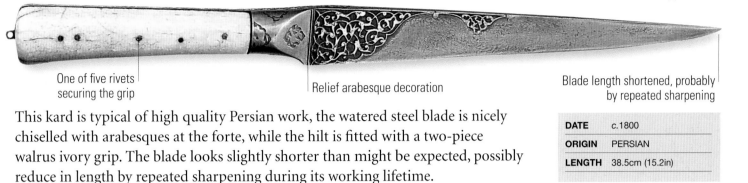

One of five rivets
securing the grip

Relief arabesque decoration

Blade length shortened, probably
by repeated sharpening

This kard is typical of high quality Persian work, the watered steel blade is nicely chiselled with arabesques at the forte, while the hilt is fitted with a two-piece walrus ivory grip. The blade looks slightly shorter than might be expected, possibly reduce in length by repeated sharpening during its working lifetime.

DATE	c.1800
ORIGIN	PERSIAN
LENGTH	38.5cm (15.2in)

Afghan "Khyber knife", early 19th century

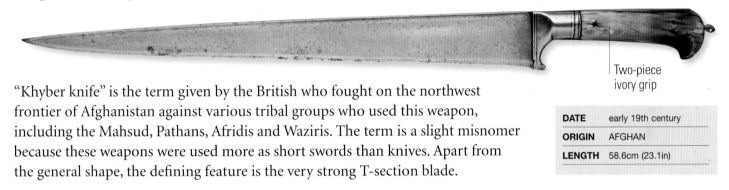

Two-piece
ivory grip

"Khyber knife" is the term given by the British who fought on the northwest frontier of Afghanistan against various tribal groups who used this weapon, including the Mahsud, Pathans, Afridis and Waziris. The term is a slight misnomer because these weapons were used more as short swords than knives. Apart from the general shape, the defining feature is the very strong T-section blade.

DATE	early 19th century
ORIGIN	AFGHAN
LENGTH	58.6cm (23.1in)

Persian/Turkestan kard, early 19th century

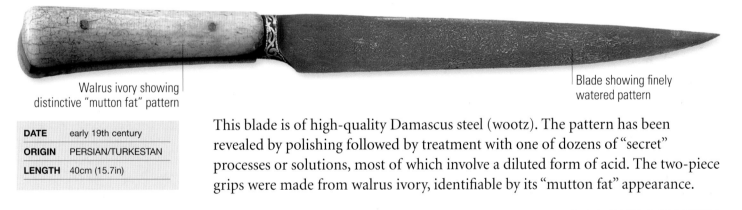

Walrus ivory showing
distinctive "mutton fat" pattern

Blade showing finely
watered pattern

DATE	early 19th century
ORIGIN	PERSIAN/TURKESTAN
LENGTH	40cm (15.7in)

This blade is of high-quality Damascus steel (wootz). The pattern has been revealed by polishing followed by treatment with one of dozens of "secret" processes or solutions, most of which involve a diluted form of acid. The two-piece grips were made from walrus ivory, identifiable by its "mutton fat" appearance.

Indo-Persian kard with green jade hilt, 18th century

Finely watered blade

Jade hilt

DATE	18th century
ORIGIN	INDO-PERSIAN
LENGTH	37cm (14.6in)

The back edges of kard blades are slightly convex. This blade is made of crucible steel and shows a "watered" pattern which is an intrinsic property of the metal. The blade could have been made in either India or Persia, whilst the tapered jade hilt was probably made within the Ottoman Empire or in India.

Indian kard, early 19th century

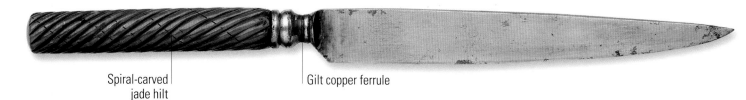

Spiral-carved
jade hilt

Gilt copper ferrule

Lahore is situated in the middle of the Punjab, and was an important centre of weapons production, particularly for the Sikhs. The unifying feature of Lahori arms production is the gold koftgari in geometric patterns, or a repeated foliate and floral motif often incorporating arabesques.

DATE	early 19th century
ORIGIN	INDIAN
LENGTH	unknown

Indian kard, early to mid-19th century

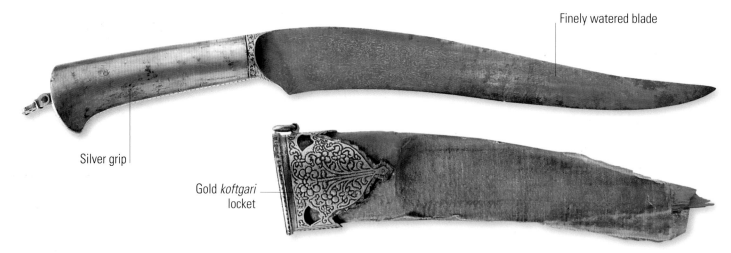

Finely watered blade

Silver grip

Gold *koftgari*
locket

The shape of this fine-quality dagger from Rajasthan is testament to the care and skill of its maker. The recurved blade is made from finely watered wootz (crucible steel) and the grips are silver. The remaining mount (locket) of the sheath is decorated with gold koftgari. Rajasthan has a number of cities famed for the excellence of their swordsmiths and edged-weapons production.

DATE	early to mid-19th century
ORIGIN	INDIAN
LENGTH	31cm (12.2in)

Indian silver-mounted kard, early to mid-19th century

Lion's-head pommel

Fairly crude blade

This silver-mounted Indian kard was probably made for a departing member of the Raj, and is quite an appropriate metaphor for the British who were soon to leave India. The lion looks both comic and bedraggled, a spent and forlorn force whose time has come. The blade is the work of a smith rather than a cutler, whilst the silver hilt and sheath have both been hastily fabricated.

DATE	early to mid-19th century
ORIGIN	INDIAN
LENGTH	unknown

Turkish kard, early to mid-19th century

Faceted jade grip | Gold false-damascened inscription | Watered wootz steel blade

DATE	early to mid-19th century
ORIGIN	TURKISH
LENGTH	26cm (10.2in)

This Turkish kard has been made with a jade hilt and the blade is of oriental Damascus steel (wootz). At the forte, next to the silver ferrule, it has been false-damascened with a gold inscription, typical of many kards and bichaqs produced in considerable quantities within the Ottoman Empire during the 19th century.

Afghan "Khyber knife", mid-19th century

Horn grips

DATE	mid-19th century
ORIGIN	AFGHAN
LENGTH	71cm (27.9in)

These short swords are always found with meticulously sharpened blades. Enormous strength was given to the blades by their T-section. The bolsters and grip straps were manufactured from steel or brass, and the grips, though normally of horn, were sometimes made from ivory or wood.

Afghan "Khyber knife", mid-19th century

Horn pommel

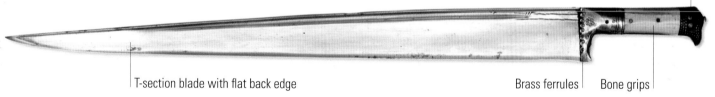

T-section blade with flat back edge | Brass ferrules | Bone grips

DATE	mid-19th century
ORIGIN	AFGHAN
LENGTH	72cm (28.3in)

The hilt of this "Khyber knife" is quite distinctive; there exists a matching smaller dagger which was probably carried through the same belt or sash. The grips are made from horn, though occasionally ivory was used, and the black buffalo-horn pommel is decorated with fine nail holes into which zinc foil has been pushed.

Turkish kard, c.1870

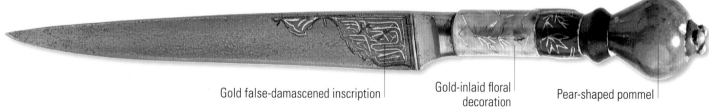

Gold false-damascened inscription | Gold-inlaid floral decoration | Pear-shaped pommel

DATE	c.1870
ORIGIN	TURKISH
LENGTH	35cm (13.7in)

The hilt of this Ottoman Turkish dagger is made from polished sections of hard stone which have been inlaid with gold in a floral pattern. Frequently daggers with this type of hilt are found to incorporate cylindrical sections of the *munal* (mouthpiece) from a discarded *nargil* (water pipe), often with undecorated pommels.

Indo-Persian peshkabz

These daggers are common to Persia and northern India. They have single-edged blades which can be straight, curved or recurved. They are normally encountered with a T-section blade which imparts considerable strength. These daggers are found in a multitude of different qualities, from the refined and exotic court workshop productions to those produced by the Pathan tribal smiths in Afghanistan.

Indian peshkabz, mid-18th century

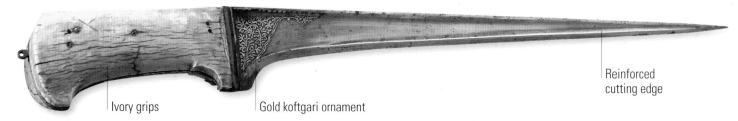

Reinforced cutting edge

Ivory grips

Gold koftgari ornament

This Indian peshkabz is fitted with a blade of wootz steel which has been decorated with gold koftgari at the forte. The two-piece ivory grips show signs of cracking due to age. The slightly thickened cutting edge further reinforcing the strength of the blade can be clearly seen.

DATE	mid-18th century
ORIGIN	INDIAN
LENGTH	48cm (18.9in)

Persian peshkabz, c.1800

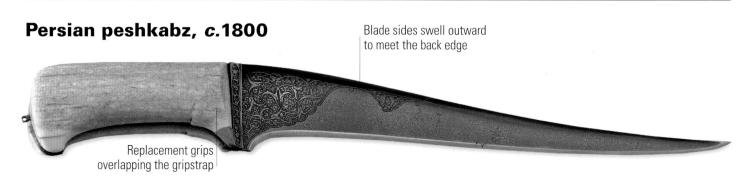

Blade sides swell outward to meet the back edge

Replacement grips overlapping the gripstrap

The recurve-shaped blade is made from finely watered steel, and the sides swell sharply outward before meeting the broad back edge. Chiselled arabesque decoration adorns the forte. The replacement two-piece walrus ivory grip overlaps the gripstrap; the original grip would have only reached the edge of the gripstrap.

DATE	c.1800
ORIGIN	PERSIAN
LENGTH	42cm (16.5in)

Indian peshkabz, early 19th century

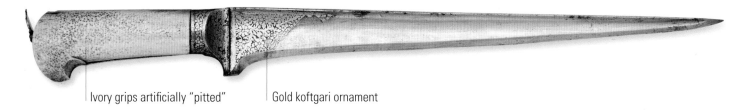

Ivory grips artificially "pitted"

Gold koftgari ornament

The blade of this peshkabz is probably the most lethally efficient of any stabbing dagger ever devised. It derives its strength from the T-section which extends almost to the point. Such a blade would be perfect for penetrating the riveted links of a mail shirt. The ivory grips have been typically "pitted" to provide a firm hold.

DATE	early 19th century
ORIGIN	INDIAN
LENGTH	43cm (16.9in)

Rajasthani gold-inlaid peshkabz, early 19th century

Button unscrews to reveal a hollow grip

Chiselled lotus flower in low relief

DATE	early 19th century
ORIGIN	INDIAN (RAJASTHANI)
LENGTH	34.5cm (13.5in)

The button surmounting the pommel of this all-steel dagger from Rajasthan unscrews and the pommel hinges to reveal a hollow grip which could be used as a container. Similar but more elaborate examples contain small instruments, while legend has it that the space was used for more sinister purposes by would-be poisoners. The hilt is well chiselled in low relief with a repeated lotus flower pattern.

Indian peshkabz, early 19th century

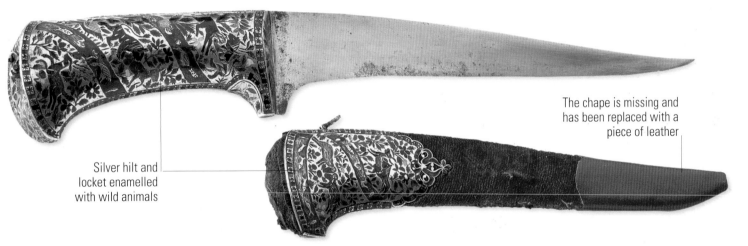

The chape is missing and has been replaced with a piece of leather

Silver hilt and locket enamelled with wild animals

DATE	early 19th century
ORIGIN	INDIAN
LENGTH	31.5cm (12.4in)

During the 18th and 19th centuries, Lucknow was famous for, amongst other crafts, its enamel work. The silver hilt and locket of this peshkabz are decorated with diagonal bands inhabited by assorted wild animals in multicoloured enamel. The predominant colours associated with Lucknow are blue and green.

Indian peshkabz with gilt copper hilt, *c.*1850

Foiled glass, or pastes

Gilt copper mounts (not gold)

DATE	c.1850
ORIGIN	INDIAN
LENGTH	35.6cm (14.1in)

The hilt of this dagger is its most impressive part. It is made from gilt copper and is set with pastes of various colours. The overall effect is one of great richness, which has been achieved at limited expense. Such daggers were produced with matching sheaths and were made to satisfy the demand from well-off foreign buyers.

Indian knives, daggers and bayonets

The diversity of weapons found on the Indian subcontinent reflects the influences this area has absorbed from invading peoples throughout history. They include Persians, Greeks, Hindus and Muslims, with European influences later on. Apart from the excellence of their manufacture, it should be remembered that many weapons were invested with a spiritual or religious dimension by their owners.

Mysore bichwa, 18th century

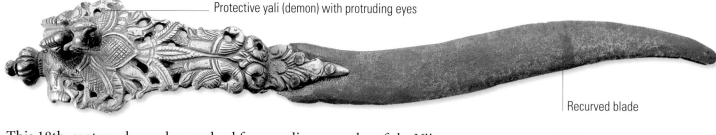

Protective yali (demon) with protruding eyes

Recurved blade

This 18th-century dagger has evolved from earlier examples of the Vijayanagaran Empire (14th–16th centuries). A typical dagger from Mysore, the protruding eyeballs of the *yali* (demon) with their stepped, conical sockets are redolent of southern India. The looped bronze or brass hilt has a narrow integral grip.

DATE	18th century
ORIGIN	INDIAN (MYSORE)
LENGTH	32.5cm (12.8in)

Mysore socket bayonet (sangin) of Tipu Sultan, late 18th century

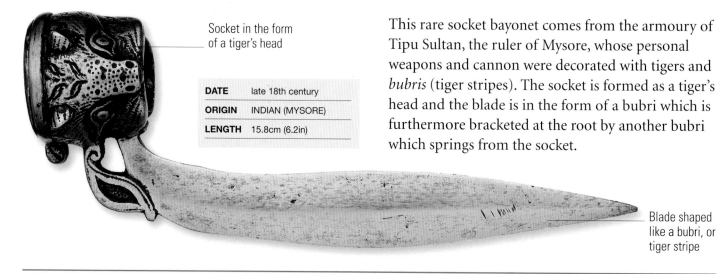

Socket in the form of a tiger's head

DATE	late 18th century
ORIGIN	INDIAN (MYSORE)
LENGTH	15.8cm (6.2in)

This rare socket bayonet comes from the armoury of Tipu Sultan, the ruler of Mysore, whose personal weapons and cannon were decorated with tigers and *bubris* (tiger stripes). The socket is formed as a tiger's head and the blade is in the form of a bubri which is furthermore bracketed at the root by another bubri which springs from the socket.

Blade shaped like a bubri, or tiger stripe

Indian plug bayonet signed by Anvar, late 18th century

Silver koftgari decoration

Ivory grip

Short cross piece

The European plug bayonet design was later used as a model for hunting knives in France and Spain in the second half of the 18th century. This example is a southern Indian interpretation of one such hunting knife. The blade and cross piece are decorated with silver koftgari and signed *'amal Anvar* ("the work of Anvar").

DATE	late 18th century
ORIGIN	INDIAN
LENGTH	57cm (22.4in)

Indian bichwa with double blade, *c.*1800

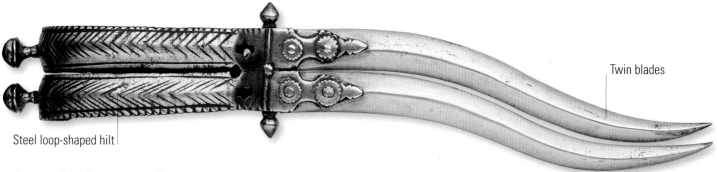

Twin blades

Steel loop-shaped hilt

The word *bichwa* means "scorpion" in Hindi, and these dagger blades are supposed to have gained their name from their likeness to the tail of a scorpion or from their ability to "sting". The steel hilt is loop-shaped and the knuckle guards are cut with chevrons. There are bud-shaped finials to the pommel, and two buds protrude laterally as short quillons, or guards. This example is quite uncommon in having two blades and probably comes from Hyderabad. Being relatively easy to make, the bichwa has persisted into the 20th century as a decorative dagger.

DATE	*c.*1800
ORIGIN	INDIAN
LENGTH	32.8cm (12.9in)

Nepalese kukri, mid-19th century

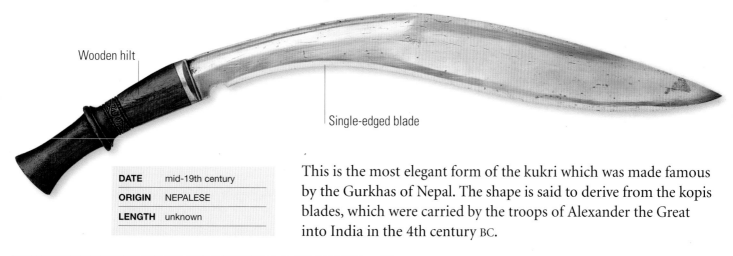

Wooden hilt

Single-edged blade

DATE	mid-19th century
ORIGIN	NEPALESE
LENGTH	unknown

This is the most elegant form of the kukri which was made famous by the Gurkhas of Nepal. The shape is said to derive from the kopis blades, which were carried by the troops of Alexander the Great into India in the 4th century BC.

Nepalese kukri, mid-19th century

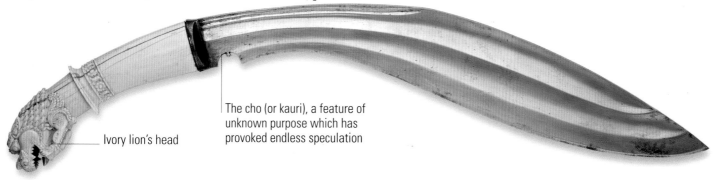

The cho (or kauri), a feature of unknown purpose which has provoked endless speculation

Ivory lion's head

DATE	mid-19th century
ORIGIN	NEPALESE
LENGTH	40.6cm (16in)

The carving of a lion's-head pommel on the ivory grip of this kukri is a very unusual feature and denotes a high-status client. The blade too is a little unusual, and carving the channels and ridges into it in such a symmetrical and aesthetically pleasing manner requires a considerable degree of skill as well as artistry. The Gurkhas have earned a formidable reputation using this weapon for their fearlessness and bravery.

Mysore "knuckleduster" knife, early 19th century

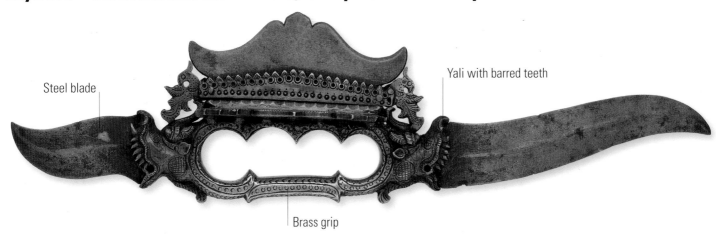

Steel blade

Yali with barred teeth

Brass grip

This very exotic-looking Indian weapon from Mysore is a "knuckleduster" with two blades. The grip is made from brass and the steel blades protrude from yali heads. The manufacture is particularly well executed. Similar weapons, without blades, are used for a type of fighting during Dasara festivities and are called vajramustis.

DATE	early 19th century
ORIGIN	INDIAN (MYSORE)
LENGTH	32cm (12.6in)

Indian "tiger-claw" dagger, early 19th century

Integral steel blade

Finger ring

Steel claws

The all-steel *bagh nakh*, or "tiger's claw", is a uniquely Indian weapon and is designed for slashing. One was famously used in 1659 by Shivaji when he killed Afzal Khan; it had been concealed until the last moment within the palm of Shivaji's hand. The two rings are for the outside fingers, and the other fingers would lie on top of the steel claws.

DATE	early 19th century
ORIGIN	INDIAN
LENGTH	unknown

Coorg Tamil knife (pichangatti), mid-19th century

"Clip back" tip

Silver hilt

Heavy blade with single edge

The *pichangatti* (the word means "hand knife") is a Tamil knife from Coorg. It has a broad, heavy, single-edged blade which turns up slightly at the tip. The hilts are often to be found made from silver, although brass and wood are also common. Most were made in the late 19th century and seem to have been used as utility knives or for chopping.

DATE	mid-19th century
ORIGIN	INDIAN (COORG)
LENGTH	unknown

Coorg Tamil knife (pichangatti), mid-19th century

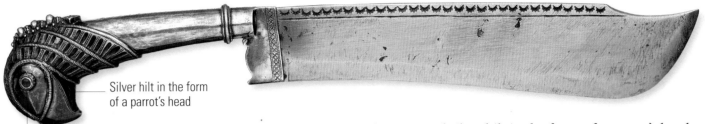

Silver hilt in the form
of a parrot's head

Red-stone eye

DATE	mid-19th century
ORIGIN	INDIAN (COORG)
LENGTH	25.5cm (10in)

This pichangatti has a somewhat unusual silver hilt in the form of a parrot's head; the eyes are made from red stones. The Coorgs carry a chopper-like weapon called an ayda katti in a metal carrier called a todunga, and this is held in place by a belt. The correct position for the pichangatti is in the front of this belt. The sheath of this knife is bound with silver and from it, suspended from a chain, is a small kit of personal grooming tools for cleaning nails and ears.

Assam dagger (dha) with carved horn hilt, mid-19th century

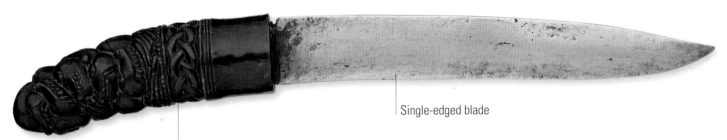

Single-edged blade

Carved horn handle
incorporating a demonic figure

DATE	mid-19th century
ORIGIN	INDIAN (ASSAM)
LENGTH	23.6cm (9.3in)

This type of dagger, called a dha, is the classic Burmese form and is often found with a carved ivory hilt. The blades are slightly curved and single edged. This particular example has an unusual, carved buffalo-horn hilt, and is said to have come from Assam, close to Burma but sufficiently distant to have developed a somewhat unusual hilt. Formal Burmese dha hilts are carved with an assortment of demonic figures, sometimes in contorted poses.

Mysore bichwa, mid-19th century

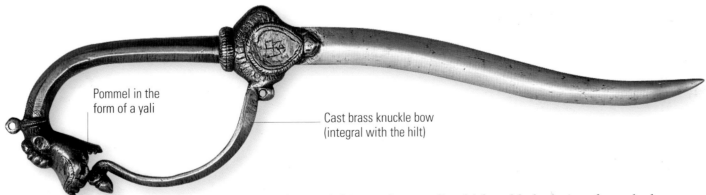

Pommel in the
form of a yali

Cast brass knuckle bow
(integral with the hilt)

DATE	mid-19th century
ORIGIN	INDIAN (MYSORE)
LENGTH	unknown

The recurved shape of this southern Indian bichwa blade derives from the horn daggers made by the Dravidians (aboriginal inhabitants of India), who made their daggers from lengths of animal horns. The brass hilt has been cast in one piece and the pommel is in the form of a yali. The root of the hilt, however, is of such confused and debased design that it is likely to be of quite a late date.

Indian katars

The Indian katar is a punching dagger and, as such, the design is unique. It is an ancient Hindu weapon which was adopted by the Muslims. Usually made of all-steel construction, the hilt commonly consists of a pair of handlebars at right angles to the sides which extend upwards parallel with the user's arm. The triangular-shaped blade is normally cut with a number of fullers, although in the 16th and 17th centuries it became fashionable to fit katars with European blades which have parallel sides.

Indian katar, 17th century

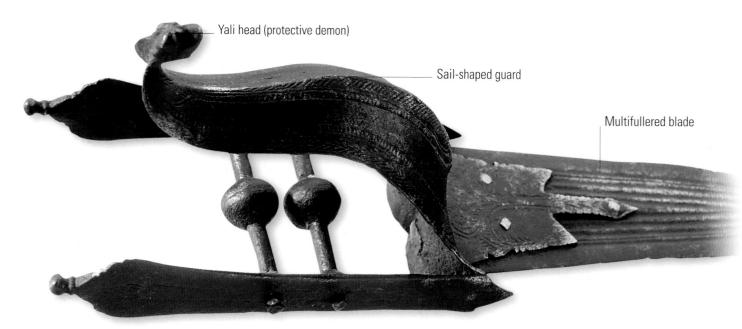

Yali head (protective demon)

Sail-shaped guard

Multifullered blade

This form of katar, with its sail-shaped guard and multifullered blade, comes from the Vijayanagara Empire, which lasted until 1646 but whose power declined after a defeat in 1565. The twin-ball shapes inbetween the handlebars are hollow, and the sail-shaped guard that protects the back of the hand has a finial in the form of a yali.

DATE	17th century
ORIGIN	INDIAN
LENGTH	56.5cm (22.2in)

Northern Indian katar, late 18th century

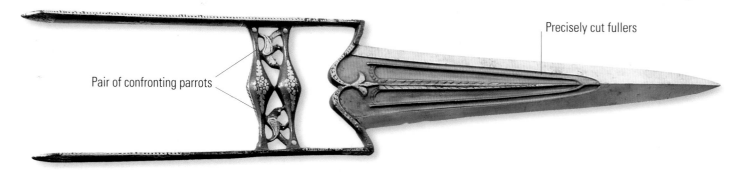

Precisely cut fullers

Pair of confronting parrots

The thickened tips of katar blades are often referred to as being "armour piercing". It is likely that only slender blades like this would stand a chance of performing that function. The twin handlebars are separated by a pair of confronting birds and the hilt retains traces of gold koftgari decoration. The fullers on the blade have been well cut.

DATE	late 18th century
ORIGIN	NORTHERN INDIAN
LENGTH	42.5cm (16.7in)

Rajasthani katar, 1800

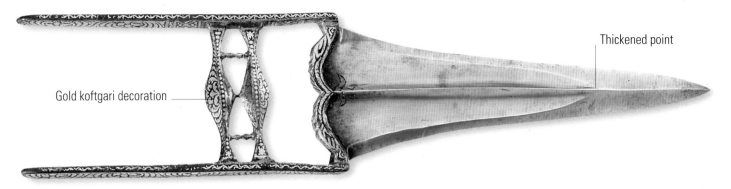

Gold koftgari decoration

Thickened point

DATE	1800
ORIGIN	INDIAN (RAJASTHANI)
LENGTH	30.5cm (12in)

This is a classic Rajasthani katar which has seen much use. The thickened point is clearly visible, and the irregular and "waisted" outline of the cutting edges are testament to the vigorous and persistent sharpening that it has undergone. The hilt is thickly covered with a conventional design of gold koftgari decoration.

Indian katar with scabbard, early 19th century

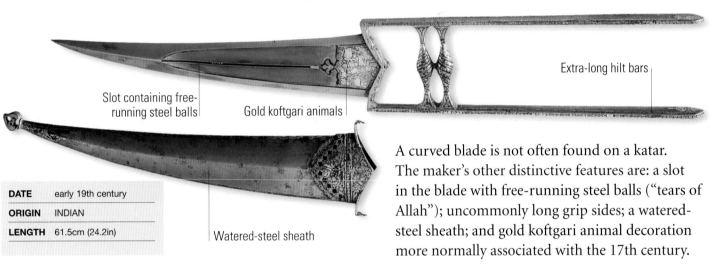

Slot containing free-running steel balls

Gold koftgari animals

Extra-long hilt bars

DATE	early 19th century
ORIGIN	INDIAN
LENGTH	61.5cm (24.2in)

Watered-steel sheath

A curved blade is not often found on a katar. The maker's other distinctive features are: a slot in the blade with free-running steel balls ("tears of Allah"); uncommonly long grip sides; a watered-steel sheath; and gold koftgari animal decoration more normally associated with the 17th century.

Rajasthani katar with elephant's head, dated 1849

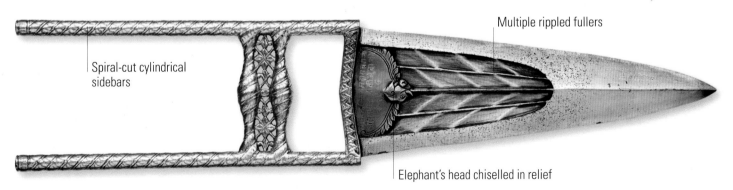

Spiral-cut cylindrical sidebars

Multiple rippled fullers

Elephant's head chiselled in relief

DATE	1849
ORIGIN	INDIAN (RAJASTHANI)
LENGTH	40.4cm (15.9in)

This katar belongs to a distinctive group of katars produced at Bundi in Rajasthan during the 18th and 19th centuries. This example is dated 1907, Vikrama era (AD1849), and belonged to the Maharajah of Bundi. Hand-forged, beautifully finished and with a hilt covered with gold foil, it was exhibited at the Great Exhibition of 1851 in Crystal Palace, London.

Indian katar, mid-19th century

Produced well into an era when such weapons had almost become redundant, this katar is nevertheless of reasonable quality. The hilt is decorated with gold koftgari, and the steel sheath is pierced with a pattern including pairs of confronting parrots within foliage, all of which is enhanced by further gold koftgari decoration. The extremes of both heat and moisture encountered in India would have rendered steel a most unsuitable material for a dagger sheath.

DATE	mid-19th century
ORIGIN	INDIAN
LENGTH	40.5cm (15.9in)

Parrots and foliage decoration

Twin handlebars

Indian katar with two percussion pistols, 18th to mid-19th century

In order to embrace "modern technology", a good-quality 18th-century Indian katar has been refurbished during the middle of the 19th century. A pair of percussion pistols has been added to the hilt sides, and the whole hilt has been covered with silver-gilt koftgari. The resulting ungainly weapon provides a strange foil for the beautifully carved Mughal iris flowers at the root of the blade.

Fabric-covered sheath

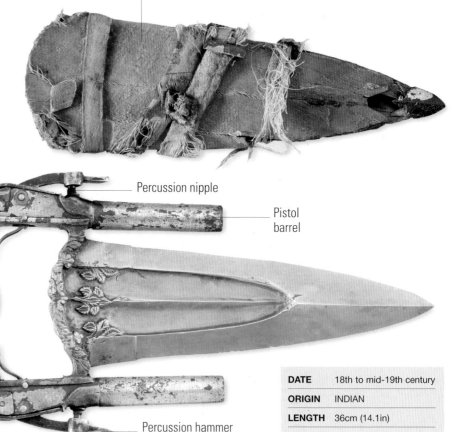

Percussion nipple

Pistol barrel

Trigger

Trigger

Percussion hammer

DATE	18th to mid-19th century
ORIGIN	INDIAN
LENGTH	36cm (14.1in)

Indian scissors katar, late 19th century

Silver koftgari decoration of the poorest quality

DATE	late 19th century
ORIGIN	INDIAN
LENGTH	41cm (16.1in)

The scissors katar is mechanical and when the twin handlebars are squeezed tightly, the main hollow blades hinge open to reveal a shorter blade within. These were contrived for a European market, and however impractical, they appealed to the same sentiments as those invoked by Q's special weapons for James Bond.

Indian scissors katar, late 19th century

Two hollow blades hinge open to reveal another blade within

Handlebars, when squeezed, cause the blade to open

DATE	late 19th century
ORIGIN	INDIAN
LENGTH	36cm (14.2in)

This is another example of the scissors katar. A very similar example was given to the Prince of Wales during his tour of India in 1875–76 by the Raja of Mandi (in the Punjab). They are normally decorated with silver koftgari and their survival rate in the west, and in Britain in particular, seems to have been quite high.

Indian scissors katar, late 19th century

Hollow blades in the open position

Handlebars in the squeezed position

Inner blade

DATE	late 19th century
ORIGIN	INDIAN
LENGTH	40cm (15.7in)

Evidence that the design is fatally flawed is provided by the fact that the blades cannot be made to open once the katar has been thrust into a body, and if the katar were to be used with the blades in the open position the force on the outer blades would have to be absorbed by the hinge pins at the root of the blades.

Indian chilanums and khanjarlis

The chilanum is an all-steel dagger with a recurved double-edged blade. The blade shape probably developed from the Dravidian horn dagger which was made from a longitudinal section along an animal horn. Examples occur from the early 16th century in Vijayanagara, and were used by Hindus (Marathan) and Muslims (Deccani) alike. The dagger evolves in easily recognizable stages into the khanjarli, whose defining characteristic is the large, lunette-shaped pommel normally made of ivory.

Vijayanagaran chilanum, c.1600

This all-steel dagger represents the earliest form of chilanum in this group and the design can be seen in miniature paintings dating from the 16th century. It is made from a single piece of steel, and the grip and pommel button are both lathe-turned. Miniature paintings from the various Indian courts are an invaluable source of information for the student of Indian weapons. Although the artistic conventions result in images quite different from their European counterparts, details have been rendered with astonishing fidelity.

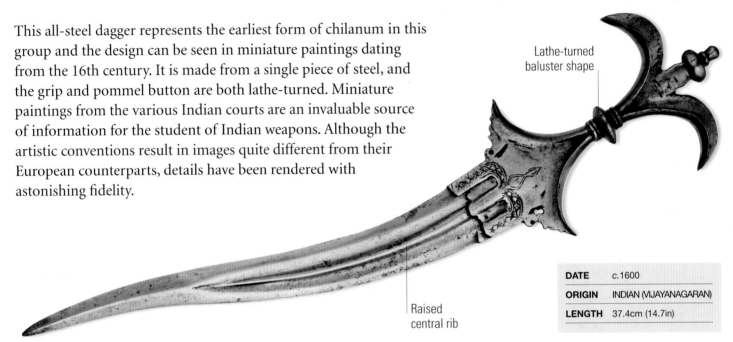

Lathe-turned baluster shape

Raised central rib

DATE	c.1600
ORIGIN	INDIAN (VIJAYANAGARAN)
LENGTH	37.4cm (14.7in)

Deccani chilanum with spiral decoration, early 17th century

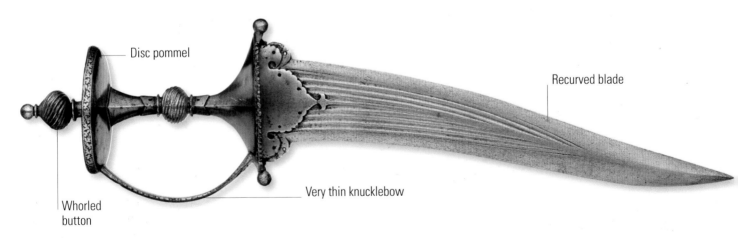

Disc pommel

Recurved blade

Whorled button

Very thin knucklebow

A group of chilanums of identical design made of polished steel exist in Bikaner in Rajasthan. Probably originating in the Deccan, they are distinguished by their circular pommels, whorled buttons, and by their slender knucklebows which appear to be almost an afterthought. This example is unusual in having gold-damascened (koftgari) ornament; those in Bikaner are perfectly plain. It is not certain whether the decoration is contemporary or from a later period.

DATE	early 17th century
ORIGIN	INDIAN (DECCANI)
LENGTH	42cm (16.5in)

Indian Mughal dagger with knucklebow, *c.*1625

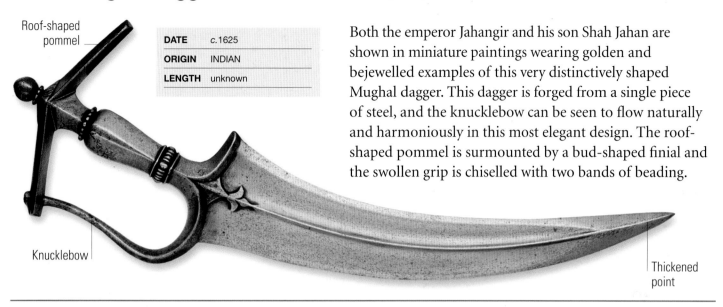

Roof-shaped pommel

Knucklebow

Thickened point

DATE	*c.*1625
ORIGIN	INDIAN
LENGTH	unknown

Both the emperor Jahangir and his son Shah Jahan are shown in miniature paintings wearing golden and bejewelled examples of this very distinctively shaped Mughal dagger. This dagger is forged from a single piece of steel, and the knucklebow can be seen to flow naturally and harmoniously in this most elegant design. The roof-shaped pommel is surmounted by a bud-shaped finial and the swollen grip is chiselled with two bands of beading.

Deccani chilanum, mid-17th century

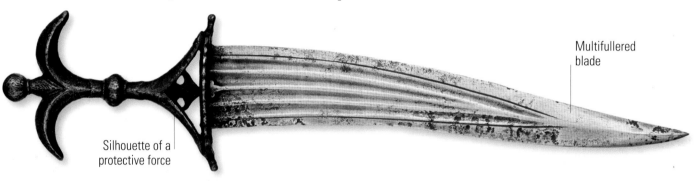

Multifullered blade

Silhouette of a protective force

DATE	mid-17th century
ORIGIN	INDIAN (DECCANI)
LENGTH	39cm (15.4in)

Representing a classic and fully accomplished all-steel chilanum, the hilt of this dagger sits easily on the blade. The multifullered blade is reminiscent of katar blades from the same period. The pierced silhouette at the base of the hilt is a representation of a protective force.

Indian khanjarli, *c.*1700

Traditionally associated with Orissa and the Hindus of Vizianagram, khanjarli daggers probably come from a much wider area. Their defining design feature is the large lunette-shaped ivory pommel, the ivory grips, and the recurved blade which betrays their common ancestry with the chilanum. This example has a slender knucklebow.

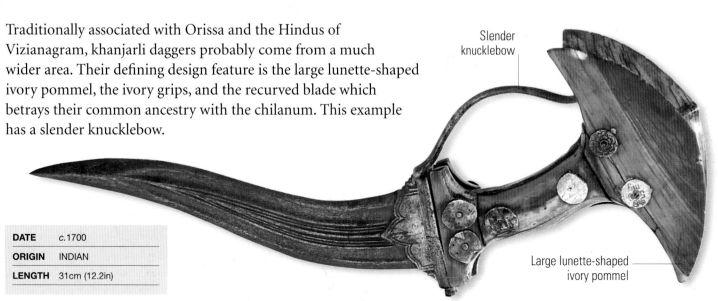

Slender knucklebow

Large lunette-shaped ivory pommel

DATE	*c.*1700
ORIGIN	INDIAN
LENGTH	31cm (12.2in)

The Indonesian kris

The pre-eminent Hindu dagger from Indonesia is the kris. Examples from the 14th-century Majepahit Empire are not uncommon, and their lineage probably goes back to the Bronze Age Dong-Son era.

The smith would use iron from more than one source, one of which traditionally came from meteoric ore which had a high nickel content. The resulting blade patterns and carved hilts are highly regarded.

Sumatran kris, *c.*1800

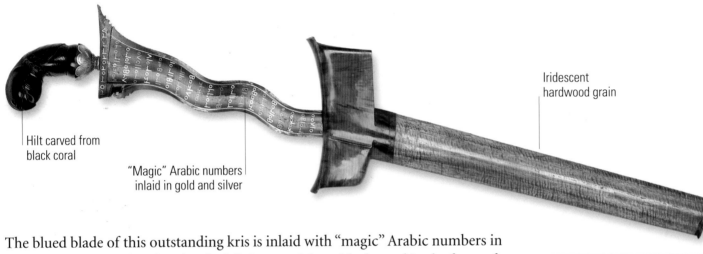

Hilt carved from black coral

"Magic" Arabic numbers inlaid in gold and silver

Iridescent hardwood grain

The blued blade of this outstanding kris is inlaid with "magic" Arabic numbers in alternate gold and silver bands. The hilt is carved from black coral in the form of a stylized parrot. The hardwood sheath has an iridescent grain. So heavily is the kris invested with legend that some believed a kris thirsty for blood had the power to leave its sleeping owner, kill someone, clean itself and return to its sheath.

DATE	c.1800
ORIGIN	SUMATRAN
LENGTH	49.5cm (19.5in)

Javanese kris, mid-19th century

The carved wooden hilt of this kris is intended to represent the god Raksha (or Raksasa), who is usually depicted with a long flowing coiffure. He is enveloped in foliage and his presence wards off evil spirits. The *pendok* (metal sheath covering) is made from nickel and chased with foliage. The armorial device engraved on the pendok was most likely introduced into Indonesia by the Dutch colonial power.

Wooden hilt carved with the god Raksha

Nickel pendok with engraved decoration

DATE	mid-19th century
ORIGIN	JAVANESE
LENGTH	35cm (13.8in)

Malayan kris, mid-19th century

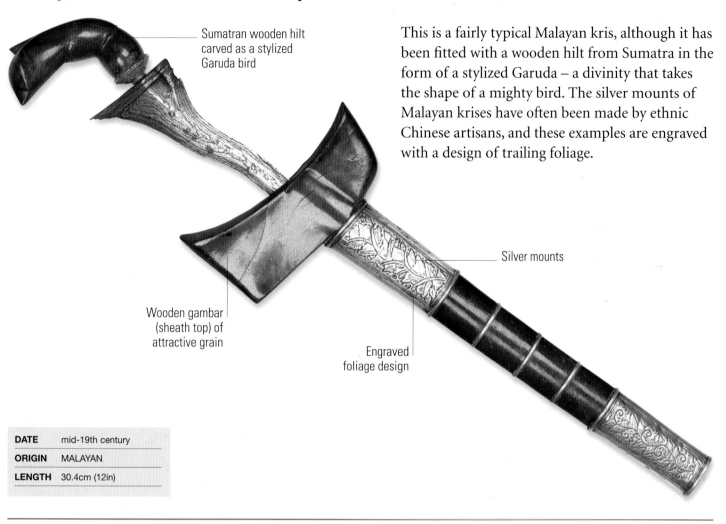

Sumatran wooden hilt carved as a stylized Garuda bird

This is a fairly typical Malayan kris, although it has been fitted with a wooden hilt from Sumatra in the form of a stylized Garuda – a divinity that takes the shape of a mighty bird. The silver mounts of Malayan krises have often been made by ethnic Chinese artisans, and these examples are engraved with a design of trailing foliage.

Silver mounts

Wooden gambar (sheath top) of attractive grain

Engraved foliage design

DATE	mid-19th century
ORIGIN	MALAYAN
LENGTH	30.4cm (12in)

Maduran kris, mid-19th century

The ivory hilt of this kris is typical of those carved on the island of Madura. The top of the blade exhibits the *pamor*, or watered pattern, created by the smith who forged iron of differing composition. The silver *pendok* (stem cover) is elaborately embossed with a Bonaspatti mask, the face of a popular Hindu divinity.

DATE	mid-19th century
ORIGIN	MADURAN
LENGTH	41.9cm (16.5in)

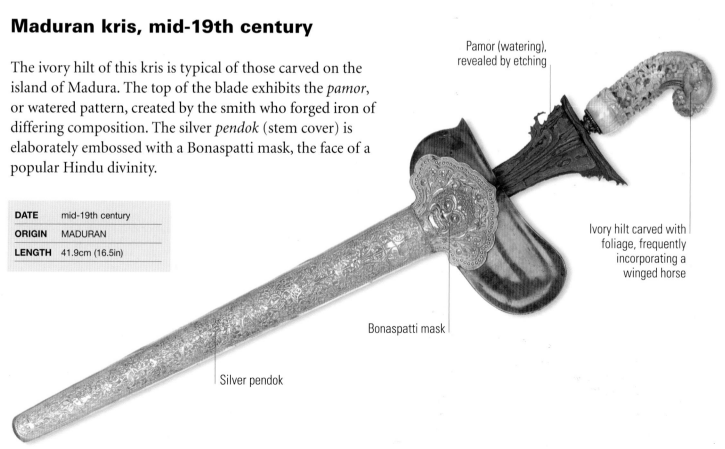

Pamor (watering), revealed by etching

Ivory hilt carved with foliage, frequently incorporating a winged horse

Bonaspatti mask

Silver pendok

149

Malayan bade-bade, mid-19th century

Ferrule of gold

Hardwood sheath stem

Hilt carved from a
sperm whale's tooth

The bade-bade is the classic Malayan knife. It has a slightly curved, slender blade
sharpened on the inside edge. The hilt is carved from a whale's tooth, the sheath
from hard wood and the top from ivory. Although mainly a cutting implement,
the bade-bade could be used as a dagger.

DATE	mid-19th century
ORIGIN	MALAYAN
LENGTH	22.8cm (9in)

Malayan kris, mid-19th century

Malaya is rich in exotic timber, and very fine-
grained woods have been chosen to manufacture
this kris. The blades of such krises are often
cleaned with lime juice, which relies on its citric
acid content to etch the blade. They are then
wiped with sandalwood oil for protection.

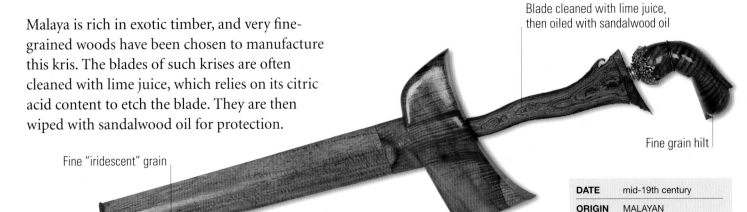

Blade cleaned with lime juice,
then oiled with sandalwood oil

Fine grain hilt

Fine "iridescent" grain

DATE	mid-19th century
ORIGIN	MALAYAN
LENGTH	33cm (13in)

Malayan kris, 19th to 20th century

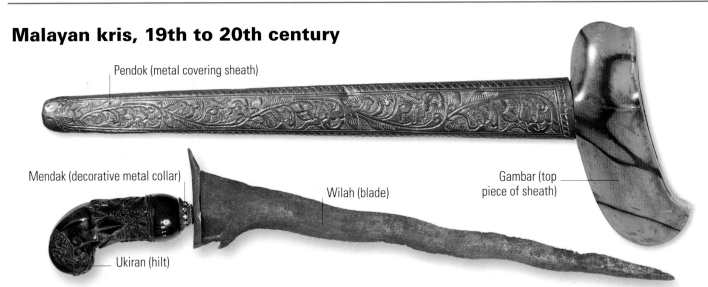

Pendok (metal covering sheath)

Mendak (decorative metal collar)

Wilah (blade)

Gambar (top
piece of sheath)

Ukiran (hilt)

No Malaysian or Indonesian would wish to own a kris that might not be propitious
for good health, good fortune, wealth or good luck. Consequently, the *lok* (waves)
of the blade are each counted by a would-be purchaser. An odd number is
considered auspicious to some, an even number to others. The blade of this Malay
kris is 19th-century in origin but the hilt and sheath are 20th-century.

DATE	19th to 20th century
ORIGIN	MALAYAN
LENGTH	unknown

Javanese kris, *c.*1900

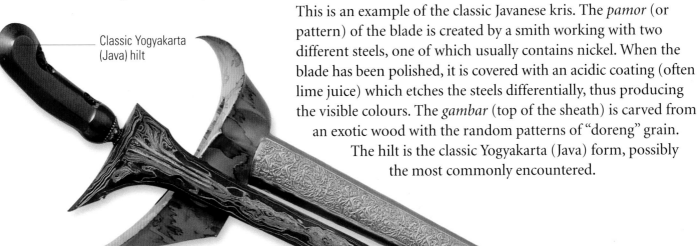

Classic Yogyakarta (Java) hilt

This is an example of the classic Javanese kris. The *pamor* (or pattern) of the blade is created by a smith working with two different steels, one of which usually contains nickel. When the blade has been polished, it is covered with an acidic coating (often lime juice) which etches the steels differentially, thus producing the visible colours. The *gambar* (top of the sheath) is carved from an exotic wood with the random patterns of "doreng" grain. The hilt is the classic Yogyakarta (Java) form, possibly the most commonly encountered.

Pamor (pattern)

DATE	*c.*1900
ORIGIN	JAVANESE
LENGTH	47cm (18.5in)

The kris stand

Traditionally, the kris was kept on a wooden board, which was often carved and sometimes painted. Only a very few antique sculptural kris stands of the type shown here are known. However, when Bali became popular as a tourist destination in the 1960s, a market developed for these extraordinary objects and production was revived. Skilfully carved from a single piece of wood, they are mostly in the form of brightly painted Hindu divinities. Typical figures include Ganesh (the elephant god), Hanuman (the monkey god) and Wayang figures (shadow puppets). Each figure is ostensibly designed for a kris to be held in the hand. The degree of skill used in the manufacture of some of the stands is very great indeed. The krises which the stands support also continue to be made and some are highly sought-after; the most exquisite specimens are very valuable.

RIGHT The stand on the right holds an "executioner's kris". The victim was tied to a chair and the long, slender blade thrust downwards into the heart.

Japanese daggers

The Japanese blade and its fittings represent the highest artistic achievement of the bladesmith anywhere in the world. They are regarded with the same reverence others hold for a great painting and its frame. Blades may be recognized as productions by different schools or individual smiths, and each will vary slightly in detail. Any comprehensive approach requires some understanding of Japanese and the swords and daggers themselves. To fully appreciate a blade's qualities, it must be held in the hand.

Japanese yoroi toshi, *c.*1400

Peg hole (mekugi-ana)

The blade of this yoroi toshi dagger is intended to pierce armour so is quite thin in width, broad across the back edge and almost straight. The tang (*nakago*) is pierced with a hole (*mekugi-ana*) to receive a bamboo peg which secures the hilt. The remains of an earlier such hole shows the blade was originally longer.

DATE	c.1400
ORIGIN	JAPANESE
LENGTH	30.6cm (12in)

Japanese aikuchi, 1625 and later

Hoshi mon (family badge) representing three stars

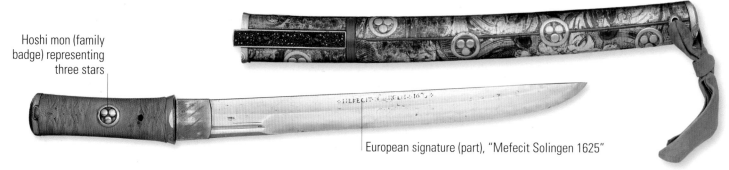

European signature (part), "Mefecit Solingen 1625"

The aikuchi is simply a Japanese dagger mounted without a guard (*tsuba*) to protect the hand. This dagger is almost certainly unique: the blade was made in Solingen (Germany) and is dated 1625. The rest was made later. It has been re-used by a Japanese smith and mounted for the Sanga family who used the *hoshi mon*.

DATE	1625 and later
ORIGIN	JAPANESE
LENGTH	48.7cm (19.2in)

Japanese tanto, late Edo, *c.*1840

Guard (tsub)

Pommel cap (kashira)

Grip ferrule (fuchi)

The attractive copper-alloy (*shakudo*) mounts of this tanto are decorated in relief with gold and are typical of the late Goto School. Warriors form a perennially favourite motif, and those here are worked in high relief against a granular ground (*nanako*) made with a punch that produces a tiny hemisphere.

DATE	late Edo, c.1840
ORIGIN	JAPANESE
LENGTH	39cm (15.3in)

Japanese ken, late Edo, *c.*1850

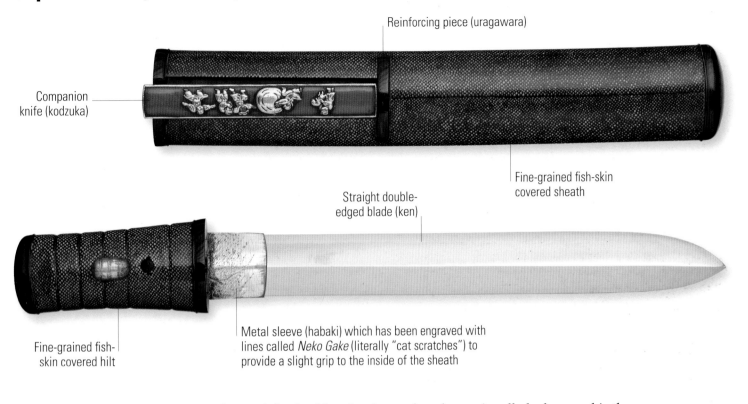

Reinforcing piece (uragawara)

Companion knife (kodzuka)

Fine-grained fish-skin covered sheath

Straight double-edged blade (ken)

Fine-grained fish-skin covered hilt

Metal sleeve (habaki) which has been engraved with lines called *Neko Gake* (literally "cat scratches") to provide a slight grip to the inside of the sheath

DATE	late Edo, c.1850
ORIGIN	JAPANESE
LENGTH	30.8cm (12.1in)

The straight double-edged sword or dagger is called a ken, and is the weapon carried by some Buddhist divinities. It originated in China from whence the sword (and Buddhism) was introduced into Japan during the 7th and 8th centuries. Consequently many such ken were made for temple presentation.

Japanese tanto, late Edo, *c.*1860

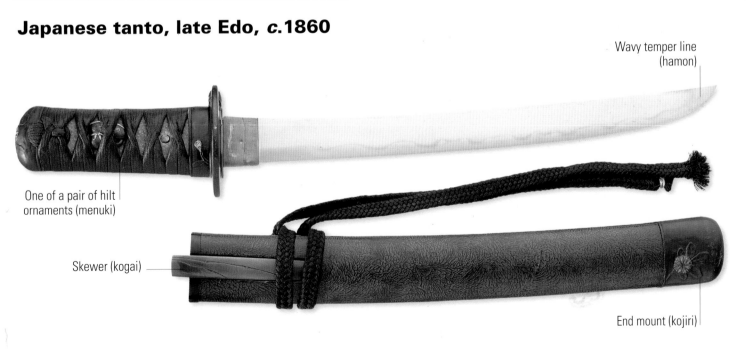

Wavy temper line (hamon)

One of a pair of hilt ornaments (menuki)

Skewer (kogai)

End mount (kojiri)

DATE	late Edo, c.1860
ORIGIN	JAPANESE
LENGTH	43.3cm (17in)

The hilt (*tsuka*) of this tanto is bound with silk tape, although sometimes string, leather or even baleen was used. The grip is covered with ray skin (*same*) and fitted with two small ornaments (*menuki*) before being bound. The menuki provide a more secure grip. The sheath is fitted with an end mount (*kojiri*) intended to protect the sheath, but in practice it is merely a vehicle for further ornamentation.

Japanese aikuchi, late Edo, *c.*1860

Silk strap (sageo), used to tie the sheath to a belt

Brass skewer (kogai)

Mouthpiece (koi guchi, meaning "carp mouth")

Lacquered hilt with brass mount

In this example of a Japanese aikuchi, the mounts (*koshirae*) are made from brass (*sentoku*), while the hilt (*tsuka*) and sheath (*saya*) are beautifully lacquered. This particular dagger was made in the second half of the 19th century during the late Edo period. The *kogai* (skewer) was carried in a slot in the scabbard.

DATE	late Edo, c.1860
ORIGIN	JAPANESE
LENGTH	33.5cm (13.1in)

Japanese tanto, Meiji, *c.*1870

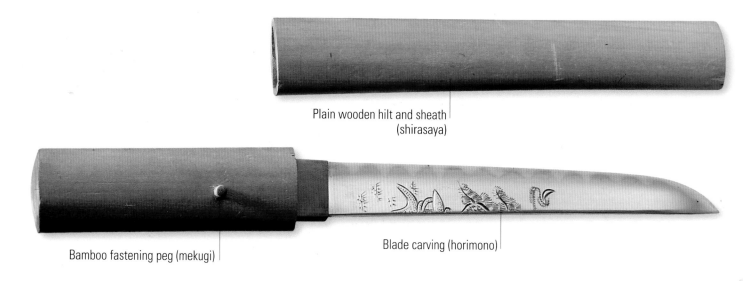

Plain wooden hilt and sheath (shirasaya)

Bamboo fastening peg (mekugi)

Blade carving (horimono)

This blade is contained within a plain wooden hilt and sheath, usually made of magnolia wood, known as a *shirasaya*. It is entirely devoid of any fittings, and even the *habaki* has been replaced by a wooden equivalent made as an integral part of the hilt. The shirasaya is intended to protect the blade and to provide a suitable method of storage; it is not intended to be used. This blade has a carved decoration called *horimono*.

DATE	Meiji, c.1870
ORIGIN	JAPANESE
LENGTH	32cm (12.6in)

Japanese tanto, Meiji, blade date 1877

Utility knife (kodzuka)

Metal sleeve (habaki)

The beautifully lacquered, curved and segmented sheath of this tanto dagger probably betrays the maker's intention to sell it to a foreign (*namban*) buyer. The blade is dated 1877, and although some very fine blades were produced at this time the majority were intended for foreign consumption. The European "aesthetic movement" of the late 19th century was partly informed by Japanese art, and both Europe and the United States evinced a seemingly boundless appetite for Japanese art and artefacts.

DATE	Meiji, blade date 1877
ORIGIN	JAPANESE
LENGTH	41cm (16.1in)

Japanese dagger, early 19th century

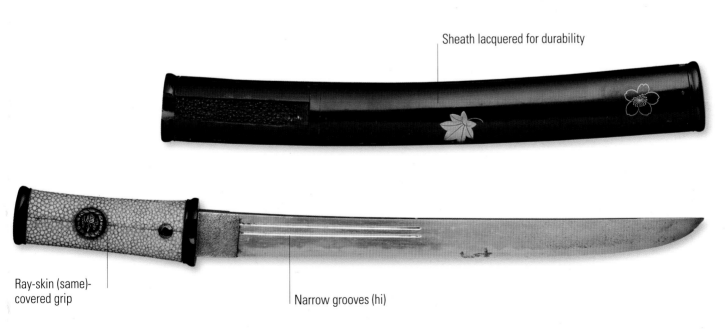

Sheath lacquered for durability

Ray-skin (same)-covered grip

Narrow grooves (hi)

A blade which has been formed with no ridges on either side has a shape called *hira zukuri*. This particular example has been cut with a pair of short shallow grooves called *hi*. The mounting is tasteful and of good quality. The sheath is covered with lacquer which provides a very durable finish; it is made from the ground-up wing cases of various beetles.

DATE	early 19th century
ORIGIN	JAPANESE
LENGTH	43cm (16.9in)

Glossary

Aikuchi Type of Japanese dagger with a handle but no guard.

Antennae dagger Dagger with a pommel that is shaped into a pair of curved arms.

Bagh nakh The Indian "tiger claw". A crossbar pierced for the fingers fits over the knuckles; curved blades are attached and hidden inside the palm.

Ballock (kidney) dagger A medieval form of dagger with a hilt shaped like the male genitalia.

Baluster-turning Method of decorating metalwork, commonly used in the 17th century to decorate stiletto hilts and ricassos.

Baselard Type of dagger or shortsword with a hilt shaped like a capital "I".

Bayonet Dagger or fighting knife designed to be fitted onto the end of a firearm to convert it to a stabbing weapon for close-combat.

Bhuj Indian weapon comprised of a stout, single-edged cutting blade attached to an axe haft. Also called a "gandasa".

Bichwa Short Indian dagger with a long, narrow looped grip to which is attached a narrow undulating blade.

Blarka ngirdi Style of southeast Asian pattern-welding, producing a blade with the distinctive "palm-leaf" design.

Bowie knife Large fighting knife said to have been invented c.1827.

Butt The end of the handle of an edged weapon, having no pommel.

Byknife Small utility knife made as a matching companion to a sword or dagger, held in a small sleeve built into the scabbard of the larger weapon.

Chape Metal mount fixed over the tip of a scabbard.

Chilanum Indian dagger with a slightly curved blade and a hilt incorporating a pommel section with broad narrow arms.

Choil Unsharpened, rounded cut-out section of the blade on some knives, separating the sharp edge from the ricasso, or cut into the ricasso itself.

Cinquedea Type of civilian dagger or shortsword popular in Italy during the late 15th and 16th centuries.

Coutiaus a pointe "Stabbing knife" – a medieval term used to describe a narrow, stiff-bladed dagger designed specifically for stabbing with the point.

Coutiaus a tailler "Cutting knife" – a medieval term used to describe a wider bladed dagger, often single-edged.

Cross guard Shaped bar of metal between the blade and the top of the handle, mounted at right angles to them and designed to protect the hand.

Cross-hilt Hilt incorporating a simple cross guard. Also called "cruciform" hilt.

Cultellus Medieval Latin for "dagger".

Damascening The process of inlaying soft metal into a hard metal to produce intricate patterns.

Dirk Word used to refer to various types of dagger. Mostly commonly used in reference to the long dirks carried by the clansmen of the Scottish Highlands.

Dudgeon dagger Late Anglo-Scottish ballock knife of the 17th century, the handle of which was carved from a single piece of box-tree root or "dudgeon".

Ear dagger Form of dagger that probably originated in Spain in the 14th century. Characterized by the two large disks that make up the pommel section.

Ersatz bayonet Emergency bayonet, often rudimentary, made to fit a rifle for which it was not originally intended.

Escutcheon Small shield-shaped plate mounted on an object, usually to display the coat of arms or device of the owner.

Falchion Short, and usually curved, wide-bladed cutting sword popular in Europe during the Medieval and Renaissance Periods.

Ferrule A metal ring or short tube that is employed to join two shafts together, or to cover a join.

Fire-gilding A decorative technique for covering iron, steel, copper, silver or bronze with a thin layer of gold.

Foible The upper, weaker half of a sword blade.

Forte The lower, stronger half of a sword blade.

Frog stud A small metal button or knob mounted onto a scabbard for fastening it securely into the "frog", a tab of leather mounted to a belt.

Fuller Groove cut or hammered into a blade to reduce its weight without weakening it.

Ganja The narrow guard of the Southeast Asian kris.

Gladius The famous shortsword of the Roman legionary, with a hilt of carved wood and a stout double-edged blade.

Granulation A form of decoration wherein a surface is ornamented with tiny closely-set beads or spheres.

Grip The handle of a weapon, usually made of wood and often covered with textile or leather, or bound with wire.

Guard The hilt structure of bars and/or plates that protects the wearer's hand.

Hilt The area of a dagger, knife or sword that is held in the hand, usually comprising a pommel, a handle and some kind of guard for the hand.

Holbein dagger Type of dagger popular in Germany and Switzerland in the mid-16th century, having a wide double-edged blade and a wooden hilt shaped like a capital letter "I".

Jambiya Arabic for "dagger".

ABOVE British L1A3 bayonet for L1A1 SLR, 1957.

Kard Persian for "knife".

Katana Japanese longsword, larger than the wakizashi (short sword) but smaller than the tachi (two-handed sword).

Katar Form of push dagger common in India. Also called a "jamdhar".

Katzbalger Type of shortsword used by German mercenaries in the 16th century.

Khanjar Arabic for "dagger".

Khanjarli Type of Indian dagger with a strongly recurved blade and a wide half-moon-shaped pommel.

Knucklebow A curved bar on the hilt of some edged weapons that protects the fingers.

Koftgari Indo-Persian term for false or counterfeit damascening.

Knurling Method of decoration involving a series of small beads, knobs, ridges or hatch-marks.

Kogai The Japanese byknife.

Koshi-gatana "Waist-sword", a long Japanese dagger or shortsword with no guard, worn with the *tachi* (two-handed sword).

Kris A distinctive type of Southeast Asian dagger of asymmetrical design, with a pattern-welded, often wavy blade.

Kukri Wide-bladed axe-like knife, the signature weapon of the Gurkha people of Nepal.

Landsknecht dagger A modern term referring to three distinct types of 16th-century European dagger: the "katzbalger" shortsword; a rondel dagger variation with a drooping guard; or an early type of ring-hilted dagger.

Locket Metal mount fitted over the throat of a scabbard to protect it.

Main gauche Mid-17th-century Spanish and southern Italian parrying dagger.

Mokume-gane "Wood-grain metal", a Japanese form of pattern-welding.

Navaja Type of folding fighting knife that originated on the Iberian peninsula in the 18th century.

Parry A defensive movement and the primary function of the parrying dagger.

BELOW Dutch bayonet, Beaumont-Vitali rifle, Model 1871/88, 1888.

Peshkabz Type of Indo-Persian dagger with a straight or recurved blade of T-section.

Pipe-back blade Type of blade found on 18th- and 19th-century military bayonets and swords, where the unsharpened back of the blade is given a rounded or tubular cross-section.

Plug bayonet The earliest form of bayonet – a dagger, usually with a double-edged blade, fitted with a handle that tapers down to a very narrow end.

Pommel A metal weight, often spherical, ovoid, or wheel-shaped, fixed to the end of a sword or dagger to counter-balance the blade.

Pugio Short wide leaf-bladed dagger of the ancient Romans.

Push dagger Dagger having a grip set at a right angle to the blade, so that the weapon is held in the fist with the blade projecting along the line of the arm.

Quillon Post-medieval term referring to one of the arms of the cross guard of a sword or dagger.

Rapier Type of predominantly thrusting sword worn in everyday life in 16th- and 17th-century Europe.

Ricasso The unsharpened area of a blade immediately above the hilt.

Rondel A medieval term denoting any circular plate used to protect a part of the body.

Saw-back blade A blade, the back of which is toothed like a saw though otherwise unsharpened.

Scabbard A sheath, usually made of metal, leather or wood, inside which the blade of an edged weapon is placed.

Scramasax (seax, sax) One of the primary edged weapons used by most north and west Europeans during the Early Medieval Period. Made in a wide range of sizes, from extremely long sword types (*langseax*) to very short ones (*handseax*).

Sgian dubh (skean dhu) Small knife worn with formal Scottish Highland dress from the 19th-century onwards.

Shell guard A small rounded plate of metal incorporated into the guard of some types of sword and dagger to give additional protection to the hand.

Side-ring A small ring of metal mounted on the outside of the cross guard of most 16th- and early 17th-century parrying daggers.

Socket bayonet A bayonet generally with no hilt, just a narrow tube or socket of metal, onto which is attached the narrow, often triangular section blade by means of a short curved arm.

Stiletto (stylet) Small stabbing dagger dating from the end of the 16th century.

Sword bayonet Very long type of bayonet having a sword hilt and wide cutting blade.

Tang Unsharpened end of the blade, over which fits the hilt or handle.

Tang button The end of the tang that is hammered (peened) over the top of the pommel, adding stability and strength. Some tang buttons are screwed into the pommel and attached to the tang.

Tanto Japanese dagger with diamond-sectioned blade.

Telek The northwest African arm dagger. Also called a "gosma".

Trumbash The sickle-knife of the Mangbetu people of the Congo.

Tsuba The guard, usually round or oval and beautifully decorated, of most Japanese daggers and swords.

Volute A spiral or circular motif often found in 16th-century weapons.

Ukiran The carved handle of the kris.

Yataghan Turkish or Eastern European short sword with a recurved blade.

Yoroi doshi Specially-thickened armour-piercing Japanese dagger or tanto.

Index

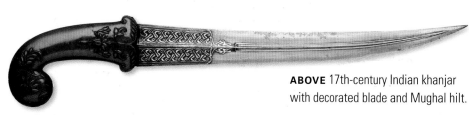

ABOVE 17th-century Indian khanjar
with decorated blade and Mughal hilt.

ABOVE Czech VZ/24 knife bayonet, *c.*1926.

BELOW Japanese aikuchi dagger. The blade is dated 1625, the rest was made later.

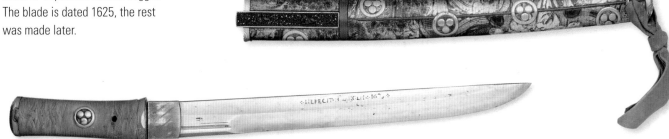

Picture credits

The publisher would like to thank the following for kindly supplying photos for this book: AKG: 7t, 22b, m, 115t, 144b,m, 79b; Barrett, Jonathan: 19ml, mr; Berman Museum of World History, Alabama: 8br, 9tr, 11bmr, 25t, 56m, 58b, 64b, 68mb, mt, 70b, t, 71b, t, 72bb, bt, 73m, t, 76m, 94t, 96m, 101t, 102m, t, 107m, 108b, 109t, 119t, 131t, 140m, 150b, 151br; Bridgeman Art Library: 11tm, 21t, 22t, 23b, m, 24t, 26t, m, b, 27t, 30b, 33b, 49b, 61b, 123b; Corbis: 25b, 73b, 106b; Ernest, PJ: 114b; Getty Images: 93b; Hermann Historica Auctioneers, Munich: 11mlt, mrt, tl, 12b, m, 13b, 15m, t, 17bb, bt, tl, tr, 21b, m, 24m, 27m, 28t, 37m, 38b, t, 40b, 41b, m, 42t, 45mt, tt, 54m, 55m, 63b, m, 68b, t, 69m, t, 71m, 88b, m, 89m, 98t, 99m, 117b, 120b, m, 121b, m, t, 122b, t, 123t, 124b, 125b, 126b, 127t, b, 128b, t, 129b, t, 131b, mb, 132b, t, 133mb, t, 134b, m, 135b, mt, t, 136m, t, 137mt, t, 138t, 142b, t, 143m, t, 144b, t, 145b, m, 147b, 151t, 152b, 153b, 154b, t, 155t; Kenney, DX: 27b; Stephens, Frederick: 105t, 107t, b; Royal Athena Galleries: 17mb, mt, 20b, m, t, 24b; Wallis and Wallis Auction Gallery: 9tl, 18tb, tt, 57m, t, 58m, 59b, m, t, 60b, m, t, 61t, 88tt, 89b, t, 91bb, 116b, m, t, 117t, 148b, t, 149b, t, 150m, t, 151 bl; All other images from the Royal Armouries, Leeds in England. All artwork by Peters & Zabransky Ltd.

Every effort has been made to obtain permission to reproduce copyright material, but there may be cases where we have been unable to trace a copyright holder. The publisher will be happy to correct any omissions in future printings.